Also by Lucy Irvine

CASTAWAY

RUNAWAY

Runaway

LUCY IRVINE

RANDOM HOUSE NEW YORK

Originally published in Great Britain by Viking in 1986. Copyright © 1986 by Lucy Irvine.

Grateful acknowledgment is made to the following for permission to reprint previously
published material:

Random House, Inc.: Excerpts from "Anthem for St. Cecilia's Day," from *Collected
Poems* by W. H. Auden. Reprinted by permission of Random House, Inc. Canadian rights
administered by the British publisher, Faber and Faber Limited, London.

Warner Bros. Music Limited: Excerpts from "Horse with No Name" by Dewey
Bunnell. Copyright © 1971 by Warner Bros. Music Limited. Used by permission of
Warner Bros. Music Corp. All rights reserved.

Library of Congress Cataloging-in-Publication Data

Irvine, Lucy, 1956–
    Runaway.

    1. Great Britain—Description and travel—1971–
2. Irvine, Lucy, 1956–   . I. Title.
DA632.I47   1987   914.1′04858   86-20198
ISBN 0-394-54510-9

Manufactured in the United States of America
24689753
First American Edition

TO "MARIANNE"

CONTENTS

PART ONE

Sunny Day

A green field in England on a sunny day. It was early summer, the time of dog roses and fallen fledglings along country lanes. The sun, now high, would last until early evening and then give way to a sudden chill. Yet again, I would miss all but the last half hour of it. And that would be wasted hanging round the bus stop listening to talk of teachers, homework and the cost of aniseed balls.

I craned forward to catch a glimpse of the stream. Light tickled ripples hide-and-seeking in the reeds. How good to be beside the water now, or better still floating on it, dipping a hand to break the play of beams. I drew my head back. Julia Fosdyke's ponytail was in the way.

Miss Eccleston's voice crackled out, weary, automatic: "Turn to page two hundred and forty-two, exercise five. Caroline Austin, begin, please."

Caroline's effortful voice stumbled among the phrases full of *silvae*, *agricolae* and soldiers laying waste. Miss Eccleston's gray head wobbled as she shook it. The sunlight caught a fall of powder from her jowls.

"Next."

Slowly up and down the rows of small, blond-wood desks, chairs scraped back and hesitant voices, some earnest, some bored, pushed on through the woods and wastes. A bee droned against the window, exhausted. Finally he knocked himself out. He would never escape. I looked at the timetable for the afternoon: R.I., Maths, Singing. Then the bus to 309, tea, homework, television, bed. School again tomorrow. And so on until I was eighteen. I looked again toward the water and the field.

Miss Eccleston's eyes fell on my raised hand.

"Yes?"

"Please may I be excused?"

"You should have gone at breaktime."

"I know. I'm sorry I didn't."

"Go along, then."

I left the classroom quietly, closing the door behind me.

In the corridor I pulled off my shoes and, holding them in one hand, sprinted silently past all the classrooms until I reached the top of the stairs where, breath held, I listened for footsteps below. Not a sound. I tiptoed down and with a sudden surge of confidence took the last four steps at a bound, sliding expertly on the polished floor below. In the cloakroom I emptied all the textbooks out of my case and replaced them with gymshoes and a blank exercise book. I left my blazer but remembered to grab my beret at the last minute. It was forbidden to be seen outside in school uniform without a beret and its absence from my head might attract more attention than my absence from class if I bumped into anyone.

Clear of the pupils' exit, I stood for a second looking across the field. My feet were on the grass and I was no longer just wishing, but there. One small dream realized. Careless of eyes that might be following, I plotted a clear diagonal to a gate in the far corner and walked out into the sun.

Outside the gate I stopped to work out the next move. If I went to 309 now there would be nobody in. Good. I could get rid of the school clothes and find some useful things to put in the case. Then I would let Richard, my father, know I had left. We always told each other about important things in our lives. Absently, as I crossed the bridge over the school stream, I took off my beret and tossed it in. It spun as it floated away.

The bus was slow, packed with women lugging shopping, and when I reached 309 I had to rush to avoid meeting my mother. She would be upset and not understand. It would cause a messy delay. Upstairs I changed quickly and ripped a small blanket off my bed. On the way through the kitchen I swept four apples into the case and swiftly downed a glass of milk. I looked around for the cat to say goodbye. She was curled up on the grand bishop's chair in the hall. Lifting her warm body I kissed the surprised old face once, then plonked her back on the chair, where she began to sneeze. It was the last sound I heard before I banged the front door and set off down the road.

Richard's office was in Kensington, St. Mary Abbot's Place. I expected him to be on the telephone when I arrived, or at a meeting. Instead he was sitting sideways in a leather chair, munching bread and honey and talking to a smart woman in a green pant suit. She had a lot of rather exciting red hair. He stopped in mid-munch when he saw me, eyebrows raised.

"Hello, no school today?"

I looked him straight in the eye.

"I've left."

He finished his mouthful and said lightly, "Have you? You don't think it might be a bit soon?"

I shook my head. Twelve seemed old enough to me. The smart woman went out quietly and I thought they exchanged a look over my shoulder. Richard jabbed the bread and honey gently in my direction. I took a bite and we both chewed for a minute, looking at each other. His casual reaction to my announcement did not surprise me. Richard's reactions were usually different to those of other grown-ups. That was what made him so special.

"Listen," he said, "I'm doing some filming at Windsor Horse Show tomorrow. Do you want to come?"

"I might."

I knew I would not but he was being so nice I wanted to show willing. The phone rang suddenly and he picked it up. He talked for what seemed a long time and when he had finished, said he had to go out.

"We'll talk later, hmm?"

I nodded noncommittally, knowing that "later" would be no good. But at least he knew now that I had left and I trusted him not to do anything embarrassing, like call the police.

Back on Kensington High Street I took a 73 bus and changed in Richmond for one that went to Kingston, knowing I had to go through there to get out on to the road south. Kay, my mother, always used to say this was the worst part of the journey. That was when Richard kept his boat near Chichester and we used to go down at weekends, a family of five with a dog and a cat.

I had never hitchhiked before but I knew how it was done. I had seen people do it on the motorway when we drove up to Scotland. Sometimes, if it was two girls, Richard would joke: "Not pretty enough" and drive on. He frowned if it was long-haired youths.

It struck me that the middle of Kingston was not the best place to start, so I followed the main street until I was past the last shop, then stuck out my thumb. I held it out for a long time. A number of cars went by and several passers-by stared. Then two cars passed with the passengers grinning and waving. I blushed. I was not being taken seriously.

Waiting until there were no pedestrians approaching—I did not want anyone to think I was giving up—I started to walk, head down and arm well out. I swung my thumb vigorously and was concentrating so hard on technique that when the window of a parked car rolled down and a man spoke, I jumped.

"Where are you trying to get to, lass? You'll never get a car stopping here."

He had a northern accent and a blotchy, sincere kind of face. I bent down to the window.

"I'm trying to get out on the road to Dorking. Actually I'm heading for somewhere near Chichester."

"Well, you've got the wrong road for a start, unless you want to go via Guildford. Tell you what, hop in and I'll put you on the road you want."

"Thank you."

I sat in the front with the case on my lap. The driver was chatty and I realized, as I felt my way cautiously round his questions, that it might be an idea to evolve a few stock replies. It was not long before the matter of age came up.

"Bit young to be doing this, aren't you? How old are you? Fourteen, fifteen?"

Not wanting to push credibility too far, I said fourteen. He raised his eyebrows and with admonitions to "Take care, lass" let me out on the Dorking road.

After only a few minutes a truck stopped. The engine was noisy and I shouted above it, one foot on the step of the cab.

"Dorking?"

The driver nodded and I scrambled up. I liked the way his red, knobbly hands manipulated the controls of the big truck and his eyes stayed businesslike on the road. I gazed out of the window, happy on this warm, swiftly moving day. Briefly, as my stomach gurgled, I thought of what they would be having for lunch at school. Friday: fish fingers. I was not missing much.

The truck went fast and soon the driver was pulling into a lay-by and saying that my best bet was to try for a lift here without getting mixed up in the town. He handed down my case, waved, and was on his way.

The next lift came quickly but the man warned that he was only going as far as a village outside Horsham. Was that OK? So long as it was in the general direction of Chichester, that was fine with me. I was learning fast. In years to come I was to find that a dead set on the final aim but flexibility on the way was a healthy policy for most things.

This driver was annoying. He fiddled constantly with the radio, talked over it, and a jacket he had hanging in the back swung around on a squeaky hanger. I asked him "what he did" and was irked when he hedged around. It seemed a very adult question.

"Guess, go on, what do I look like?"

I thought he looked like an office sort of person and said so. He laughed and pulled a pamphlet from the mouth of an open briefcase beside him.

"There you are, that's me—a traveler in baby powder—or if you want to be more down to earth about it, a sales rep."

He offered me a free sample but I refused. I did not want anything unnecessary in my case.

He dropped me on a small road where there was hardly any traffic and there followed a period of walking. Two cars went by without stopping and one man made a silly face. A woman on her own shook her head and looked angry.

I took out an apple and crunched it as I walked along. The sun was still high and I felt good. The last of the apple was still in my mouth when an elderly man in a small van stopped. I went through the routine of making sure he was going the right way. He spoke stiffly.

"If you don't mind going by the small roads I can take you nearly all the way. I've got to pick something up in Petworth, but after that I'm going straight on down. I live that way."

I climbed in. Petworth rang a bell. My sister, Marianne, had a friend whose parents had a country cottage near there. We had gone there for a weekend once and had had two midnight feasts in one night. I thought of Marianne. She would probably be in the school toilets now, dodging Games. She had done that ever since she started getting thin; ever since Richard and Kay's silent war started to get louder. The driver's voice, sounding stern, broke into my thoughts.

"I don't know what a young girl like you is doing taking lifts. You want to be careful. You don't know what might happen. I don't generally stop for anybody but I thought I'd better pick you up before somebody not quite nice came along. Lot of funny folk around these days."

I told him I had been very lucky with lifts so far.

"Doesn't matter," he said. "Only has to happen once. I wouldn't have any youngster of mine taking lifts on the road."

A lecture in exchange for the ride seemed fair enough, but I hoped it would not happen too often.

The stop in Petworth was brief. He left the engine running while he went to the back of a house and picked up a box of vegetables. When he got back into the van he put five little apples on the seat beside me.

"There you are, put them in your bag. I like to see young people eating what's good for them."

Gratefully, I fitted the apples into my case and we drove on. He took me so near my destination I could walk the rest of the way. I knew this last part of the journey well.

Birdham Pool lay next to Chichester yacht basin, much smaller and less grand. Rows of boats, mostly small yachts with one or two motor launches dotted tubbily among them, sat quietly on the water, tall masts swaying gently, making occasional whirrs and pings. In the days when Richard and Kay brought me and Marianne and our brother James here, there had been swans, a whole family with cygnets, sailing elegantly round the boats hoping for crumbs. In the evenings they would retire among the reeds at a shallow end of the Pool, smooth vees in the water marking their passage as the sun went down. We always had crusts to throw and Richard used to imitate their funny sideways looks, making us all laugh. The swans were not there now.

Across the road was a big, marshy lake, and it was something in the woods on the far side of this I had come to find. Slowly I made my way round the lake, following the muddy path where I used to go with Marianne. This was where we had found a lame duck. We had adopted her for a while, called her Martha. Leaving the path, I pushed into the woods, feet sinking into layers of mashed leaves. Twigs caught in my hair and there was a dark moss stain on one trousered knee.

Suddenly that knee came up hard against something large and I grabbed a tree so as not to fall. I had stumbled on what I was looking for. Joyfully I set to work clearing away branches and long grass. It was warm and I rolled up my sleeves, bending over with legs braced, hair in my eyes. But as my treasure was revealed, enthusiasm ebbed. The little dinghy I had hoped to paddle to the farthest reaches of the lake—maybe even round the coast if the weather were fair—was nothing more than a bottomless shell. Two winters had eaten away the planking, ferns had grown under the rowing seat and where I pulled at a section of gunwale, it came apart in my hands. I tossed the broken pieces away and stood looking out through the trees at the calm water.

I very much wanted to be out on it, floating, to complete the realization of the morning's classroom dream.

On Birdham Pool I had noticed a small tender lying in the mud not far from where the swans used to glide when the sun went down. Determinedly, I stomped back along the muddy path. On the other side of the road I checked to see there was no one about, then took off my socks and shoes and rolled up my trousers. I left the case behind a tree and made straight for the white tender. I had to rock it a few times to break the suction of the mud but after that it slid easily. One good push and she was afloat.

For an hour, perhaps two, I drifted around in that little boat. I could not go far—there was not far to go—but that did not matter. There was a spidery tangle of overhanging branches along the bank. For a while, as the boat rocked gently in the reeds, I lay and looked up through a mesh of twigs at the sky. It was very big, making me and my world look very small. There was something about that I liked. The words and tensions that cluttered life at 309, and made it hard to concentrate at school, slid away to nothing in that big sky.

When the sun went in and there were sounds of cars and children, I sat up. Friday-evening families had begun to arrive, unloading cars piled high with provisions for a boating weekend. Just as we used to in the old days. It made me feel strange to watch them and soon I put the boat away.

Back on the road, like an old hand, I began to hitch. It was time I found somewhere to stay the night.

Chichester always seemed a grand place to me. This was where the family had come for major shopping, when more was needed than could be found at Birdham Pool store. I must have been to the town center dozens of times but I was thoroughly lost now and it did not seem so grand. I stopped in front of a café and put down my case. I wished I could see in to tell what kind of place it was but the front was all smoked-yellow panes covered with whorls and dimples and luncheon voucher signs. I tweaked my plaits to straighten them before walking in.

A loud jangle announced my entrance but the woman behind the steaming cylinders of the coffee machine did not look up. Voices and the tinkle of cutlery floated up from below. I wondered if I could get past the service counter without having to buy anything. With her pink powdered face and frizzy yellow hair, the woman looked like a sleazy version of my old Geography mistress. I would not have been able to get past her. But I made it safely to the top of the stairs and there was a momentary lull in the voices as I walked down.

In a corner behind a post there was one empty table. I moved toward it but knew that if I sat down I would be stuck. I would have to order something and pretend that this was what I did every day. Standing where I was, I fixed my eyes on an advertisement pinned to the post. It read: JOLLY JACK TAR SEABOOTS: THE BEST BY FAR. I gripped the handle of my case more tightly. The eating faces were a blur beyond the seaboots.

"Excuse me"—my voice would have won top marks for clarity in an elocution class—"does anyone know where the nearest, cheapest dosshouse is?"

As soon as the words were out I knew I had made a mistake. There was dead silence in the café. Still staring at the seaboots I felt my cheeks flame. I fled up the stairs and into the street, shutting the jangling door on the frizzy-haired woman's face, her mouth wriggling sound-lessly in surprise.

Charging along furiously, smarting inside and out, I zoomed past shops and lampposts and across roads without any idea where I was going. My legs, in my newest, most grown-up trousers, took enormous strides.

It was some time before I realized I was being followed. A man, trotting to keep up, was trying to attract my attention from behind. I did not stop but slowed down enough for him to come alongside. He was young, with dark hair, wearing a flecked fisherman's sweater. His face had an anxious-to-be-friendly expression on it.

"You were in the café just now, weren't you?" he said.

I said nothing, and kept on walking.

"I didn't want to say anything in there, but look, if you're looking for somewhere to stay . . ."

My pace slackened again subtly.

". . . Me and some friends, we've got this place in Littlehampton. You'd have to sleep on the floor."

That'dbeallright."

I shot the words out as though they were one and followed quickly with a question.

"Is it far?"

"Not far, no, but we'd have to take the train. I was on the way to the station myself."

He slowed down and stopped. I stopped with him.

"It's the other way," he said lamely and we turned round and set off again.

"How much will the train be?" I asked. I had a pound note and twelve and six in change.

"Oh well," he said, "I usually dodge the guard."

I flashed him a sharp look.

"It's all right," he said, "it's easy. Just do what I do."

I said doubtfully that if we got caught I would probably be able to pay.

"Naah," he said disparagingly, "you don't want to waste your money."

The guard-dodging went smoothly, although I suffered in suspense as a white-haired guard, punching tickets rhythmically, moved up the carriage toward where we were.

"What are we going to do?" I hissed. The young man put a finger to his lips and said to follow him. While the guard's back was turned we casually walked past him and up to the end of the carriage which had already been checked. I was amazed that he did not pursue us. My companion shrugged.

"Can't be bothered," he said. But I did not relax until we were off the train.

That hurdle safely over, I became curious about what sort of place we were going to, what the friends he had mentioned were like. Here on the streets of Littlehampton, his home territory, our positions were reversed. Now I was the one trotting alongside asking questions.

"Oh," he said vaguely, "you know, it's just a place where we doss. Sometimes there's two of us, sometimes seven or eight. I think there's about three now, so should be room for you. Got a doss bag?"

I told him about the blanket.

"Doss bag's better. I'll lend you mine—we could share it if you like."

He said this last as a joke and I put on the man-freezing expression which made Richard laugh.

"Only kidding," he said, "you're safe with us." Then he added, as if it explained everything, "We like bikes."

It seemed a long walk from the station. In the sun, earlier, I had been too hot in my jersey, but now the day was drawing in and I was glad of its warmth. Littlehampton looked all gray. Wind, smelling faintly of sea, rushed around corners on to wide gray streets, blowing up newspapers and chasing gray dust swirls along gutters. We stopped at a small shop.

"Hope you like beans," my companion said.

"Baked beans?"

"What else?"

I didn't, but kept quiet. He also bought a loaf of white sliced bread—the sort Richard would call cottonwool—and a bottle of Tizer.

"I've got some apples," I offered, wanting to contribute.

"Never eat apples," he said as we swung back into stride.

We turned into a long road at the end of which was the sea. It was distant, gray as the town, but I loved the sharp tang on the air and the faraway whisper of breaking waves.

"That's us. One or two of the boys around, I see."

He gestured ahead to a small two-storyed house. What distinguished it from similar houses on either side was the jumble of machinery in the front garden. There were four motorbikes drawn up in neat formation in the road outside.

"What's your name?" he asked as we went in. "Mine's Bill. You don't have to tell me your real one."

"Susan," I said promptly. Unwittingly, Bill had laid the foundations of a habit that was to stay with me for years: when among strangers I always gave the first name that came into my head, rarely my own.

Bill's companions greeted me with casual nods. I nodded back, doing as in Rome. One of them I found impressive. He was tall, with rather long fair hair and a mauve scarf knotted at his throat. It contrasted pleasingly with the rest of his outfit which was heavy and black. I noticed that they all wore black, except for Bill with his fisherman's sweater. They sat around and chatted, using expressions I did not always understand, until someone said it was time for eats. Bill pulled out a camping Gaz ring from under a bed—we were sitting upstairs—and started to open a can of beans.

"Here, Susie, butter some of this, will you?" He tossed me the loaf and I buttered carefully, stacking the slices in face-together piles on a square of paper. There seemed to be a shortage of plates.

"Run away from school then, did you?" said the tall one conversationally as the bean pot went round.

"Yes."

"First time?"

"Yes."

"Cops aren't after you, I hope?"

I finished my mouthful before replying. The beans tasted all right here.

"No cops, no. I told my father I had left."

"Did he give you a row?"

"No."

There was a pause and a hint of surprise before he dismissed the subject.

"Well, lucky, aren't you? Do you like bikes?" Motorbikes were not something I had ever really thought about but I said yes.

"All right, we'll give you a ride tomorrow if you're good."

He seemed to be the boss. Later, when he was leaving, I heard him say to the others: "Keep your old ladies downstairs while that kid's around."

"He's nice, isn't he?" I said to Bill.

Bill reflected for a moment, then agreed.

"Yeah—got the best bike in the gang."

I spent the night on the floor, comfortable enough in Bill's sleeping bag, but I did not like being so close to the grubby carpet or the smell of smoke that clung to my hair. In the morning I was sent out to buy more beans. That was to be my job while I was with the boys. They called me Susie the Bean.

The others were there again when I got back and as the morning went on the row of motorbikes outside the front door grew. It was another sunny day and I sat contentedly in the machine-strewn garden, sleeves and trousers rolled up, watching all the new arrivals. Then somebody brought a radio and there was loud, angry-sounding music. A girl with greasy hair and torn jeans turned up with one of the boys. She smoked all the time with her head hanging down and I wondered why her hair did not catch fire. I hoped the fair-haired leader had not forgotten about my ride. I hung around while he did things to his bike and when he looked hot, went indoors and poured him a glass of Tizer. I was fascinated by a tanned section of belly that appeared as he moved around under the bike and his shirt wriggled out of his jeans. I could not tell whether it was hair or dirt that made his belly button so brown.

At last they were ready. A dozen leather and denim legs were thrown over saddles and starters were kicked. Nobody talked any more. They all knew what they were doing. The level of noise mounted as one after another the engines erupted into life. The boys were putting on headgear. A few wore crash helmets but most had blue or black peaked caps. One had a German army helmet and goggles. The leader, to my surprise, had a red beret not unlike the one I had recently thrown into the school stream.

As some of the bikes began to circle in the road, angry faces appeared at the windows of neighboring houses. A door was banged meaningfully. Nobody paid any attention. Just as I thought they were about to go without me the leader said, "Jump on then, we'll give you a spin."

I jumped on and as the big machine vroomed into the road my casually dangling arms leaped around the jacketed waist and my knees gripped the seat hard.

The ride began slowly. In three lines of four we cruised down the road toward the sea, a loud black and silver phalanx. When we reached the esplanade there was a pause and the lines broke. The bikes wove slowly between each other, tracing figures of eight. A few day-trippers further along stopped to watch; a woman hustled her little boy away. Then, one by one, the bikes left the group and rolled down a steep slope on to the beach. Some of the riders used their booted feet to steady their machines through the dry sand, others took the slope at a graunching zig-zag, swirling up yellow clouds. The bike I was on was last to go and I screwed up my eyes and clung tight as we crunched and slid among the clumps of marram grass and spraying sand. Once on the level again I sat up straight.

Out on the water there were a few boats. A man in a dinghy with red sails flapping stared curiously as singly and in pairs, the bikes milled, revs gathering. Then, rearing in unison, the first two shot away. The leader held back, watching the others go, one foot on the sand, the machine under us moving backward in small curves as though it were alive.

Suddenly, launched in one dynamic motion, we were off, cutting like a chainsaw through the stillness of the day. The noise and the speed, ever rising, seemed to take us into another dimension where all the wind and sound in the world was our own. Passing the others now, tires gliding on the hard-packed sand near the water, the machine achieved its final level of speed. Eyes in visor slits against the wind, I saw the sea flash by as a silver frieze, the line of foam at the edge a wild, white whiplash.

The end came with no cessation of noise. First at the finish, where a jetty blocked the way, the leader revved and wheeled while one by one the others swept in and swerved into triangular formation. Dazed, I dismounted, the flesh still fluttering on my thighs where I had gripped the seat so hard. The leader held the bike still beside me for a moment and playfully tugged one of my plaits.

"Like it?" he mouthed, inaudible above the engine roar.

I nodded. I had more than liked it. It had been something new: fear and elation fiercely combined.

"OK, stay here."

I moved back and flopped down against one of the jetty legs, bottom squirming into the sand, elbows on knees, as I watched them go. They were doing tricks now, performing hard-practiced stunts, rigorous in their attention to detail. Over and over they spun and jumped, using a thin plank and a drum as a ramp, and then each other's bodies as obstacles. High into the air they flew and then wove between an evenly spaced line of men. They hardly spoke, going through the routines like soldiers carrying out a familiar drill. When the black and silver missiles flew straight at them they did not flinch and their faces were empty of all expression. Finally they lined up to race, engine noise rising to a blurred howl as the invisible flag went down. Then all I could see was the wavering mirage of their exhausts and the wrecked sand after they had gone.

Left suddenly in silence I got up and stood with my feet in the sea. The line of foam was back to normal now, bubbles breaking and spilling over my toes. I climbed on to the jetty and walked to the end. After the thrill of the ride my mind felt pleasantly numb. The sea winked, becoming one with the sky on a hazed horizon.

The sun was low by the time they came to fetch me, just three of them, gliding at top speed in single file. Quickly I took my place and once again felt wonder surge as we passed the mad brink of that other dimension, seeming, in our hurtling flight, to slice the pinkening sky in two.

Back in the house, the evening followed the pattern of the day before: baked beans, smoking and the same strange, jargoned talk. They had their music going, music that snarled and jerked and made it impossible to think. It was exciting and disturbing at the same time. I did not sleep well that night, wishing there was a bath, that the music would stop and the smell of smoke go away.

On Sunday they took the bikes out again but this time I was not invited. There were jokes, something about things I should not see. The leader said he would take me for another ride on Monday. He was wearing a different hat today, with DAY-TRIPPER inked in jokey writing on the brim. I nodded and said OK. Upstairs I looked at the room with the sticky Gaz ring, the rumpled bed and Bill's doss bag on the floor and knew I did not want to stay there any more. My world and theirs only overlapped outside, on the bikes. There was nothing to pack in my case; it held the same as when I arrived—minus a few apples.

The day was not so warm, the sun an intermittent yellow splurge, the sea a weakened blue. I found a pebbled bay where I was alone and there, forcing myself to crouch in knickers and teen-bra under the cold waves, I bathed. I had no towel and the blanket I used instead was gritty. I spread it out on the rocks to dry but it was still damp at the end of the day when I put it back in the case. I had opened the blank exercise book once during the afternoon and closed it again a little later, still blank. It was chastening to find I had nothing to say.

When it was too cold to sit any longer I walked back toward the town. I had noticed a row of tiny cottages behind the railway. One of them had a Bed and Breakfast sign.

The woman who answered the door was old and very small. She stared at me through misty bifocals and shot words in quick succession out of a mouth like a knitted buttonhole.

"How many nights? Cooked breakfast or Continental? Twelve-an'-six all in."

The buttonhole closed and the misty glasses raked me for a reply. Behind her in a cramped hallway a terrier was mauling a rubber rat.

"Yes, please, one," I said vaguely and to cover up the inadequacy of the answer smiled briskly in a way that Kay did at shopkeepers and men who served her in the garage. I was shown up to a bare room with a bible on the windowsill and a chamberpot under the bed.

"Lavvy's outside. Breakfast at half past seven. Payment in advance."

I counted out the money and thanked the old woman politely. Her tiny mauve-veined hand stuffed the coins into an apron pocket and she backed on orthopedic shoes to the door. Just before she closed it she gave a startlingly pretty smile.

"Shall I bring a drop of hot water up in the morning so's you can have a warm wash? I don't bother for the gentlemen."

I said that would be very kind. Later, snuggled in the big bed, I reflected. I had never been to an outside toilet or stayed in a house without a proper bathroom. But then I had never walked out of school before or left home. With those two doors closed behind me a whole new set had opened and there were different lives going on behind each one. I pulled the covers higher, reveling in the warmth but knowing that tomorrow I would have to come up with a plan. Beyond the borrowed doss bags and the Bed and Breakfasts of Littlehampton was a big, mysterious world I had chosen to confront alone.

2

But that confrontation was postponed, for the next day curiosity and a desire to experience once more the crazy, other-dimensional thrill of a bike ride landed me firmly back in the lap of adult care.

I lay stunned in a white cocoon of quiet while again and again, the same short scene repeated itself in my mind: high, twisted iron arches, spiraling verticals, elegant fleurs-de-lis; my arms stretching up to fly; a woman in a brown skirt with a gaping mouth; a sharp pain in the jaw, then blank.

At first, I thought I was at the dentist's. There was that same circular drilling motion ending each time with a savage yank. But it was somewhere on the outside that it hurt, not a tooth. Something was pulling at my chin. My hand explored cautiously and found a big square of plaster. As I traced the edges my fingers were taken and held. I opened my eyes and the first thing I saw was the back of my exercise book in somebody's hands. It was open, being read.

Indignation cut across confusion. I did not know where I was, did not know who these people were, but I did know they had no business to be reading my diary.

"Hey!" I cried, and the plaster on my chin stretched painfully.

"Stay quiet, dear. You don't want to break your stitches."

I looked up at the speaker, a stocky woman in a black uniform. It was she who was holding my hand.

"Nurse," she called, "young lady here is with us again."

The man reading my diary closed it. There was another man standing back a little, a cap in his hands. Police. A nurse came bustling over.

"How are we feeling? Got a nasty little cut on your chin, you did, but otherwise you are a very lucky girl. How's your head?"

I moved my head on the pillow. It seemed all right.

"All right."

The man with my diary stepped forward.

"Now young lady, since you seem to be none the worse for wear, I'd like a few words with you. Perhaps you'd like to tell me just what you think you've been up to."

"As you've read my diary," I said clearly, "you know."

I was furious. It had been a long entry made just that morning while I was waiting for the old lady to appear with my hot water.

"I'll tell you straight away," said the man, who had outsize ears and yellowish bags under his eyes, "there's no point taking that attitude. You've caused a lot of worry all round."

Had he been in touch with Richard and Kay? How did he know where to find them?

"Whose motorbike was that you were on?"

"I don't know."

It was true. I did not know the leader's name.

"Well, whose ever it was isn't going to be very pleased. It's a mess."

The black-gate scene flashed through my mind again, but this time I remembered more of it.

I had met some of the bike boys shortly after leaving the Bed and Breakfast place and jumped at the offer of a ride straight away. I did not notice until I was on the back of the leader's bike that they were all in a strange mood, laughing a lot, with goggling, bloodshot eyes. I heard one of them say he had not stopped tripping since last night. I wondered where he had been. We did not go to the beach this time but cruised around the backstreets of the town. It was not the same and I began to fidget. I muttered that one day I would like to drive a bike myself. The leader said he would give me a go.

We came to a quiet place where there was a path with an expanse of grass on one side, houses on the other. First he put me on the seat in front of him and drove along slowly with my hands on the controls under his own. He showed me how to use the accelerator. Then we stopped by the others and he got off. They all seemed very tired, lolling on the ground and grinning. I sat on the bike with the engine running. One of them said, "Go on, take her round on the grass."

Nervous, because I knew the bike was too heavy for me to steady with my feet, I clutched the rubber handgrips tightly. The bike lurched crazily and the leader jumped to his feet, shouting. Looking to see where the brakes might be, both my wrists went down. There was a terrible noise and the bike flew forward jerking, then shot in a straight line along the path. Sound and speed were chaotic, a mad cacophony, but my understanding of what was going to happen was perfectly clear.

The path was not long. There were big wrought-iron gates at the end. I was going to hit them.

I tried to do things with the handgrips to make the machine and the madness stop but it only went faster, thundering, screaming. I stared at the top of the wrought-iron gates rushing closer, noted the curves of the high, twisted arches, the spiraling verticals, elegant fleurs-de-lis. My arms stretched up to fly and I saw the gaping mouth of a woman in a brown skirt. Pain in the jaw then blank. And here I was with a plaster on my chin and that man holding my diary.

The memory produced an inner slump. I was just a silly little girl. My defiance collapsed and I answered the man's questions flatly, letting things take their course. When a woman took his place I answered her questions too. They had already telephoned 309, the address was on the inside of my school case. I could imagine the expression on Richard's face when he heard. He would not be angry, but puzzled. What had I been up to? What was the idea behind this escapade? And looking back over the events of the last few days, I had no good answer. It all seemed silly now.

They put me on a train back to 309. A social work woman came with me. She kept saying how Mummy and Daddy would be pleased to see me back safe and sound. I turned away and stared out of the window at the drearily whizzing countryside. I was so bitterly ashamed of the mess I had made of things I did not even want to see the cat.

When I walked out across the school field that sunny day I failed to appreciate both the glamour and the iniquity of my crime. Ideally, when shunted back, tail between legs, I would have liked to retire to some quiet corner, nurse my injured pride and brew up a better plan for next time—something which covered such contingencies as scarcity of funds and nonguaranteeable sunshine. This was not to be. From the moment I walked in to 309 and saw the delighted, conspiratorial gleam in Marianne's eyes, I realized that my status had undergone a major change. Things would never be the same again.

"Mummy's been livid," she said as soon as we were alone.

"You've got to see Stew."

Stew was what we called the headmistress of the school I had left, Miss Margery Stewart-Grange.

"Why's Kay been livid?" I asked.

"Because you went and told Daddy before her."

"Ah."

Marianne, who was fifteen months older than I, followed other people's relationships closely.

"Does James know?"

James, our little brother, was five years my junior.

"Sort of—he doesn't really understand. What are you going to say
to Stew?"

The prospect of my audience with the head intrigued her.

"I don't know. I'll see at the time."

"You'll have to wear your uniform to see her."

"Why?"

"It's a school rule. Have to wear full uniform on the premises."

"I don't go to that school any more."

I had to stand in the corridor until Miss Stewart-Grange was ready
to receive me. The timing was unfortunate. Thirty seconds after the
break bell rang, the corridor was aswirl with girls, many of them from
my year. Those who dared hissed things as they passed.

"Latin was fantastic after you'd gone. You should have seen Eccleston. She thought you'd fainted in the loo."

"You'll never be allowed to be form captain again, even if we vote
you, I heard them say . . ."

But the most repeated remark was: "Golly, you're not in uniform!"

I was glad when they had gone. The girl I had been closest to had
not said anything. Now that I was not one of them any more, I found
I had nothing to say to her either.

At last I was told I could go in. Miss Stewart-Grange stood erect
behind her desk, dignity drawn smoothly round her like a robe. The
lecture she delivered had two parts, the first based on the words "surprised" and "disappointed." ("We are surprised and disappointed by
your behavior.") The second was more complicated, dealing with the
charity of forgiveness. It sounded like a speech we had been reading
in English recently—"the quality of mercy'—and ended on a mag-
nanimous flourish.

"It has been decided that owing to your promising reports up to this
time, and the fact that we understand there have been difficulties at
home, you are to be allowed to return to school immediately."

My eyes left her face and traveled down to the tip of one polished
shoe. The mention of "difficulties at home" disturbed me. Its inclusion
as a reason for my being forgiven somehow sounded deprecating to
my family, making them into a mitigating circumstance. I remained
silent.

Miss Stewart-Grange's last words were: "Don't ever let me see you out of school uniform on these premises again."

"No, Miss Stewart-Grange."

I did not mention that she was never going to see me in it again, either.

Although it was accepted that I would not go back to that school, it was required by law that efforts were made to continue my education somehow. Richard, seeing what was expected of him, spoke dutifully of the occasional need for "compromise" in one's attitude. I think the word sounded as strange to him as it did to me. When people talked about him they used words like "single-minded" and "determined." Sometimes they said "ruthless," too, which I thought sounded rather thrilling. Kay, more conventional and anxious to steer me back on to the rails, equipped herself with a thick blue book listing hundreds of different schools. It was felt that a boarding establishment might be best and for a while my bedtime reading consisted of long academic records and parochial triumphs of the field in brochures bright with crested photographs of formidable-looking buildings in attractive settings. The dining rooms always looked spartan and the dormitories huge. There were invariably long lists of uniform.

As efforts were continued and I remained polite but unyielding, patience began to fray. There was an undercurrent of tension in the house which sometimes simmered to the surface and burst in snappy bubbles off Kay's tongue. Although I knew I was only partly the cause, I felt I must do something soon.

Often I was tempted to fill my case with books and apples and take to the road again. Having once tasted the ease of mobility, it was hard to discard as a way out, however temporary. But the lessons learned on that first walk into the sun had gone deep. The indignity of having my diary read and the misery of the train ride with the social worker were still vivid. I realized that stabs at an independence for which I was not yet equipped were not only damaging to self-esteem, they were dangerous. To maintain what little freedom I had gained I must remain as uninvolved with the authorities as possible which, in effect, meant cooperating to some degree. In a moment of frustration the words "approved school" had been flung at me. Although my quiet, non-delinquent behavior did not qualify me for such measures, I took heed of the warning. The last thing I wanted was to have my options restricted by law.

One day a brochure arrived which was different from the others. It showed an artist's impression of a place neither grand nor stately, but rather a cluster of houses set in grounds which looked encouragingly unkempt. There were boys as well as girls in the photographs and none of them wore uniform. It came under the heading "progressive school." I had to do something. I would give St. Paul's a try.

There were few possessions to which I was greatly attached but one thing I did not leave behind when packing for St. Paul's was my music. From the age of six, when I began to learn, I had had an ambivalent relationship with the piano. Publicly, I disliked practicing and shrank from the rigors of scales and theory, but privately, I was very drawn to certain pieces. There was satisfaction in making the music say things I felt but could not describe in words. I also had a lot of respect for my music teacher, a dedicated, highly principled woman who disapproved of me strongly but saw potential behind my capricious moods. Under her guidance, I took and passed the practical and theory examinations up to grade seven. Then suddenly, I balked. That was around the time Kay and Richard started to be more open in their hostilities to one another. Without any explanation to anyone, I stopped playing altogether. Nevertheless, into the bottom of my St. Paul's case went Heller, Paderewski and Beethoven, graffiti'd indelibly with my teacher's annotations in green ink. Those tattered sheets of music were the first objects of conscious nostalgia in my life, representing a brief era of discipline, security and achievement gone forever.

St. Paul's, I soon discovered, was not the place to be reintroduced to the benefits or otherwise of discipline hailing from the adult world. Although, paradoxically, one of the main ideas behind the school was to nurture the talents of the individual, there was a slant toward the communal way of living which isolated me from the start. Only ever at ease in groups when way out in front or so far behind as to be off the map, I was an unhappy misfit in a system where everything was "fair." Democratic was a word frequently used.

And, with the special "free" structure of the school, there was a whole new set of rules to learn. These were not rules made by the staff, they were the unwritten decrees as to what constituted good and bad set up by the children in the absence of any other code. "Freedom" as a catchword was held aloft and waved like a militant banner. To the pupils of St. Paul's, freedom meant extremism. It was their way of coping with a concept too daunting to handle. Using the conventional mores of the establishment as a wall to kick against, they formed a solid anticulture which bristled with as rigid a set of values as those they claimed to despise.

I was welcomed as a shining example of antiestablishment when it was learned that I had run away from my last school. But as it became clear that, far from having a tearaway attitude, I was quiet and spent a great deal of time reading, respect dwindled and I was labelled dismissively as a goody-goody. Not even getting into trouble for the sin of eating sardines under the bedclothes helped: freedom for animals meant we all had to be vegetarian.

"How *could* you?" I was asked.

"I like sardines."

A well-meaning girl, who was nearly fourteen, tried to make me understand.

"Don't you see how wrong it is to eat those poor little fish? What right have you to take their lives?"

"I'm a bigger fish."

"That's a really fascist remark!"

She turned to the rest of the dorm and there were nods. Now I was a goody-goody *and* a fascist. It all seemed very complicated. I went on quietly eating sardines.

One afternoon Richard came to see me. We made the arrangement on the spur of the moment by telephone and, to avoid wasting any time, fixed to meet outside the school grounds. Richard was as bored at the thought of going through the usual formalities as I was. After lunch recess, instead of getting changed for Netball, I slipped unnoticed through an opening in the hedge and walked along the road to our rendezvous. He had a Bristol at the time, a big, sleek bomb of a car, and I felt proud as he turned up right on time with a rich slur of tires on the verge.

We went for a drive in the country and talked. Or rather he talked. I was only dimly aware that this was for him as well as me a period of major changes. He was not specific, but hinted that things would be different from now on. There was talk of sailing a new boat up to Scotland, selling this car. I knew without asking that he would not be sailing with Kay and it crossed my mind that it might be the lady with red hair from his office who was to be the crew. I nodded as I listened to him, catching the thread of his enthusiasm and spinning visions of my own. It had been too long since he had said those exciting words: "I've got a plan!"

He smiled in a special way that was just for me and him and told me "not to breathe a word." Then, as if just checking, he said, "You like Scotland, don't you? Remember those holidays we had? The cottage? The sea?"

I remembered, and knew then that I was not being cut out of his plan.

When we stopped for tea at a deathly silent hotel, where Richard made me giggle by imitating the sour-faced waitress behind her back, he broached the subject of how I was getting on at St. Paul's. "I'm not," I said flatly, only ever afraid to hide the truth from him. For a moment he looked irritated, then sighed, searching for something positive to pull from this confession which would no doubt cause problems for us both.

"Well, I suppose it means I won't have those exorbitant fees to pay any more."

He looked down at the tea tray with its fussy white doily. There was one biscuit left on the plate.

"Do you want that biscuit?"

I shook my head and he popped it whole into his mouth. I loved the way he ate so neatly and with such relish, dabbing up the last of the crumbs with a finger.

As he drove me back to school I reflected that I had never once heard him speak of a plan without it being put into action sooner or later. He was a *doer*, and I wanted to be a doer too. I could not imagine that anyone could ever take his place in my heart.

Richard's failure to go through the proper channels before visiting gave rise to a disturbing confrontation. Shortly after I got back to St. Paul's I was summoned to the houseparents' quarters.

Housemother was a square woman: square shoulders, square bust, square frown. Her husband was taller but similarly angled, a rectangle. They both faced me, standing, in the kitchen of their apartment. Housemother began.

"How can we be expected to do anything for you youngsters when parents set an example like this? How were we supposed to know where you were? For all we knew you could have been kidnapped."

She leaned her square buttocks against a dresser and folded her arms. Housefather chipped in.

"What is he? In films or something? Same old story. Half the messed-up kids here come from theatrical families."

The disparaging way he spoke startled me. He had got it all wrong.

I began to explain that Richard made commercials and fishing documentaries but was cut short.

"Whatever he does, he has behaved irresponsibly and encouraged you to do the same. There are plenty like that. Coming here in their big cars and filling their kids' heads with all sorts of fancy ideas, then going off and leaving them flat for God knows how long. Happens all the time and we're in the middle of it, supposed to be doing a job."

I did not care about this man's job and Richard was not going to go off and leave me flat for God knows how long. "Leaving me flat" was an expression I had heard Kay use, and it scared me. Angry that I could not bring myself to glare into their faces, addressing instead a stain on the wall behind, I blurted, "If it weren't for *people like my father, people like you* would not even have a job. He pays for you."

My taunt could not have been more unfortunate. Housefather was quick to bite back.

"Oh no, girlie, that's just where you're wrong." He rocked a chair at the kitchen table with his long arms and his blockish face loomed close. "What we do we do because we believe in it. Getting paid has precious little to do with it." There was a grunt of agreement from his other half. "And besides, if I am not mistaken, your dad has had more than one reminder about fees due before the beginning of term . . ."

Housemother put out a restraining hand. This was perhaps going too far. I took in nothing of what was said during the rest of the interview, conscious only that the voices were placatory and an arm around my deliberately stiffened shoulders was meant to be sympathetic. I shook it off.

Back in the dormitory, relieved to find myself alone, I flung on my anorak and felt in the pocket for the two half-crowns Richard had given me. One had vanished and as I descended to the ground via the fire ladder, I cursed the thief with a word once torn from Kay's lips in a moment of fury. I knew who the culprit was. It was that girl with the tapeworm who dyed her hair and kept dope in a Tampax tube. I muttered the word again and when a fat boy called out to ask if I wanted to "go to Winkley"—the standard St. Paul's formula for a fumble—I turned my venom on him.

He grinned appreciatively and bounced it back.

"Bugger off!"

"Bugger off!"

"Bugger off!"

"Bugger off!"

It went like a chant with the rhythm of my stride and the blotting ugliness of it canceled all other thought and made me feel strong.

In the High Street of the local town the shops were beginning to close. I slipped into Woolworth's just as a man with a swab bucket was about to lock the doors, and for seven pence halfpenny equipped myself with a lump of pink and white slab cake the size of a brick. St. Paul's could keep their nut rissole supper. Moments later I regretted the indulgence when I learned that a half-fare bus ticket to anywhere within ten miles of 309 cost two and sixpence. If I had wanted to go badly enough I could have hitched, but I did not. I did not know what I wanted. Richard probably would not even be there.

Aimlessly, I wandered back into the High Street and started to munch on the slab cake. Only when a woman wheeling a pramload of groceries stared did I realize that tears were running down my cheeks, making salty trifle of the crumbs.

That Easter it was suggested that I spend the holidays with my godmother in France. I leaped at the chance, not caring where I went so long as it was away. I knew I would not be going back to St. Paul's.

3

I came back from France armed with a sort of mental carapace—it was a word I had recently learned—which shielded me from the worst chunks now beginning to crack off my parents' marriage. I had enjoyed the foreignness of the holiday. A limited understanding of the language made me see people from a distance and observe their behavior dispassionately, as if I were a fly on the wall. I took refuge in this point of view now, turning it on my family and myself. As a defense system it was only partially successful.

This term my name was on the register of a local grammar school and I was also, perhaps belatedly, putting in appearances at a child guidance clinic where a gracious lady in maroon gave me coffee and inkblot tests. She asked me to tell her what games I liked and I told her about being a fly on the wall, and Chatter.

Chatter was a game Marianne and I used to play when we shared the Big Room at 309—a room at the top of the stairs which Richard could cross with one magnificent leap when he came to say good night in an exuberant mood. The rules of the game were flexible and developed in pace with our own minds and bodies. We called it Chatter in honor of frequent yells from below to ''Stop that chatter!'' It went on for years.

Immediately after Lights Out one or other of us would whisper, ''Up to?''

This was the signal to begin. Our principal character was stolen from a TV serial about a horse. The horse's owner, Joey, was our hero. In fact we discovered that on close examination Joey was not up to much as a hero, so we made improvements of our own, giving him more height, changing his American accent to King's English and toning down the loud check of his lumberjack shirts. We also dealt fairly summarily with the horse, putting it out to grass after it had served its purpose in the initial episode and allowing it to age gracefully while Joey got on with his adventures. For Chatter was an endless saga of how Joey got himself into and out of a wide variety of challenging situations.

The other characters we chose to bring into Chatter were selected from books, films, history and our own social circle. At first we surrounded Joey with animal friends, allowing him to steal Long John Silver's parrot and somehow having Guy the gorilla and King Kong produce an endearing miniature called Little Ho, after Horatio Nelson. A small, ugly dog by the name of Benji went everywhere with Joey and was a constant source of embarrassment. He turned up in a suitcase when Joey, in a reckless fling with Peter Pan's Wendy, eloped to Penang. (I had just started reading Somerset Maugham.) The dog's squeaking, puddling presence ruined the romance of the occasion and sent Wendy rushing back to Never-Never Land, while Joey sat on the balcony sipping a manly stengah with David Copperfield, who was having similar trouble with Dora. They both decided they were better off without girls and Copperfield was shortly replaced by Dick West, the Lone Ranger's sidekick, who was tanned and dashing and always had sandwiches in his saddlebag.

Gradually, as our early adolescent curiosities became defined, we placed Joey in situations where, through him, the questions in our own minds could be aired. What did it feel like to be a grown-up woman? Briskly we thrust upon Joey a pair of breasts, a tight skirt and high heels, making him, for the sake of continuity, the temporary victim of a surgical slip. The result was disappointing, lasting only one episode. After he had dressed up and done his hair differently a few times, been shopping and had a giggly candlelit dinner with Dick, we could not think what else to give him to do—beside the washing up, and Joey certainly wasn't going to do that.

Being a baby lasted longer. Both Marianne and I found the concept of infant helplessness fascinating. Imagine knowing what you wanted but not having any way of expressing it except by crying. The thought was appalling. Time after time we forced babyhood upon Joey, surrounding him with adults who sometimes listened but never fully understood his needs. We could imagine no worse hell than being entirely at the mercy of grown ups. Eventually even this palled and Joey reverted to his original, enviable form: a young man in charge of his own life who did not have to depend on anyone for anything. For that, before puberty stepped in, was how we wanted to be.

The game recalled a time when Marianne and I took the closeness of each other for granted and when our parents and the future were solid, unquestionable things. I told the lady in maroon about Chatter but not about what happened when that, and so many other things in my life, suddenly came to an end. I did not tell her how Marianne changed, overnight it seemed, into someone who was always ill; how I ran away, was brought back, left again; how the cat was run over and Marianne's Doberman puppy, gone wild because she was no longer strong enough to take it for walks, ate my pet hen and savaged the last of our rabbits. I said nothing of the evening Kay appeared with a black eye saying she had fallen against a door knob or of how, when I tiptoed down to Marianne's room, I found Richard with her, white-faced, rocking her thin body against him. They were both crying.

After that Richard often came home from work too late to say good-night. And sometimes he did not come at all.

If I missed Marianne sharing the Big Room or Richard's long good-nights, I did not admit it. I cried many times, secretly, when Perdita the cat died, but when Kay sat on the end of my bed and told me unhappily that things were going on between her and Richard which I could not be expected to understand, I felt curiously little interest. Knowing that some kind of sympathetic response was being solicited, I would nod with appropriate gravity and offer noncommittal comments from inside my carapace. As soon as she had gone I would dive back into the book I was reading, taking advantage of the fact that in her present state of mind she was more lenient about Lights Out time.

It was different for Marianne. When Kay went to talk to her she listened with her whole being, her eyes, ever-widening as her face grew thinner, alive to every nuance, every hint as to what was going on. And when Richard sat with her she gave him the same breathless attention. She also gave him a small ocean of childish loyalty and everything she knew of love.

I had accepted from an early age that Marianne was not only brighter than me—described as "the academic one"—but also more attractive. Dark and fine-boned with pale, clear skin and glossy brown hair, she was like a pretty Arab pony, beside whom I remained for years a scruffy Shetland—what bones I had lost beneath cheeks stubbornly rosy and round. The change that came over Marianne when the family began to divide was profound, and she used every ounce of her considerable intelligence to conceal it from the rest of the world.

It began when she announced that from now on she would make her own breakfast. She went down ahead of the rest of the family, fed Annie, the little mongrel who outlived and outsmarted all our more exotic pets, and made herself a piece of toast. The first morning I found the toast, still warm and unbitten, under a scrumple of paper in the dustbin, I was mildly surprised, but after a while it become automatic to check it was there. Sometimes I ate it. Marianne's plate, knife laid across a strategic scattering of crumbs, was left by the sink with a mug in which milk had been swirled. Tacitly loyal, I said nothing about this regular waste either to Marianne or the grown-ups. But I wondered at it all the same.

Avoiding lunch was not difficult for her. She simply tipped the contents of her lunchbox down the school lavatory. And at tea, as soon as Kay's back was turned, she shoveled everything she did not want into our brother James's eager mouth. It was Richard, with his casual habit of offering a bite of whatever was especially good on his plate, who presented the only real problem, and in dealing with this Marianne employed her most subtle tactic: she accepted. Richard did not know for a long time that the odd nibbles she took from his hand were often the only nourishment she had. When he did not come home to supper, she starved.

Weeks, perhaps months, went by while her crusade continued undetected. It was only when she started to avoid Games at school, hiding in the cloakrooms because she knew she was too weak to run, that people began to wake up to what was going on. By then it was almost too late to arrest the downward trend. And inside her shrinking body other insidious things were happening.

Words had always interested me. Now there were several new ones around. *Anorexia* was repeated often enough to become ordinary sounding after a while. Then there was *duodenal colic* with a question mark, followed by *psychosomatic* and then *peritonitis*, no question mark, and finally *peritoneal abcess*. Somewhere here the nonmedical term *adultery* slipped in and somewhere here, too, Kay, under pressure miles beyond my ken, gave vent to a revelation for which, with childish brutality, I punished her for years.

It was after the grown-ups' supper and James was in bed. Marianne was in her room, ill, and Richard had left the house after a row I had not heard. I went into the dining room, where Kay was slowly clearing the table. Her movements were wooden and her face frighteningly sad. The paisley apron she wore for washing up hung over the back of a chair. She put it on now, carelessly flattening her hair. I hesitated by the door, wanting to go through to the kitchen for a glass of water but not wanting to get involved with Kay. I guessed there had been a row and knew there was very little safe to say.

"Can I just get some water?"

I hovered with my glass, poised to bolt through. Kay pulled a plate toward her, rucking the tablecloth.

"What?" she said, the word a small, bitter explosion, "are you talking to me? Of course you can get some water. Do what you like. You all do what you like in this house."

I started to walk past the huge painting on the wall, Madonna and Child with fruit. The baby in it looked vacant and old and the mother had a sixth finger half erased. Kay held out a pile of plates.

"Take these with you as you go."

Her voice sounded brittle, as though it would break if she allowed it to soften. The dishes she was collecting slithered together and a fork fell to the carpet, strewing an arc of cold gravy. She asked me to bring a cloth.

In the kitchen I found the cloth screwed up in a ball beside the sink. A few days before I had seen her kill a spider with it, a spider I had pointed out because I liked the way it walked. She used it now on the bread board with slow, crumb-crushing swipes. Her eyes, cold with misery, stared ahead unseeingly.

All at once I no longer wanted to escape but to smash this mood I had seen so often. I knew she was in pain but I did not care. I plowed in pitilessly with a line guaranteed to make her explode.

"Where's Richard? What did you say to make him go away?"

Her hands gripped the bread board, holding the knife slotted down one side.

"What did I say? What did *I* say? Why don't you take a look at your wonderful father for a change? What do you think he is doing right now—thinking about you, thinking about Marianne up there half dead because of him? No, I'll tell you . . ."

I hated the writhing shape of her lips.

"Shut up, shut up!"

One of Kay's hands flew out from the bread board. The knife was in it.

"Don't you dare tell me to shut up! Who the hell do you think you are? If it wasn't for a hole in a condom you wouldn't even be here— I never planned to have you so soon after Marianne. Don't you think I had enough on my plate?"

"Well, I *am* here!" I shouted, grabbing the bread board and leaving her waving the knife. "I *am* here! And if I was an accident"—I looked at the spilled gravy, the rumpled cloth—"I bet it was your fault. I bet you used an old *thing*!"

"Get out of my sight, you little bitch!"

I went.

As usual, I felt ashamed for having deliberately baited Kay, but from the detached, fly-on-the-wall point of view I was intrigued. The bit about the condom was new. Her words conjured up a film-strip image of myself in miniature, boxing my way through a hole in the void to burst upon the universe with fists raised.

"I am here!" I thought again excitedly, as I stood on my head before going to bed that night. And the knowledge that I had entered the world uninvited made me feel fierce and special.

"I am here!" I thought again and again. "I am alive!"

For a long time Marianne was in hospital. When she came out, her bags were taken into a downstairs room, Richard's old studio. I was called to come and say hello. Pleased that she was back I bounded down the stairs, bursting with things to say. Just inside the door I stopped short, every word eclipsed.

A set of clothes had been made for her while she was away, a skirt, waistcoat and jacket in green tweedy material. Marianne had just finished putting it on when I came in. And that was the only reason I believed it was her. From beneath a short pudding-basin of thin, mouse-colored hair, one side of her mouth twitched upwards. Lines like pencilled algebraic symbols broke out where a dimple used to be.

"Hello, duck."

It was our private greeting. At least her voice was her own. Very slowly, as if her body were a jumble of glass coat hangers, she stooped to pull up her tights. Thick nylon mesh was bunched in wrinkles over each transparent ankle. Her calves were bowed out and flattened like stripped wishbones. There were heavy suede shoes on her feet. I sat down on the edge of a big lounge chair watching as her white fingers tugged at the laces.

" 'lo, duck. Why are you wearing those old-lady shoes?"

"Mummy bought them specially. They're 'sensible.' "

"Sensible" to us meant boring and unattractive. Teachers were sensible. There was a knock on the already open door and Kay came in smiling, her brightness painfully strained. She had a friend with her in the lounge and had made coffee. There was a mug for each of us and a plate of ginger biscuits. In a moment she bustled out and we heard the tail end of a sentence—"leave the girls to get on with it"—as she went in to join her friend. I wriggled under the formality, feeling like a visitor.

"Shall I get Annie?" I said, thinking the presence of the dog might help.

"Not allowed," said Marianne, indicating a Kay decree with a familiar movement of her head.

"Do you want her?"

There was a nod and a tiny hint of the old conspiratorial gleam. I opened one of the windows on to the garden. It was easy just to step out. Annie was very excited to see Marianne and her cries of welcome had to be stifled with a cushion. When she was calmer we sat her on a chair and threw ginger biscuits for her to catch.

"Was it horrible?" I asked, meaning the hospital and everything.

"Yes," said Marianne, and then rather proudly, "I've got lesions."

There was a pause as I wondered how best to respond to this.

"Foreign lesions?"

We giggled. Suddenly I found myself telling her how I had been kissed for the first time on my last day in France. It was in a lift and the man had put a lot of spit in my mouth and I did not know what to do with it.

"So what did you do?"

Marianne's great eyes were right there with me in the lift.

"Pretended to bury my face in his chest and dribbled it down his jumper. It was awful, left a great wet stain."

Marianne laughed, a lovely, tinkly sound. I wished I did not think of glass coat hangers every time her bones moved.

"Tell me more," she said, "more, more, more."

And telling true stories of things that happened to me became the role I played with Marianne: the more details of faces, dialogues and scenes I remembered, the more raptly she listened. It was like a living version of Chatter: I had stepped into Joey's shoes.

The day came for me to meet "the other woman." We had all known there was one for some time. I furrowed my brow at Richard when he made the suggestion.

"What on earth will we talk about?"

He looked wicked for a moment, screwing up his eyes in imitation of Annie at her most prima donna'ish, wagging an imaginary tail and saying, "Me!"

Then he sat up properly and thought for a moment.

"Horses. You're both mad about horses. She used to teach riding."

Oh no, I thought. I was not mad about horses, I was terrified of them; had only endured the years of Saturday-morning hacks in Bushy Park to keep up with Marianne.

"And she's done quite a lot of acting," he went on. "She was in a feature film when she was twelve."

Worse and worse. When I was younger, keen on dancing and reciting poetry, I had announced that I wanted to be an actress. This had made Kay bite her lip and lit Richard's face with a smile which said: "I've been waiting for this," but that ambition was out of date now. I wondered if I ought to wash my hair before visiting Edwina.

In the end I went as I was, in an old brown duffel coat with a book in each pocket; the *Odyssey* and a James Bond. Arriving early, I sat against some railings near her flat, reading until it was time to go in. I was still mentally lashed to the mast as Odysseus' ship passed the island of the Sirens when Edwina opened the door, and I gave a jump when I recognized her.

If I had been expecting a familiar face at all it was that of the woman in the green pant suit. But this was another, a girl glimpsed fleetingly on an occasion when I played a part in one of Richard's commercials. The impression then had been of a tall, wind-ruffled figure always in a hurry. She looked different now, much more sophisticated. The flat she lived in was very tidy. The only thing that matched the former dashing image was a huge colorful bedspread woven of subtly matched silks. I fingered its rich texture while she was out of the room. From the kitchen she called to ask if I would like to hang up my coat. I did, noticing that she had a duffel coat too, then I wandered through to watch her arranging tea things on a tray. Her hands were businesslike. The teapot had been properly warmed.

We sat at a low table in the main room. The minutes while the tea brewed seemed very long. Edwina brought in some shortbread still warm from the oven.

"That smells good," I said, and sought for the right descriptive word, ". . . homely." An unfortunate choice.

Edwina poured, holding the lid on the teapot. The weewee gurgle of the sound brought a hysterical lump into my chest. I was enormously relieved when it stopped. It was not a good moment to giggle.

"Do you like cooking?" asked Edwina pleasantly.

"Quite. I can make fudge."

She offered me a piece of shortbread. The inside of it was exactly the same color as the jerkin she wore, which complemented her dark hair well but looked as though it were made out of a blanket.

"Richard says you're a good cook," I said, keen not to let the conversation die, "and very economical."

Edwina gave a loud neigh of laughter, long eyebrows moving up and down merrily. She was not wearing any makeup and her face had little natural color. It was the dark eyes and wide, laughing mouth that made her attractive. I wanted to know how often she washed her hair, which shook like a mane. That reminded me of the horses. We both started speaking at the same time.

"I gather that . . ."

"Richard says that . . ."

There was a silly moment of confusion while we both apologized. Then Edwina completed her sentence first.

"I gather you're keen on horses."

I decided to risk the truth.

"Actually," I said, with what I hoped was a confiding look, "I'm scared stiff of them."

"Really? But I thought . . ."

I nodded and out it all poured. It was Marianne who was—who used to be—the keen rider. She was very good, always given the most difficult pony in the stables and sent to canter ahead while I, clinging miserably to the pommel when no one was looking, skulked at the back, wishing I did not exist. The mud flying, reins slapping and hot snorting so horrified me that sometimes I would hurl myself deliberately into the stinging nettles just so it would be over. Once I broke my wrist doing this but was so ashamed I got back on and kept quiet until the whole arm swelled so badly in the night I could not get my pajama top off or on, and eventually had to go to hospital with the sleeves wrapped embarrassingly round my neck.

Edwina seemed very understanding about all this.

"What you need," she said, "is a quiet pony you could get used to by yourself."

I agreed. To give up altogether would be an acknowledgment of personal weakness, the thing I most feared in myself and others. Weak people got left behind by strong people like Richard.

When Edwina and I said goodbye we smiled a lot and if I had been a boy we would have shaken hands. As it was I ducked my head in friendly farewell one last time and went out into the street hands in pockets. At the bus stop I found out what had happened to Odysseus

—he survived the blandishments of the Sirens by stopping his ears with wax—and started on a James Bond.

Kay, Marianne and Edwina. One thing they all had in common was Richard as a focal point in their lives. And who was that actress with the kitten playing in a forest of black hair—he described her on the telephone, all husky and vibrant and come-and-see-me-soon—and the tall, fair one who was so beautiful and had a Swedish name? Would I ever meet the Indian lady who wooed him from his dark moods with solo performances of Bach on the violin or the one who bought him bedroom slippers and a dressing gown, which made him run away?

No, that era was over. There would be no more commercials, no more pretty actresses, no more family holidays and no more after-supper rows. The dreams Richard had sketched when he visited me at St. Paul's were now becoming realities. He did sail to Scotland but instead of buying a small croft to write in, which had been the original plan, he bought a hotel.

For a short period after Richard left I moved into an open residential unit on the advice of the Child Guidance people. The lady I had talked to about Chatter thought a supervised break from the home environment might ease pressures all round. Marianne was slowly recovering— physically at least—but things were difficult for Kay and my presence did not help. Once, after angry words, I banged the back door so hard all the glass shattered. Kay was convinced I had done this deliberately with my lacrosse stick which happened to be lying near by. The implication that I was being untruthful so enraged me that I smashed every piece of furniture in the Big Room and announced that *that* had been done on purpose but the back door was an accident. From that time on I slept on a mattress on the floor and found pleasure in the clarity of the empty room. Kay wept and raged at my behavior but callously I ignored her. I could not help blaming her in some way for having let Richard go.

Then one day the call I had been waiting for came. It was always a special event when Richard phoned. Kay would speak to him first in her bedroom, then Marianne, huddled over the extension in the studio. Occasionally James would have a few words upstairs under Kay's eye and then it was my turn and I would stand in the hall and speak loudly so everyone could hear. On this occasion he said simply, ''Come,'' and I said, ''Yes.''

Afterwards he and Kay talked for a long time and Marianne, who had been listening on the extension, told me they had been discussing the problem of my education. Apparently I was going to have private lessons and there was also mention of another school where I might board next year. I wrinkled my brow significantly at Marianne.

"I shouldn't worry," she said. "He sounded as though he was only saying it to keep Kay happy."

Since Richard had gone she had begun calling Kay by name, but when she woke sobbing in the night the cry on her lips was always: "Daddy, Daddy, Daddy!" She would be seeing him again after her term of private lessons had come to an end. For Marianne, too, had turned her back on conventional education. None of us knew then how finally the child in her had died.

4

"Look."

I looked.

Lead-colored mountains pressed back in a bunch against the evening light, old and proud as veterans in a reunion pose. A still loch threw off a shallow glow, uneven edges soaking into bogland and waterlogged reeds.

Before, the landscape had been a dim, grand scene in the distance. But here, on the fifteen-mile single-track road leading to the coast, it was bang in front of us and all around. Our left front wheel mashed a tuft of yellowish fleece into a line of sheep droppings and Richard began to talk again.

It was late March, almost a year to the day he had visited me at St. Paul's. This time he was driving a mud-spattered Land-Rover loaded with straw and sacks of animal feed, swinging it round blind bends on the Highland road with the same casual virtuosity he had handled the Bristol. March for him meant less than a month before the opening of the hotel. My imagination blinked as he made rapid verbal sketches of half-a-dozen already burgeoning schemes. He leaped from one topic to another—goat husbandry, kipper smoking, pigpen building— creating an image of a hotel quite unlike any other I had seen. That was his vision too.

In the middle of an enthusiastic monologue on the virtues of producing methane gas from pig manure, he broke off suddenly and said, "I want you to think of this place as home." Then he was off again.

As we drove on with the glimmering loch on one side and rocks close enough to touch on the other, I hugged his words to me. That was what he was doing: digging, planting, building—he was making a home, something 309 had not felt like since I was too young to know the difference. A warm bubble of anticipation rose in me and I gazed out at the mountains and smiled. They were crazy shapes. The crazy shapes of home.

*   *   *

I had not expected there to be a car park or for the sea to be only two fields away. There were islands out there, dark hummocky clods like gingerbread spilled from a pan. Inland, beyond the row of houses straggled above the road like knots in a string—the hotel the biggest knot—there were mountains and sky, mountains and sky. We did not go into the car park—that was for when the guests came—but up a small side road with a sign at the top saying PUBLIC BAR. Richard swerved to avoid a fat puppy which waddled forward to greet us wagging its entire body.

"That's Caillach," he said. "She hasn't learned about cars yet." The name means something like little old lady in Gaelic.

The kitchen door was open. Edwina stood before an enamel sink as long as a trough straining hot liquid through a triangular sieve. I had never seen a sieve that shape before. Nor had I ever seen Richard and Edwina kissing. I looked at the sieve. When they were detached, Edwina said a cheery hello and got on with what she was doing. Richard showed me to my room and told me that supper was at seven-thirty.

There were two single beds in the room. Automatically I chose the one nearest the window and looked out. There was not much to see: just a wall and a rickety sort of pen closed in at one end. I let the net curtain fall and set to unpacking. The room, which had looked dark and blank at first, improved as soon as my duffel coat and dressing gown were hanging on the door and my prune-stone and walnut necklace looped over the mirror. I was sitting on the bed dreaming of how I would gradually collect things to cover the blank surfaces when Richard's stride came along the corridor.

"Supper," he called, drumming three fingers lightly against the door, and strode away again.

Soup was already on the table in the kitchen. There were five places set and as I hovered, wondering which was mine, two men in work clothes came in and sat down opposite a place which was clearly Edwina's, near the stove. I sat on the smaller of the two stools left and immediately wished I had not as it made me lower than everyone else. Richard came in last and ate quickly to catch up. Edwina had the main course dished up before the first soup spoon went down. Everyone had exactly the same on his plate and although I was not sure what it was, it was good. Richard said so and Edwina hrummphed absently. She was making notes in a large diary while she ate. The workmen responded with polite och ayes to comments Richard made concerning dwangs and spirit-levels. Otherwise there was no sound but the scraping of steel on china and occasional glops and rattlings from a pot on the stove. Edwina poured mugs of tea to go with pudding, which was a serious steamed affair, then the plates were collected and the table cleared. I was impressed by the efficiency of it all. Should I offer to do the washing up? But Edwina was already at the sink. The drying, then.

"Oh, I usually leave it to drain."

Her arms plunged about briskly in the soapy water. It was clear she did not need any help.

Richard was at the back door, talking to the workmen. It was dark outside. Not knowing where else to go, I went to bed. I looked forward to becoming part of things so that I would not feel strange any more. After all, this was to be my real home.

In the middle of the night I was woken by a loud noise. It was a straining, pressureful sound, as though something of great weight were trying to rub its way through a barrier. It sounded close. Feeling for my torch I crawled to the end of the bed and cautiously pushed up the window. The beam shone on to a nude mountain of hairy flesh moving back and forth systematically and with evident pleasure. Embedded in the flesh was an ecstatically slitted eye fringed about with short blond lashes. Without interrupting the rhythmic rubbings of its body, the eye widened and stared unflinchingly into the light. I withdrew my head from the window but continued to watch, riveted. My neighbor, a pig bigger than I ever could have imagined, was clearly engaged in very private business.

A new sound added itself to the creaking and straining—a succession of low, hoarse breaths cut off sharply at the peak of each rise. I crouched motionless on the bed, staring at bliss and listening to agony. Until I realized the agony was bliss as well. The new sound came from indoors.

I dropped to the floor and crawled across to sit with my head locked tight against the door. Through the thin walls of the corridor between Richard and Edwina's room and mine the dragging gasps shuddered and swung. The volume rose and the seconds between breaths grew shorter until there was no space and one hoarse whoop crashed into the next, gathering at last to one continuous braying din. When I knew it could go no further, I felt my face flush and clapped my hands over my ears. Just too late to smother the final cry of "Richard!"

Breakfast was punctually at eight. Porridge with thick Jersey cream, followed by eggs with yolks as bright as ox-eye daisies. Edwina had already milked the cows and fed the hens. I watched covertly as she moved around the big kitchen, mane of hair scraped back, tweed-covered hips businesslike. Her breasts, neatly harnessed under a dark sweater, did not swing as she worked. She wore the ultimate in "sensible" shoes.

After whisking the table clear she gave her cheery smile and took me on a tour of the domestic facilities. Here was the place to leave dirty laundry and this was where the Hoover lived. Aprons were in a cupboard in the hall and all boots and outdoor shoes went into the drying room. Clean linen was upstairs—please use only those sheets and towels marked Staff. I would find toothpaste and shampoo in the downstairs bathroom. Anything else I needed, I was to ask. Picking up a bucket and a can of paint stripper, she strode away to attack a room. I thanked her disappearing back and plodded off to fetch my boots.

Richard was talking to the pig outside my room, scratching its back and muttering under the bristly flap of an ear. I went out to join them.

"It's huge," I said, standing with hands firmly in pockets as the rude snout snuffed wetly at me through the chicken wire. I did not tell him about its performance in the night, because then he would know I had heard the other thing, too.

"He's called Hairy Hans," said Richard. "Come and meet the girls."

We walked down past the bar and car park into the field below the road. Wind rattled the gate behind us. I noticed the islands looked greener by daylight, and not so far away.

The three young sows were named Freeman, Hardy and Willis, after a shoe shop. Richard explained that it was the first shop he had passed when bringing them home.

"Willis is chief wife. She'll be the first to produce. The other two are more like concubines." He tickled Willis's ear and she rubbed her long, slobbery jaws against his leg. "When Hairy Hans turns into bacon next year we'll have to go on to AI."

He noticed my questioning look.

"Artificial Insemination. I'm going to learn to do it myself. But you won't mind, will you, old friend?"

Willis did not look as if she would.

Richard introduced me to the cows: a big, buttery Jersey with pool-brown googoo eyes and a smaller one called the Heifer. There should be a calf in June. In another field were the goats, Linty and Emma. Emma nibbled his sleeve and playfully butted him with her small, snub-horned brow but when I stretched out a hand she backed away.

"They'll soon get to know you when you've milked them a few times. Watch Edwina this evening. She'll show you how to do the hens too. You'd like to have a shot at doing the animals, wouldn't you?"

"Yes."

But I was sure I would never be as good as Edwina.

The animals were a crucial part of Richard's plans for self-sufficiency. He talked to them, scratched their backs, made houses for them and treated them as friends, but not one of them was there without a purpose. While learning to tend the animals I learned the relationship between field and kitchen, animal and man; while one hand kills to feed, the other feeds to kill. When the time came to test the culinary use of a hen which had gone off the lay, it was I who fed it, Richard who broke its neck and Edwina who cooked it. We all ate it and after the bones had been boiled for stock they went back to the hen field in the next feed bucket. Bonemeal was good for strengthening eggshells.

I did not mind squelching up to the hen field to scatter potato peelings and feel in the straw-lined beer crates for eggs; I had no objection to driving the dawdlesome cows from byre to field and back again; even Linty's tridirectional squirting teats did not bother me once I had mastered the art of keeping her back legs out of the milking bucket—but I would have given almost anything to avoid taking the swill down to Willis and Co.

The trouble began when Hairy Hans was moved in with the girls to perform his conjugal duties.

"Is he safe?" I asked Richard as I lifted the heavy buckets of swill.

"Of course he is," said Richard, impatient at any sign of cissiness. As I set off he called after me with a grin, "Just don't let him get on top of you!"

That was exactly what I was afraid of.

The minute they heard the clomp of my boots and the slop-slap of swill spilling into the tops of them, every pig in the field came charging toward the gate. Every pig except Hans. He was waiting by the trough and all I could see of him as I sloshed down the field, yelling at Freeman, Hardy and Willis as they shoved their faces into the buckets, was his long, pink, imperiously questing snout. As the distance between us narrowed I could hear above the squealing of the girls cozy, expectant little grunts rumbling up from somewhere in his huge gut. Then he would emerge.

The first time I saw his erect penis I dropped both buckets and ran. It was about two feet long, twizzled like a corkscrew and *multicolored*.

I had to go back for another look. I wondered what sort of connection there was between his brain and the end of that thing to enable him to aim straight. It must be very difficult if Willis was not helpful.

After a few weeks a letter from the education authorities recalled Richard to the arrangements he had made for my continued schooling. This coincided with the arrival in dribs and drabs of ground and hotel staff, and when I returned from my first lesson I was not unduly put out to find Edwina going through the animal routine with a stranger. The new girl was huge and could handle seventy-pound feeding sacks with ease, but she still cried buckets when Hairy Hans bit her in the thigh one morning. I sympathized from a safe distance when Richard implied that it had only happened because she failed to understand the pig's character. It irritated all the staff that none of the animals ever bit him.

If efforts to rechannel me into conventional education had been half-hearted before, they now became token in the extreme. Once a week I went to the head of the local junior school for tuition in basic Maths, and a lady in a cottage above the fishing pier made patient attempts to civilize my French. There was talk of History and Geography but neither went further than a run-through of ground already covered. The most instructive study period came on a Sunday afternoon when I walked a mile to the house of a local lady artist and joined her for a session of painting and tea.

Her house, standing alone on a flat stretch of moorland, smelled cozily of mold and old coffee grounds. She was very English and very much a lady and her crystal-clear enunciation of every syllable delighted me. She waited for the kettle to boil with a faraway expression and ash from an expertly cocked cigarette flaking gently over mannishly cut trousers. Her eyes dropped in a sad lost way whenever she mentioned her late husband. I liked to think how happy the house must have been when he was alive.

We took our tea in the studio or in the garden if the weather were fine. I showed my appreciation of her excellent cake by eating a great deal of it. She paid me the compliment of talking as though, at fourteen, I were as much a woman of the world as any of her old companions at the Slade. We got on very well and I quite enjoyed the painting part too.

Initially, to avoid meeting people on the single village road, I walked to all my lessons over the hills. Feelings toward Richard among the local people were ambivalent. On the one hand he was admired for applying himself to the backbreaking task of transforming their modest old guesthouse into a uniquely self-sufficient hotel; on the other he was viewed with skepticism as an upstart Sassenach who would soon lose heart and go home to the soft South. As his daughter, I was looked upon as an extension of him who might provide interesting material for gossip. I found the frankly probing stares of Kirk-going women and watery-eyed old crofters hard to take, so I used the hills, which they only used for sheep, as a refuge. I did not know how readily their curiosity could turn to friendliness.

I had memories of long trudges in the Highlands, dating from the times Richard and Kay rented a holiday cottage near Lochinver. We went there several years running, accompanied by different au pairs, and sometimes Richard was with us and sometimes he was not. After the last time, when school had started again and everyone had to write essays on what they did in the holidays, I had to squeeze my imagination hard for impressions of Scotland other than chapped thighs and midge bites, Marianne being sick in the car and Kay getting in a rage because three-year-old James kept chanting "fuckfuckfuck' with a beatific smile. He had learned the word from her when she dropped a tray on the cottage floor. Pressed for a description of scenery, I conjured up an image of a long, snaky road with a lot of squashed frogs on it and a high rock ledge over a sandy bay which Marianne dared to jump off and I did not. The fields were more brown than green and several had Aberdeen Angus bulls in them. The mountains were tall and brown and looming.

It took the secret joys and loneliness of puberty to open my eyes to the mysteries of that brown, looming land.

To begin with I kept my head down while walking to avoid twisting an ankle between tussocks. Even so I fell down often: town-bred limbs wobbling, stiff-booted feet sliding on the banks of hidden burns. Then my hands would fly out, clutching air, and I would land with a thump, momentarily winded, and lie still, feeling the black ground press its moisture through my clothes and hearing the soft crackle of heather stalks crushed against my palms. Sprawled like that, I heard for the first time the sound of sheep munching grass, the squeaky pull of stems breaking, the whispered creak of earth forced to yield. I lay and listened to it, idly tracing fissures in the black bog surface which had already begun to crack under the first spring sun.

There was a rock part way to the lady artist's house from which, after the first few journeys, I could judge the timing of my descent accurately. The hill was strewn with rocks, as though some giant had crumbled the mountain tops and played a lonely game of marbles with the debris, but this one was special because it was the first stop from which no human habitation could be seen. There was just the sea before me, the sky above and an endless hinterland of brown valleys and gray hills. But gradually I learned that each of those vistas had only one constant, and that was change.

My nose became familiar with the warm smell of peat, my cheeks with the scratch of heather, my toes with the iron-cold kiss of a mountain burn. When I rubbed at the patterns of yellow-gray lichen on rocks, my fingers came away with an ochre stain. From other rocks the stain was bread mold blue. Through trial and error, and sodden thighs, I learned to distinguish the alluring emerald of bog moss from the matt shades indicating firm ground. Many a time I lay prone at full-belly stretch to grasp a fistful of silken strands from a pink hummock in the center of a treacly pool. I would slip and stumble yards up a rushing burn to press palms against the living resilience of tiny moss islands, dark and soft as moles. The damp brown hills were a feast for hands just beginning to learn the beauty of feel.

And as I walked a little further every day, my clumsy limbs began to strengthen. I grew confident about the width of burns to be taken in stride, challenged myself to leap others. Coming down the hills I learned to zigzag, running; flexing my hips to keep the pace light, swiveling my upper body with arms outflung for balance. I felt my young breasts jump and I laughed for no reason. Near the hotel the geese honked as I ran past their field and Caillach the labrador puppy squirmed up reproachfully to lick my hands. She had her walk in the evenings with Edwina, a never-changing tramp down the road to the postbox.

At that early stage in the evolution of the hotel, Richard and Edwina were experimenting on all fronts. Neither had worked in a hotel before and neither had smoked kippers or kept pigs. But they had a vision of what as guests they would like to see and their standards were uncompromisingly high. Edwina, naturally pale, acquired the blanched look of a prisoner who rarely sees the sun. I had never seen anyone work so hard and when I saw her arm snake over Richard's shoulder as he stood anxiously studying a list, or watched them together, digging foundations and shoveling manure, she seemed to me like a white Amazon beside whom anyone else would look small. It was impossible to resent the fact that under her thrall the hotel would flourish but never be a home in more than a mechanical sense for the three children of her lover. We were an overhang from the past. The luxury of regular meals and a meticulous laundry service hardly compensated for this, but it helped. And perhaps Edwina saw more than I knew for she gave me the means to explore deeper into my own developing personality, as well as the hill which I was growing to love. She gave me a pony.

Before anything else, though, for every individual involved in the hotel, came work.

For a month my name was down on the duty roster for breakfast and dinner service, which included laying up the dining room before and Hoovering and glass polishing afterward. This left the middle of the day free, ostensibly for studies. Like all the other waitresses, I was equipped with a neat little Black Watch kilt and instructions to treat the guests as though they were special visitors in my own home. If, feeling more like a stranger in theirs, I saw any irony in this, I did not express it, concentrating all my attention on doing the job as well as, if not better than, the older girls.

Soon I learned how to tackle the two most daunting installations in the kitchen: the washing-up machine and the chef. Both were capable of giving vent to odious torrents if mishandled. The chef was a large, purple-lipped Liverpudlian called Gordon. He had an impressive chimney hat and an unpleasant habit of wheezing through his teeth while taking half-inch drags of cigarettes he was not supposed to have in the kitchen. His breath was strong and fishy and I avoided close contact with him, grabbing the dishes he set down with a forbidding expression which was transformed into a charming smile in the brief space between kitchen and dining room.

Breakfast waitressing, I found, was more enjoyable than the dinner shift. The guests came wandering into the dining room from seven-thirty onwards, blinking in sleepy appreciation of the morning-lit vista of sea and islands. Thermoses would appear on tables if the day looked promising and I would note down requests for boats on lochs and packed lunches, along with porridge and finnan haddies. It was a matter of pride to me that everyone got their order promptly and I took pleasure in the subtle rapport established with each table. It was funny how differently people behaved in the evenings, dressed up and talking with louder, less friendly voices, not always returning my smile. That all changed when Richard, keen to use any potential not going in an academic direction, carved out a special role for me which upped my status considerably. But that did not happen until after Dossan and I spent the best part of many a day "studying" on the hill.

Dossan means fringe or forelock in Gaelic and because that was the first thing one noticed about my pony, that was what she was called. Her body was soft dun with a smudgy dorsal stripe running the length of a well-upholstered spine. Edwina had not forgotten that I was afraid of horses and had deliberately chosen one which was not too lively. But sure-footed and strong, Dossan was a true garron and Richard had his eye on her for hauling stags at the end of the season. By that time, however, she had unlearned most of her civilized ways, for I rode her bareback, unshod, and sometimes with only a rope in lieu of reins.

There was nothing miraculous about the transition from timorous pommel-clinger to bold bareback rider. Day after day I led Dossan out of sight of the hotel and often onwards for as much as a mile before I plucked up the courage to mount. I abandoned the saddle because of a recurrent vision of being dragged over the hills with one foot stuck in a stirrup. Also, without a saddle I could jump off easily and roll away, something I practiced over and over again.

Two weeks, perhaps three, of cautious ambling and falling practice went by before the next breakthrough, which happened as a result of my being late for work. I turned Dossan's head in the direction of home and, perhaps sensing my feeling of urgency, she broke into a trot. Bouncing hectically I clung on with everything, including heels. Obediently her stride quickened and become a canter. The increased comfort of the movement came as such a relief that when I felt her slowing again I urged her on. Dossan delivered me, snorting a little after her unaccustomed leg-stretch, at our normal stopping place outside the byre. Richard and Edwina both happened to be in the yard.

"That was rather a grand entrance," said Richard, smiling approvingly.

Edwina looked at my flushed face and fingers still knotted in the mane. I blessed her for saying nothing.

Next day I forced myself to do it again, only this time under control. With Dossan's head pointing straight up the hill I leaned forward, clove to her like a suction pad and told her to go. She went, and although it would be untrue to say we never looked back, the surge of exhilaration I felt as her body answered mine marked a turning point.

And, as often happens, one small personal triumph led to increased confidence in other fields. When Richard asked if I would like to have a go at some baking for the hotel, I embraced the idea as a brand new challenge.

* * *

It began with a few modest trays of shortbread for packed lunches and progressed swiftly to fancy cakes for afternoon teas. Recipes, I found, were easy to follow and improvisation amusing. The climax was a nightly extravaganza known as Lucy's Sweet Trolley. This last appeared on the dinner menu with asterisks round it like the star-turn in a cabaret and Richard stage-managed the whole performance with all his old film-directing flair. Every evening, on cue, I made a grand entrance, wheeling before me the most extraordinary collection of desserts ever to grace Highland cuisine. Most were of my own invention, all were of my own concoction and some—Jacobite Grenades, Mocha Genghis Khan and Goat's Milk Bavarois to name a few—were undeniably strange.

It was Richard's master stroke to deck me out to match my wares and make me stop at each table and recite the name of each dish. I did not have to be told to address my remarks principally to the head of table, for I was on the cusp of feminine awakening and I knew. Staring steadily from behind a curtain of long fair hair into the eyes of the nearest most impressive male, I gravely recommended cream-filled chocolate-covered Pretender's Balls. On more than one occasion a mouth fell open and deftly I would pop one in.

I loved the way Richard stroked my hair and looked proud when some parties of men asked for second helpings and kept me chatting at their tables. It was somehow less exciting when ladies asked for recipes.

Lucy's Sweet Trolley lasted all through that season and through all the changes of kitchen hierarchy. When Gordon left, taking his bad breath and wheezes back to Liverpool, and Gilbert moved in, my position was well established. It must have been strange for a fat Aberdonian chef, most of whose experiences, culinary or otherwise, had been picked up in the merchant navy, to share a kitchen with a nubile fourteen-year-old, who leaped around in jeans and scanty blouses during the day and appeared like the prize plum in a harem at night. A barman from Glasgow joined the team at the same time and when Marianne, stronger but still withdrawn, arrived part way through the season, she and I became the butt of many a ribald exchange between the two Scots.

It was unfortunate that Marianne should choose the barman for her first virginal crush. I was intrigued to know what she did with him and when I learned that things went further than salivary kisses felt I had to look into the matter myself.

On evenings when my performance with the sweet trolley had been a particular success I found it difficult to wind down. I would lie awake, covers kicked to the bottom of the bed, squirming restlessly until Marianne returned from her nightly visit to the barman. One evening, when she came in looking more flushed than usual, I asked her straight out if she would mind if I went and had a go. She sat on her bed regarding me dully. Neither her eyes nor her spirit had ever fully regained their luster after her illness.

"I don't mind," she said at last, bending to find her slippers under the bed so that I could see how thin the hair lay over her skull. "Anyway he fancies you."

"Does he?" I sat up with a jerk, entranced by the idea. "How do you know?" "Said so." She swung herself under the covers and added, with eyes closed, "But he reckons you're out of bounds."

"What do you mean?"

"Too young."

"But you're only fifteen months older."

She was settling down to sleep, but before she turned over she said, "Makes all the difference. Age of consent."

I did not understand, had to go and find out immediately. As I pulled on my jeans I said to her still back, "Are you sure you don't mind?"

Some part of me was distantly aware of how damning the change from prettiest, brightest daughter to sad shadow must have been for her. Her voice came out flat but I was too excited to care.

"I told you, I don't mind."

The barman was getting ready for bed when I presented myself at his door. His shirt was off and belt unbuckled. I thought at once how disappointing his chest was.

"Lucy!" he said, broad Glaswegian accent full of surprise. "What can I do for you?"

I insinuated myself into the room and faced him squarely. He was standing, back to the wash-hand basin, fingering his chin. I noticed on a shelf behind him a bottle of spot-clearing lotion. It obviously did not work.

"Is it true that you fancy me?"

His fingers stopped moving on his chin. He made a sputtery sound, well sprinkled with ochs, which I understood to be mostly positive.

"Kiss me, then."

I suddenly found myself on his knee in the dressing table chair. He was rubbing acne enthusiastically into my neck and muttering about jailbait. I held him away and said, "Do it properly, like you do to Marianne."

He immediately wanted to know what Marianne had been saying and did she know I was here and did anybody else know. I fidgeted impatiently. Talk was not what I had come for. Wriggling down lower on his lap I positioned myself so that his mouth was directly above mine. My jumper had risen a little and in a moment his hand was inside it and his face was rushing down toward mine in a blur. I closed my eyes and for a few seconds everything was strange and wonderful. Then all at once his tongue was in my mouth flailing about like a wedge of wet spam. I was so shaken that for a moment I could not react in any way. There was a quality of intimacy behind that raw, visceral invasion which brought a conclusion to my mind like a slap. For this to work you had to fancy them back. You even had to like their pimples.

I pulled my jumper down and wiped my mouth on a sleeve. The barman looked ready for another go but I was already off his lap and at the door.

"What's up? Did you no' like yer wee kiss?"

"Yes, thank you," I lied, hand on the doorknob. "But I don't want another one just now."

I rushed off to report the disaster to Marianne. Years later she confided that the main reason she went to the barman's room was to escape the noises made by Richard and Edwina across the corridor. She did not think much of the wet spam kisses either.

Now that a large part of my time was taken up with the making of puddings, my hunger for the outdoors had to be satisfied with a quick run down to the sea each morning. The gorse shone brilliantly with stars of night rain and as I passed the bushes I stopped now and then to press one of the full flowers along its yellow or flame-tongued side. A tiny bunch of curled stamens would spring from a slit in the bulging pocket and hang there, trembling. Everything felt fresh and fine.

At the bottom of the first field was the ruin of a croft. The gable ends still stood, each irregular boulder slotted cunningly into its neighbor to form a solid, two-foot-thick blockade against the elements. Between them, pink-edged daisies grew beside tumbled stones and a pipit had made her nest in the rusty curve of a barrel hoop. In June I watched her flutter to and from the four chocolate-colored eggs and rejoiced on the morning they hatched. I checked on them daily, amazed by the rapidity of their growth: how from helpless, floppy, damp things they blossomed suddenly into demanding little units of life with open beaks and pin-bright eyes. I mourned angrily when, before the end of the month, a predatory gull plundered the nest, leaving great gouts of shiny turd as evidence. It made me think how rich nature must be to afford to form and destroy life so fast.

I climbed over a makeshift gate to reach the sea, my weight stretching its orange string ties a little more each day. The stones at the top of the beach were large and loud to walk on. Below the tideline, strewn with bladder-wrack and plastic bottles, were smaller pebbles, a few among them flat enough to skim. Again, early in the summer, nature thrust itself under my eyes in the form of stray lambs bleating in exhausted bewilderment by the edge of the sea. I would pick them up and bleat with them until there came an answering cry. It pleased me to deliver them safely to their yellow-eyed mothers who came galloping to the call, simulated or real, of an errant offspring. I did not mind that the little ones peed down my front, glad that their bones were not destined to join the bars of gray, sea-sucked driftwood on the shore.

The hills were littered with carcasses of ewes at that time, making birth seem a lonely, hazardous process, death easy. Shards of bleached, ancient trees poking up through the bog like more bones told of other deaths, other times. But with the sundew and bog cotton growing up on the mulch of those compressed times, it was clear that what died only turned into nourishment for more life. Finality existed only in an individual sense, which made the individual both the most vital and the most dispensable thing.

But embryonic philosophies conceived in the course of my wanderings were hard put to match the reality of the hotel kitchen. Here, matters of life and death receded before the immediate drama of having the dinner ready on time.

Besides Gilbert, there were now two other members of staff in the kitchen. One was Lena, a fifteen-year-old lass with a top half lovely as a Dresden shepherdess and white hairy legs like a split parsnip. She was employed to do the washing up and stood before the trough sink hour after hour, dreamily running a brush round the same dish until Edwina bustled up and chivvied her on to the next. The other was Jeanie, a brunette, whose soft hips blotted amoebalike over two stools while she peeled battalions of vegetables into bowls which were always too small. Her husband was a fierce marionette-limbed character whose face was almost black from some disorder of the blood. The calm pink sea of Jeanie's bulk trembled when he was near and she found no respite from masculine tyranny at the hotel, for Gilbert kept both girls in a state of jittery subservience. He treated all staff, with the exception of the barman, with the same brand of casual sadism which makes grown men kick dogs. Marianne and I, as daughters of the boss, did not escape this treatment, but it was meted out to us in a subtly different way.

Gilbert was, I sometimes believed, the reincarnation of Hairy Hans, now interred in several deep-freezers. Man and pig shared the same not-quite-pink bristly skin, the same grossness of form and, above all, the same insidious threat of crude sexual power. As an instrument to dominate two adolescent girls, this last proved highly effective. All Gilbert had to do if either of us annoyed him was approach with one thick-fingered hand held out, palm cupped exactly to match the small, innocently blossoming protuberances on our chests. Marianne invariably fled, apologized or pleaded until a cool glaze of satisfaction jelled over Gilbert's small, blond-lashed eyes and the threat passed without contact being made. But I spat and fumed against the curious force of the gesture, flushing violently as he backed me against the shelves, against walls and once so that I was bent like a limbo dancer over the stove. My words, in a high, young voice, fluttered about uselessly, never succeeding in breaking the power I could not define.

In precise opposition to its unfolding to pleasure on the hill, my body learned to deny itself, to recoil: breasts, mouth, legs freezing at his approach. I knew now that between my legs could close up with disgust as well as squeeze inside itself with secret joy. That he could make this happen involuntarily was humiliating. It made me hate him. I did not learn until late on in the season that the perfect weapon against him was not denial, but a cunningly measured degree of "come on." Gilbert, by response and unconscious direction, taught me all I would ever need to know about the art of prick-teasing.

It began with casual observation of the effect produced by clothes and movement. Stretching and swaying was good, I found, for showing off the gap between the hem of a blouse and a trouser top, and a carelessly unbuttoned shirt, disappearing into an apron bib which slipped from breast to breast, never failed to produce results. But I discovered my master card accidentally one evening when my sweet-trolley caftan was in the wash, and I was forced to wear the only other dress I had, which was as short and shocking as the other was long and demure. Bending to get the cheese off the bottom of the sweet trolley had an interesting effect in the dining room as well as on Gilbert and a gratifying backview response could be achieved by the simple act of reaching up to a high shelf for a bottle of wine. Gilbert got in a wonderfully bad temper and dropped two hors d'oeuvres on the floor. He sweated and gurgled Aberdonian curses as, smilingly, I bent down and cleared away the mess. I knew that in this mood he would never make his threatening gesture because to do that he had to stare me in the eye, something he could not do when I was waving some other part of me at him. I did not know the dangers I was courting until two incidents, occurring on the same day, brought tensions to a frightening head.

It was a Saturday late on in the season. The wind which I had gulped during my brief dawn sortie had mellowed by midmorning to a feathery breeze. I could see it from the kitchen window sifting lightly through Dossan's mane and tickling the leaves of a rowan tree. It was no time to be stuck inside. Thoughtfully, I licked a finger loaded with cake mixture and made a calculation.

Eleven minutes later the bases of six Mocha Genghis Khans were in the oven and I was up the hill. Made daring by the urgency of stolen moments I crouched low over Dossan's warm neck and hissed for her to go.

Go!

We cantered up and lolloped down the slopes her legs knew now as well as mine. We sprang across burns mowing down bog cotton, mud sucking at her fetlocks, black droplets spraying my knees. High up, where the crags began, the wind rose again and sun splashing on Dossan's teddy-bear coat turned it to gold. Jumping off for a moment, I spread myself flat below the wind and laughed with surprise when Dossan lay down too, squirming her soft striped spine into the heather, clods of bog flicking off her unshod hooves. I lay on, eyes traveling with the clouds, wanting to stop time. There was one cloud like a cuttlefish, another like an over-risen cottage loaf . . . Hah. Into my mind came the flat white face of the oven-timer, black hands ticking impassively round and round. I must go back.

There was no time to change spattered trousers, or brush the horsehairs from my arms. The timer was ringing as I ran in the back door. The cakes should not be burned if I got them out at once. I scanned the kitchen for the oven gloves. They were nowhere. A tea towel then. But they were all damp. Then I saw the gloves. They were hanging from a string around Gilbert's cylindrical middle.

"Can I have the oven gloves a minute?"

"Yiu—can—not."

His thick voice pressed out each word separately as his thumbs jabbed into a piece of dough. Check-trousered legs, buttocks wobbling through the thin cotton, blocked the oven doors. A landscape away beyond the marble table, Lena's back curved over the sink like a comma and Jeanie stemmed an avalanche of carrots with a reddened hand.

Gilbert went on pummeling his dough and the smell of cooked cake hung warmly in the air, its homeliness a sneer. Left another minute the Mocha Genghis Khans would be ruined. I stood rubbing a dusty elbow, feeling the weight of Gilbert's knowing challenge push me back from the oven. My face twisted at the thought of spoiled cakes, of failure. Edwina never wasted anything.

"Gilbert, my cakes are going to burn."

He answered in the same slow, jabbing voice.

"Is—that—so?"

And squeezed the pastry like a thigh.

Deliberately I altered my stance, allowing one hand to fall casually on a hip while the other stroked back my hair with a movement that ensured my breasts were well raised. When I was sure that Gilbert had taken all this in I turned away abruptly and sauntered over to the sink.

"It's hot, isn't it?" I said to Lena, untucking the front of my blouse and fanning it over my belly.

She agreed, taking a hand from the dishwater and running a dripping wrist over her nose. Again I felt Gilbert's eyes flick over the length of me and again I turned away.

"Look," I said, positioning myself between Lena and Jeanie, "something bit me." My fingers were parting the blouse just below my bra. The girls scrutinized the clear flesh, baffled. One of them murmured, "Aye, is it the midges?"

I heard Gilbert move on the other side of the table. He was coming toward us. I knew he would.

Without warning, I dodged past him and quick as a pickpocket plucked the oven gloves from his waist. His fat hands bumbled the air. In a second I was on the door with the oven doors flung wide. Two, four, five cakes out, one more to go. Gilbert was saying all the rude words I had ever heard as though they were one. There was a gasp from Jeanie and I leaped up in the nick of time as a wet tea-towel cracked viciously in the air where I had just been.

"Come here, yiu little houri. Come here the nu and gi' me back them gloves."

We were opposite each other, the table in between. I caught a glimpse of Lena staring, the washing-up brush frozen in mid-air. If it had not been for the one cake still to save I would have bolted.

Gilbert advanced and I scurried behind Jeanie's broad back.

"Let me just get that one cake out, Gilbert."

"I'll let yiu do nothin." Yiu gi' me back them gloves, the nu.''

I jumped up and down in frustration. The oven was still blasting out heat and I could smell the edge of a burn. Suddenly, ignoring him, I dashed round the table. My hand was almost on the cake when his damp fingers closed around the wrist. I was yanked upright and forced close to his aproned chest. His strange jellied eyes stared first into my own, then traveled slowly to the neck of my blouse, I wrenched away, the coquette in me smashed. But he still had hold of my wrist.

"I'm gonni' break yiur pinkie," he said deliberately. He said it again, but until he started bending my little finger back, I did not know what he meant.

I held myself rigid, body averted from the captured hand, eyes compelled to watch. Gilbert's concentration was absolute, like that of a surgeon. The other oven timer, the one he used, notched the half seconds between the ticking of the clock. Breath was held in the round o's of the girls' mouths. The tendon at the base of my bending finger was white and stretched like string.

"I'm gonni' break it," repeated Gilbert and his voice broke the soft, cakey air.

I continued to stare, locked more in fascination than pain. I was convinced the tendon would snap before the bone.

There was another endless ticking hush. A black knot from my brain seemed to be trying to get out of my finger. As the pressure increased the knot became a ridge, sawing in unison with my pulse. The angles of the hand were mad. It did not look like a hand.

Then a small graunching crack, like wet wood or a chicken's wing. It fell into silence sliced almost instantly by the buzz of the timer. Gilbert released me and scooped up the gloves draped over my arm. He was at the oven door when a thud like a dropped flour sack made him turn. Lena had fainted on the floor.

At lunch Richard joked about the oversized thumbshield on my little finger. Burns were common in the kitchen. Gilbert was off duty and our voices were hidden from other ears by the din of the washing-up machine. I waggled my hand, experimenting for pain. Inside the thumbshield the broken pinkie lay snug in a splint of cocktail sticks. One of the waitresses, a nurse, had helped me fit it on. I decided not to mention the incident to Richard. The whole village could talk about it but he need never know. I feared that he would guess at once—and correctly—that something more than a petty battle for oven gloves had been going on.

The second incident, which took place in full view of all the staff coming on duty for dinner, could not be concealed.

Marianne at that time was in the odd-jobs position I had held at the beginning of the season. That evening it was her turn to perform still-room duty. This entailed folding napkins, filling water jugs and winding fluted butter pats into chilled bowls. She had just started on the butter when I came in to add the final trimmings to the sweet trolley. We each sampled a meringue while I mixed the fillings for a gâteau. I had abandoned the idea of assembling the precarious edifice of a Mocha Genghis Khan with one finger out of action. Marianne knew about the broken pinkie and joined me loyally in sending wordless waves of hate through the stillroom wall to where Gilbert was stirring soup on the other side. We fooled around, making each other giggle, and Richard, not understanding our game but enjoying the high spirits, joked with us for a moment as he passed through. Marianne, busy with the coffee trolley now, hummed softly. She was always pleased when Richard paid her attention. My giggles sputtered out like a candle whenever Gilbert came into view. The sight of his blockish frame moving about casually filled me with fury.

The meringues being ready, I went into the kitchen to set them on the trolley. There was no swaying or shimmying as I walked past Gilbert. My body felt spiky as a mine.

"Will Modom be requirin' th' oven gloves this evening? Has Modom's tongue been stolen by the wee folk?"

I ignored his taunts.

The barman came in and leaned, hands in pockets, against the door. Since the failed kissing episode he had treated me with caution. Now, recognizing a weakness in my stiff bearing, he joined Gilbert in provoking me. The thought that they must have been discussing me—laughing about me—brought on a deep flush. Immediately they both commented on it. The flush grew deeper still.

"Will you look at the bonny face, Gilbert. I think the lassie fancies you. Isn't that right, hen?"

I made the mistake of answering, despising the silly tight sound of my voice as it wavered miles off the intended sarcasm.

"I don't fancy anyone."

They laughed.

"Well, isn't that a shame and just when yer cherry's ripe too!"

"Oh aye, there's a ripe wee cherry there all right!"

Marianne came through from the stillroom. She lowered her eyes before the barman. Gilbert pointed at her with the spatula he was holding.

"And another one there."

They joked for a moment between themselves, Gilbert saying something like: "Thought you'd have done that job by now."

Catching Marianne's eye I aimed a heavy hate glance at Gilbert's back. She giggled. I aimed another at the barman. Her lashes went down. It infuriated me that she should kowtow before him. He was not worthy of her. The prim old-fashioned phrase repeated itself in my mind. Not worthy. I went back into the stillroom where there was the gâteau to finish. They went on teasing Marianne.

The cream filling I had made was not quite right. In the flurry of the morning it had been left out of the fridge and was insufficiently chilled. Because it was too late for anything else I spread the slack mixture over the first layer of sponge. It blobbed messily over the edges. Richard flashed through again.

"Hmm, that doesn't look like one of your best efforts!"

"You're not meant to see it at this stage."

He disappeared and I fitted on the second layer, upset that he had seen. The voices in the kitchen took up their teasing again. Marianne's answering giggles grated. Why did she let them do it to her? Most of the cream filling squeezed out under the weight of the second sponge. I dumped on more. And as the voices grew louder, the giggles more uncontrolled, I stopped thinking what I was doing and dumped on spoonful after spoonful until the whole disaster was masked in wobbling yellow cream. There was not enough filling left for a third layer and feeling failure swell in me like the taunts next door, I lifted the plate, balancing it on the flat of my injured hand, and was about to commit it to the rubbish bin when Marianne came in. She was moving backwards, jumping from side to side to avoid Gilbert, who capered in pursuit, trying to whip her bottom with a wet towel. She was grinning, playing the game, but I felt her distress.

"Piss off, Gilbert," I said. "Leave her alone."

"Yiu mind yiur own business, yiu."

There was a delighted chortle from the barman.

"Oh ho! What's that language I hear!"

Marianne was pink, giggling feebly. I had a sudden flashback to her first tinkly laugh after she had been in hospital.

With a mechanical motion I emptied the contents of all the nearest bowls on to the mess balanced on my hand. Strawberries, pineapple chunks, custard.

"Get back, Marianne," I said.

Gilbert was less than two yards away. He must have realized my intention almost before I did, for his puffed, ugly features became a threatening mask.

"Yiu dare," he said. "Yiu just dare and it won't be yer pinkie that gets broken next time."

Marianne's face appeared over his shoulder, eyes dancing. "Throw it! Throw it!" she cried.

She urged me on. Gilbert threatened. His thick features were contorted, asking to be blotted out. My arm lifted and the dripping cake hovered in the air. Then, with full force, I flung it.

Gilbert ducked, although he need not have bothered. At the last minute I had changed aim. I saw Marianne's hands clench as though in spasm. Her lower lip, still somehow curved in a smile, shivered and then went still. Very slowly, like bits of opaque jellyfish, cream, custard and fruit slid down her poor, thin brown hair.

I ran out before the slipping sponge revealed her eyes.

My act did not go unpunished. In one way or another that summer I learned much about the strange, mixed powers of loyalty, pride, sex and shame.

When I returned from the second wild ride of the day Edwina sought me out and asked to talk for a few moments. Their room across the corridor was tidy but cluttered, containing all the personal accoutrements normally spread over a home. I noticed at once the same woven bedspread which had enriched the decor of her London flat. Only one or two things of Richard's lay in disorder: a tie dangling like a snake down the side of the dresser; a small mountain of books slipping from under his side of the bed. I found a focal point in the pattern of a dressing gown and kept my gaze fixed on it while she groped for a balance between friendliness and authority. She found the key in the mention of Richard's name, for I wriggled involuntarily when she said, after briefly pointing out the unkindness to Marianne, "It isn't easy, you know, for Richard. Having an intelligent—and attractive— daughter causing disturbances among his staff."

She had not been oblivious to my experiments at coquetry.

"You know you are attractive, don't you?"

I moved around in the chair but said nothing. She continued.

"It isn't a good idea to lead people on."

I knew that. The incident of the broken pinkie had quelled my flirtatious urges for a long time to come. I wondered if she guessed at the very different awakenings I experienced on the hill. She started to tell me—it sounded like a joke against herself—of her own behavior as a teenager. With a laugh, she described it as outrageous. Although I was interested I did not like her playing big sister, confiding, so I failed to react. After a minute I said, "I'll say sorry to Marianne."

"Good," said Edwina briskly, smiling as though something intimate had been exchanged. "And no more nonsense like that, hmm?"

Humiliated by the word "nonsense" I did not return her smile. As she opened the door to let me out, still, I sensed, hoping to establish a rapport, I was aware for the first time that even in this relationship there was room for a reshuffling of power. I could never be to Richard what she was to him, but by being blood of his blood, I was already something she was not.

5

"Intelligent and attractive, full of potential."

I was to get used to those words. They had been said at school and at the Child Guidance clinic. Now they were said by a man from the education authorities who came at the beginning of autumn to check how my studies were progressing. Luckily there had been a phone call in advance, time for Richard to get me into the lounge surrounded by exercise books. I nodded at all the man said, anxious to get back to the kitchen where I had a whole pig's head and a vat of rowan jelly on the boil.

Soon the words were repeated by a Sociology lecturer who interviewed me for a place at a London polytechnic. On the strength of that nebulous potential I was granted the place, even though, at fifteen, I was under the usual entry age and lacked the requisite number of O-levels. I made the move from the hotel back to 309 reassured by Richard's parting words: "You can always come back."

Although it had not turned out to be home in the sense I had hoped, a link had been forged between me and the land and this, coupled with my undiminished loyalty to Richard, made it a place to which I would inevitably return.

That year and in years to come, Marianne and I bounced north and south between our two nonhomes like yoyos. James, too young to have been affected by my truant example, was a more conventional child of divorce. He spent termtimes and the shorter holidays with Kay and five or six weeks of the summer up at the hotel. The first Christmas after the divorce found me at 309, Marianne at the hotel. When our paths crossed the following spring we compared notes: hers had been a strained, mock-traditional affair, with Edwina cooking a lunch with all the trimmings which was consumed in virtual silence. Mine owed little to tradition but was a rite in its own way. The time had come for me to lose my virginity.

Being a student at the poly had advantages over being a schoolgirl, but was a far cry from the independence of working at the hotel. There, my efforts had been maintained by pride alone and needed no structure beyond a self-imposed routine. Now I was faced once more with being one of a crowd. The adjustment was not easy.

My fellow students were, with few exceptions, straight out of school and still mentally stuck behind the institution/victim barriers of the classroom. When a lesson was over they would sigh with relief and rush for the door. I hungered to find satisfaction in the learning process itself, aware that the choice to be there was entirely mine. Often I lingered after class, especially by the desk of the Sociology lecturer. His honesty about the limitations of the course was disturbing and when I asked why he did not change it, he said it would mean changing the whole system. We talked a lot about that.

Finding myself distanced from my classmates, I evolved a social life of my own outside the cultural parameters of the poly. It started one evening when I was given a free ticket for a local folk concert. I arrived early and was obliged to wait in a nettle and concrete garden until the doors opened. I had been sitting there for ten minutes, idly plaiting a chaplet into my hair, when out of the top window of the house floated a series of rich, obliquely human sounds. They came from a single instrument, a saxophone, but the breath behind it gave it the force of a collective cry. The notes clung together in the damp suburban air, a song from deeper than the diaphragm which had no need for words. I listened for a long time and when the folk concert started sat through one mournful dirge and then crept out into the garden again. The saxophone was no longer audible but a hand high above me played scales along the windowsill. I went inside and silently climbed the stairs.

The door of the top room was open. A young man, very slim and pale with black hair, stood at right angles to me. It was his hand on the sill. A girl with hair to her waist, figure hidden in a long, loose robe, squatted on the floor stirring a teabag in a mug. The saxophone sat on a high stool in the middle of the room, shining and complex amid the dust and bare walls. The young man, looking out of the window, was talking to himself in a low, wondering tone. He spoke a curious, old-fashioned English and after a moment I realized he was reciting a poem.

"And this is why I sojourn here,
Alone and palely loitering,

Though the sedge is wither'd from the lake,
And no birds sing.''

The last phrase, so simple, rested on the air like its own echo. The
girl looked up and saw me standing by the door. His glance followed,
the pale and black profile turning full face. One long, catlike eye
scrutinized me unhurriedly. The other was covered by a patch.

''And here she is, it seems. Is it you?''

Not wanting to break the spell I answered carefully.

''It is me.''

At once his pose changed and he swung away, stalking across the
room to lean on a mantelpiece, cuff-booted ankles crossed like a pantomime lead.

''Hah! She knows.''

And he began to quote again.

''Pale warriors, death-pale were they all;
Who cried: 'La Belle dame sans Merci
Hath thee in thrall!' ''

The girl placed a mug of tea at his elbow and sat down to drink hers
on the floor. I took a step further into the room.

''Yes, come.''

The saxophone was taking up the only stool so I leaned on the other
end of the mantelpiece. The man and I stood looking at each other for
a long time. From this distance I could see that the cheek below the
eye-patch was roughened with pockmarks and there were thin razor
scars on his chin. Gaps in his white shirt, a hard color against the
translucence of his skin, showed a scattering of dark hairs running
together to form a shadowy line. Like Dossan's stripe, I thought, and
wondered if they would be soft like the moss on the hill. It was the
first time I had experienced the compulsion to touch another body.
Every now and then I heard the girl take quick careless sips of her tea.
The words ''his mistress'' popped into my brain.

''Or are you a Maenad?'' he said, as though continuing a thought
out loud. His lips remained delicately parted after the last word and I
had the same impulse to run my fingers over them as I had to stroke
a leaf or a butterfly's wing.

''Was that you playing?'' I asked.

He made a curious fluttering gesture with one hand and suddenly brought the knuckles to his teeth and bit them, looking right into my eyes.

"I am always playing," he said with a short laugh and lifted up the saxophone. Facing the window he blew three, four, a dozen notes, energy seeming to pour up from his feet through his flat belly and hit the air in a curve. I hoped he would go on but he suddenly laid the instrument down and said huskily, "I am thirsty for some whisky in my tea."

He felt for money in his trouser pocket, widening a tear in the seat. I thought of the needle and thread I always carried in my bag. He did not speak to the long-haired girl as we went out, but this not speaking itself suggested the existence of a code. I wished she had not been there.

For his whisky we went to a pub across the road. It was a Friday night and the place was packed. Jem—for that was his name—inserted himself deftly between two sets of sprawled elbows. I stood back. It was the first time I had been into a bar, not counting the hotel's, which I had sometimes cleaned. Somebody made a loud joke about the seat of his pants falling out and he answered back in an identical Irish accent, making the whole bar laugh. I found the mixture of arrogance, sincerity, sham and fragile pride in him more and more appealing. Outside I told him about the needle and thread.

"You mean you're offering to . . . ?"

I nodded. His good eye was nearest and the look he shot me through it was deep.

"But why? I am nothing: a gypsy, a stranger, a bad Catholic . . ."

I caught on to his poetic manner.

"It would give me pleasure."

The look became warm.

"That, dear child, is something I should very much like to give you."

"You'll have to take your trousers off."

He swerved his eye away and I could not tell if his confusion was real or a game.

Jem took his trousers off in the room at the top of the gray house. The long-haired girl was nowhere in sight. He crouched in a corner with the silk rag used to polish the saxophone draped over his manhood and entertained me with a recitation of "All the world's a stage." It was strange to hear life so summed up, a predictable drama in seven acts, from the lips of one who seemed so raptly involved with the immediate.

From time to time my fingers on the needle paused as I took in the way short, silky hairs curled on his shins and one slender foot rubbed against the other. When I gave him back the trousers he turned away to put them on and again I was surprised by a hunger to reach out and touch. It was perhaps at this moment that the ambition to hasten my own passage from "maiden" to womanhood took form.

But hastening did not necessarily mean now, and without knowing why, I suddenly felt I must go.

"I'm going," I announced abruptly, as his hands still tucked in his shirt. My back was turned, first foot on the stair, when his voice came, low and with the mildest hint of a plea.

"How will I find you again?"

I hesitated. To be searched out, to be wanted by someone was something entirely new. It alarmed me a little.

"Oh," I said nonchalantly, "*I'll* find *you*."

It seemed to take hours to get down the stairs. When at last I stepped into the garden, thoughts still bound in the top room, a scrap of paper wrapped around a piece of rubble landed on the concrete by my side. I did not open it until I was out of sight of the house. Scribbled in a small, uneven hand the message read:

> I cannot grow;
> I have no shadow
> To run away from,
> I only play. (Auden)

> And I'm only here on Fridays. (Jem)

I treasured the little ordinariness of the last line.

Back at 309 I revisited all the new feelings of the evening, smiling for no reason as I had sometimes done on the hill. When I went to bed I did not unplait the chaplet of my "Maenad" hair and Richard's old poetry books lay scattered on the counterpane.

Those first intimations of desire, the nameless hunger which in Scotland had led me to cool my cheeks on lichen-covered rocks and press my body to the earth, transformed my outlook on the world of men. No longer did I see them through the clinical, disembodied eyes with which I had judged the unfortunate barman. The conclusion that I had drawn with him, that you had to "fancy them back," now acquired real meaning. It was as though, through meeting Jem, a previously silent voice in my body had suddenly found its tongue.

The relationship developed erratically. The next time I saw him was loud with the presence of others. It was a free-for-all music night at the gray house and he stalked on between jigging folk bands and rosy-toned girl singers, breaking the easy chitchat of the audience with his forceful nose-to-toes blues. A six-foot-five Irishman, lanky as a scaffold, backed him for a couple of numbers on a double bass. He was introduced by Jem as McAllister, "a better man than I and a good Catholic." It was McAllister, as gentle and lugubrious as he was tall, who told me that Jem had once hoped to enter the priesthood. It was not difficult to conjure that pale face above a black soutane, even the eye-patch somehow fitted. I asked what had happened to make him change his mind.

"He could not keep the vow of chastity," was the reply. And although he would have looked beautiful as a priest, I was glad.

It was not, however, until the third or fourth meeting that our intimacy—endorsed on my part by much poetry reading and listening to Charlie Parker in between—had a chance to blossom in any tangible way. Meantime, my revised vision of self as related to men exercised itself in another direction.

Once a week since moving back to 309 I spent an afternoon with a man called Mr. Fox. Kay, who had always been supportive of my musical inclinations, had been delighted when I hinted that I would like to take up another instrument. Wanting to make a change of direction clear, I blew a large chunk of my summer savings on a pretty blond guitar. (Richard, going by his own laws of justice as opposed to those of state, had paid me £3 a week at the hotel.) Thus equipped, I went down the list of teachers in the local paper. Mr. Fox was the only one able to start straight away, so I went to him. Richard agreed to pay for the lessons and Kay put the money in an envelope every week and gave it to me. I gave it to Mr. Fox, who immediately sprinted down the road and bought a steak with it—most of which I ate—giving the impression that the musical part of the afternoon was free.

I liked Mr. Fox. He lived alone in a small semidetached house in Barnes and when he was not giving guitar lessons set polished stones in rings and painted portraits. His long hands, emerging from the sleeves of a comfortable old blue sweater, were clever and calm, the nails longer on the right for playing the guitar. I found this deliberate slip of symmetry appealing; the rest of him—ankles, ears and knees-through-his-jeans—was so even and clean. He made coffee using all milk and I liked the way a bit of froth he did not know about got caught in the hairs of his moustache. His eyes were brown and mild and, although I had no idea what he was thinking behind them, made me feel at ease. It was disturbing, therefore, to see him so differently after the encounter with Jem.

An observer would have found nothing different in the lesson with Mr. Fox that day. I sat across from him as usual and ran through the pieces I had practiced during the week. The encouragement he gave was quiet and practical, as was his criticism. Much of his teaching was done by demonstration and sometimes he would treat me to an entire medieval air. He played the lute, too.

The routine with the steak had become established by now and he had already made his trip to the corner shop. At around 3:00 P.M. he put down his guitar and went into the kitchen to light the gas under the frying pan. We ate in the room where he taught, not bothering to move the piles of sheet music and jeweler's tools off the table, but finding perches for the cruet and mustard pots among them.

I watched Mr. Fox eat, the hands that rippled arpeggios and drew long, shivery vibratos from the guitar casually fitting themselves to the banality of knife and fork. Quite suddenly, I had a clear picture of those long fingers doing other things. I stopped in mid-chew, stunned, the image expanding. But imagination, curbed by inexperience, faded just where the curls of my pubic hair became more dense. It was a part of me I had only recently begun to explore.

"You all right?" asked Mr. Fox. "You look a bit flushed."

I stabbed a piece of tomato and pushed the meat I could not swallow into the pouch of one cheek.

"It's O K. I just need a sip of water."

I went out to the kitchen, thankful for a moment alone. I was holding a cool glass alternately against one cheek, then the other, when Mr. Fox came in carrying the dishes.

"I was thinking," he said, "of going up to the Tate next week, which would mean canceling your lesson. But perhaps you'd like to come? It's William Blake."

This was an unexpected development and after saying yes—not too eagerly I hoped—I vanished into the lavatory to hide my rapidly re-reddening cheeks.

Before I left he said, "Come a bit earlier than usual and we'll grab a bite of lunch up there."

I was thrilled. It was going to seem a long time until next Thursday.

*   *   *

Sunday afternoon found me wandering by the Thames. Not many people were about as the day was cold. I rather liked the chill emptiness of the towpath, the age-worn cobbles near the bridge hunched together like tortoises and smooth miles of asphalt further on, stretching out by the bulging river like a flat gray hem.

I had been in the park watching a few wintry dressed couples pushing children on swings. Their faces were pinched and they did not speak much except to say, "Whee!" occasionlly or "Oh, do come on." It reminded me of Kay calling to me and Marianne when we were little. When Richard had come with us it was a special occasion and there were photographs and ice creams.

I went and sat on a miniature island where my school friend Kate and I used to come before I ran away. Now that my legs were longer and more agile from all the tussock-hopping in Scotland, crossing the wobbly log to the island seemed easy. I trod down layers of wet leaves smelling like old newspapers and crouched among them for a while, hidden. The sky through a pattern of twigs was still one of my favorite views of the world.

Continuing my ramble on the towpath I passed the high walls of great houses whose gardens ran down to the river. Some of them had railings through which I could see clipped, empty lawns. If I lived in one of those houses, I mused, I would let the grass grow and make secret grottoes filled with Mr. Fox type music and statues of people like Jem.

On the bridge I stopped for a moment, gazing at the sparse-armed willows, the gray towpath and the broad brown water curving away below. When I looked up again, I saw Jem.

My first impulse was to run. The wind, which I had enjoyed before, was suddenly a menace rumpling my hair; the cold an enemy painting unattractive colors on my nose. But I did not turn round and the same force which drew my eager, reluctant feet on, raised that black-patched face to mine.

In contrast to my fluttering state, his composure was absolute. The dark hair lifting from his brow flopped softly in rhythm with his stride. He stared straight at me. It was only when the gap between us narrowed to less than a yard, and he staggered as though shot, that I realized he had not seen me at all before.

"You!"

The exclamation in his voice was flattering. His chin was flung high and his long throat, shadowed where he had not shaved far enough down, pulsed. Below us a wavelet broke over the stone bank and above, the clouds, which had been hanging low, gave like weary knees.

The rain was like a gift to us. Without a word we headed to the bottom of the bridge where the awning outside a skating shop offered shelter. There, staring into what I now knew to be the middle distance of his myopia, Jem said, "Sweet child, I cannot bear to see you shiver. I have no right to offer, but will you do me the honor of stepping into the poor place where I rest my bones?"

His poetic manner verged on the ridiculous but I did not care. I followed him into the rain.

Jem's temporary abode was a small dry-docked cabin cruiser called *Angel II*. She was resting in a wooden cradle and to get into her we had to climb a rickety ladder. We had got into the boatyard through a gap in the fence. *Angel II* smelt of newspapers inside, like the wet leaves on my childhood island. The low ceiling made us stoop and he threw his coat over a mouldy seat and begged me to sit down. His own body he tossed like some lovely piece of rubbish on to the only bunk. Dirty portholes admitted just enough light to show the faded denim shirt he wore and his skin pale against rumpled blankets. One arm was flung above his head, fingers tapping lightly on a worm-chewed beam. Outside, the rain tapped a second rhythm against the boat's wooden sides and not far away the lapping of the river made faint accompanying chords. With a smile toward the quiet music of the Thames, Jem began to recite.

> "Break, break, break,
> On thy cold gray stones, O Sea,
> And I would that my tongue could utter
> The thoughts that arise in me."

He stopped and murmured, "And how I long to know, child, the thoughts that arise in thee."

I decided to tell him.

"Earlier, I thought of you as a statue—I thought how I would like to touch you like that."

His fingers fell into a slower tapping on the beam and then were still.

"If that is what you want of me, then that is what I am."

So saying, he straightened his legs, crossed his hands over his breast, and lay quite still like a knight in Westminster Abbey.

"Say that poem you wrote in the message," I said. " 'I cannot grow . . .' "

While he said it, I slid down between the exposed ribs of timber and knelt beside the bunk. His body stretched out before me was like a feast in a foreign country. I did not know where to begin. Finally my hand crept out and lay low on his belly between the high, articulate bones of his loins. He did not move under the touch but in the small sound he made, interrupting the poem, I felt a response.

"Go on," I said, and his voice took up the words again. I laid a thumb lightly against his throat to feel the vibration. My other hand had found its way through a gap in his shirt and was stroking the soft, dorsal line of his body hair. I watched his lips, wondering if I would lean forward and kiss them when he come to the end of the poem: " '. . . I shall never be/Different. Love me.' "

I had not known that was the way it ended. His eye fluttered open as I hesitated, unsure of the next move. Then his hand was on my neck and that eye, drinking both my own, was drawing me down.

All at once there was a crazy explosion of sound outside. Hysterical barking. Jem wriggled a finger between us and laid it on his lips.

"Don't be afraid."

I was not. I knew not many dogs could climb ladders. He said something else I could not hear and I leaned closer. The barking went on, high-pitched, a circus din.

Rr-wuff! Rr-wuff! Rr-wuff!

"You have the touch of a saint," he murmured and laid his lips against my hair.

But I drew back. I could hear padlocks rattling on their chains and imagined the dog jumping up at the boatyard gate.

Jem's eye continued to pull at me but I would not be pulled. Now that thought had had a chance to intervene, I was flurried and unsure of what I had been about to do. I ducked from under his arm.

"But wait," he cried, bewildered, as, on deck already, I pulled up my hood and prepared to climb down the ladder. "I must give you something, a token."

He plunged back into the cabin and when he emerged there were three things in his hands: a leather-covered bottle, what looked to be a rounders bat and a strange hairy bulb in a jar. "These are all I have, please take one!"

By now I was on the ground. Our voices were raised against the dog's.

Rr-wuff! Rr-wuff!

"What's that thing in the jar?"

Jem stood above me with his treasures, offering them like sections of his soul.

Rr-wuff! Rr-wuff!

"It is my mandrake, my little man," he cried. "Here, take them all!"

I was by the fence, ready to dive through.

"Give me your shirt," I called and within seconds it was in my hands, wrapped around the leather bottle, and I was through the fence and away.

We knew we would find each other again.

Monday went by, and Tuesday and Wednesday, and still I had not decided what to wear for my date with Mr. Fox. On Thursday morning, almost in despair, I rushed into Kay's room at seven, and demanded to borrow her curlers and best black top. Kay, still a little groggy from her sleeping pills, watched me fiddling at the dressing table with a smile.

"You must think a lot of this Mr. Fox to go to all this trouble," she said. "How old is he?"

"I don't know," I answered, ramming an obstinate hairpin this way and that. "About thirty, I suppose."

"Well, just you be careful!" she said, joking.

I had not told her about Jem.

The trip to the Tate exceeded my expectations. First Mr. Fox surprised me by producing a wonderful car. It was a vintage two-seater, slate blue, with a long rattling bonnet, ground-scraping chassis and huge close-together headlamps like crossed eyes. I felt proud sitting in the squashy leather seat next to Mr. Fox as we swept through Putney attracting envious glances.

Then there was lunch at the gallery, which we had straight away. Mr. Fox left me to choose a table while he collected salad and wedges of what he called "kwitch" from the counter. Over coffee he asked if I went to galleries often.

"Not very often."

I did not want to admit that this was the first time since Madame Tussaud's in a school crocodile.

"And has anyone ever done a painting of you?"

I laughed. "No!"

His asking had made me strangely excited and I checked my appearance in the cloakroom before we looked round the gallery.

At the entrance to the Blake exhibition Mr. Fox said, "Feel free to wander round at your own pace."

So I did, and although I liked some of the thundery fairy-tale creations of Blake, I strayed out into the corridor after a while and became absorbed in a display of Hogarth cartoons. I spent some time looking at other people looking at pictures too, fascinated by the dreamy, amoebalike splits and formations of couples and groups, and the way everybody's limbs moved slowly as though the air were full of invisible liquid.

When Mr. Fox came to find me to suggest it was time to go, my head was swimming and the ordinary air outside, with people moving at their usual pace, came as a shock. It was good to be snug in the car again with Mr. Fox's long fingers, clean and calm, on the wheel. I was interested in London passing by outside the window but my eyes kept coming back to his hands and before we reached the outskirts of town I was blushing again. There was no doubt left now: I badly wanted to stroke Jem, but I badly wanted Mr. Fox to stroke me.

When he dropped me off at 309 I was cartwheeling inside. We had agreed that during the Christmas holidays I would sit for some portrait sketches and in return he would give me some extra lessons, free.

Christmas was three weeks away.

Jem and I found each other again the following weekend. I saw him through the window of a pub near the gray house. Even through thick brown patterned glass that pale face cut by a triangle of black was unmistakable. I hovered, not sure enough of myself, or him, to go in. Then, as I watched his small hands talk through the mist of the pane, a plan took form: Kay was going out that evening. I could invite Jem to 309.

I hunted through my pockets for a piece of paper to write him a message but there was none. Only a penknife, some coins and a comb. The penknife gave me an idea. Slipping into an alley beside the pub, I loosened my hair and teased out a suitably wavy lock. Carefully, so as not to hack off a handful, I applied the blade. The lock looked a bit limp so I held it tightly wound round a twig for a moment, using spit as a setting aid. A scrap of torn lining from my cape made the perfect wrapping. I returned to the window, checked that Jem was still there, and accosted a stranger about to walk into the pub.

"Please, could you give this to the young man with the eye-patch?" I cast my eyes down. "I can't go in myself, I'm under age."

The stranger's mouth opened but I did not give him time to speak.

"Tell him," I said, pressing the lock into a palm that could not flinch away because it was balancing a half-rolled cigarette, "that She will be on the bridge at nine."

I gave the "She" Rider Haggardly emphasis and hoped it would be carried on with the message. Then, without waiting for a reply, I picked up my skirt and skipped off down the alley, emerging the other end on a road that led by a convenient back route to 309. On the way I ran into a shop that stayed open late and bought half a pound of mince and an onion. I was about to cook my first meal for a man.

Inside the house, having checked that Kay had gone, I slid the safety-chain on the front door, put on a jazz record and stepped out of my clothes. I planned to bathe and change before fetching Jem. But then I saw the time. Nearly eight. How long did mince take to cook? I padded into the kitchen, shimmying to the music, and turned to the index of Kay's battered cookery manual. There were recipes for mince pies, minced collops, mincemeat, but no plain mince—and what on earth was a collop? I banged the book shut and lit the oven. I had watched Kay cook Saturday lunch mince for years, and it always started in a frying pan with an onion and ended in the oven with mashed potatoes on top. I slipped Jem's shirt over my nakedness and attacked the onion. It looked quite professional sizzling away with a little oil in a pan. And the addition of a cup of sherry and some ginger with the meat made it the right color and texture. I put it in the oven to finish cooking while I bathed.

All clean and clad once again in Jem's shirt, with plaits wound into the chaplet his eye so admired, I went into the dining room to look for a candle and some fruit for his pudding. The table around which Kay and I had sparred not so many years ago—she with a bread knife, me with my child's heartless words—had been moved since the household had shrunk, but the painting of Madonna and Child was still there. I switched on the small striplight above it and was about to draw the curtains when a noise in the passage alongside the house made me pause. Cats, I thought, dismissing it. But there it was again, a persistent little scrape, not uncatlike but not quite like a cat . . . I leaned forward against the window, trying to see into the dark. There was one more scrape, firmer than the rest, followed suddenly by the bright yellow flare of a match inches from my nose. I stayed quite still, hand on the curtain, mesmerized.

Above the wavering flame two large black-rimmed lenses quested like the headlamps of Mr. Fox's car. I could see nothing beyond them but there was a voice: " 'When I consider how my light is spent,/'Ere half my days, in this dark world and wide . . .'" It trailed off.

"That is Milton, child—'On His Blindness.'"

His breath on the window made the thinning matchlight fuzzy, like a candle in a wet jar. There was a petulant "Ouch!" as the light went out, then the deep voice resumed.

"It ends: 'They also serve who only stand and wait.'" Madam, I have been standing and waiting a long time. The hour has come to serve. I beg you let me in!"

"Go round to the front door," I said. "But quietly."

It would be awkward if Kay's elderly neighbors were roused.

I ripped the curtains to before he could reply and grabbed a pair of jeans off the back of a chair, dragging them on as I ran through to the front door. How had he found me? Why was he wearing glasses? Had he seen me looking up "mince" with no clothes on? I took a deep breath before opening the door.

Jem stood a few steps back from the porch, chin raised. The patch was in place and his lips, a glisten of teeth between them, curved downward in a beautiful sneer. Had he been wearing a sword, his hand would have been on the hilt.

I stepped back without a word and in two strides he was in the porch, the door was closed, and I was backed up against Marianne's old bicycle with Jem blowing hot dragon's breath in my ear. His short black coat was open and his white skin gleamed very close. He smelled of whisky and night air. His arms, leaning against two walls, trapped me in the corner like a claw, and he was saying one word over and over again, dropping it from deep in his diaphragm on every outbreath so that it hit my neck in rhythmic thrusts: "Bitch bitch bitch bitch."

"Jem, I . . ."

He groaned as though hit in the stomach and flung away from me into the hall. As he looked around, half blind I knew, I gave a quick stage direction to the bishop's chair. Its grand carved back and arms formed a magnificent backdrop for him.

"Bitch," he said again, floating the word on velvet waves to where I had plopped down, brain benumbed, on the edge of a long divan.

"Jem, I . . ."

"Don't speak!"

His eye closed and he held up a forbidding hand. There was rather a long pause until, disobeying, I heard my own voice holding out the second verse of Shelley's "To the Moon" like an offering:

> "Art thou pale for weariness
> Of climbing heaven, and gazing on the earth,
> Wandering companionless
> Among the stars that have a different birth,—
> And ever changing, like a joyless eye
> That finds no object worthy of its constancy?"

He gave a deep, growling moan and threw himself upon me. I toppled back on the divan, Kay's white daytime handbag bumping my shoulders. His arm was under my back, clamping me to him. The hair was swept from my neck, teeth and lips sunk into my flesh, sucking, moaning, full of hot breath.

" 'Companionless no more!'" he muttered through mouthfuls of me. " 'O my America! my newfound-land!' "

I gulped, hands on his shoulders, half hugging him to me, half pushing away. His mouth was traveling lower, heat searing through the shirt which he dragged to one side in his teeth, chewing the collar with bearlike growls.

" '. . . Sweet disorder of the dress . . .'" Gimme back my shirt."

I had never felt such excitement but I was alarmed too. It was like when Richard used to tickle me and I loved it but thought I would die if he did not stop.

"Wait, please! Please!"

Jem's body was tight against me all over, pressing, undulating. I could feel the bones of his loins swivel over mine. My bare toes struggled feebly with his booted heels. A metal button at the top of my jeans caught on one of his, grinding. His hand went between us, ripping the buttons apart, then diving in where my inbreathed belly made a gap. I squirmed.

"Jem, really. Please!"

His mouth, fastened like an oyster to my chest, let go suddenly with a sharp sucking sound.

" 'For Godsake hold your tongue and let me love.' "

Now I pushed at his shoulders in earnest.

"Please be gentle. I haven't . . . I haven't"—that mouth descended again—"*I haven't done this before!*"

Instantly he was still. After a long, long moment he sighed with his whole length and lifted himself from me. Hunched over, head in hands, he murmured, "Dear God, what a fool I have been!"

I sat up, disengaging my hair from the handles of Kay's bag.

"Can you forgive me?" he said. "I am nothing but a clumsy, loutish fool—and a little drunk."

I knelt by him and patted his shoulder cautiously. A strong wave of meaty ginger vied with the dying cold-air smell of his coat.

"It's all right," I said. "Look, I've just remembered something. Wait."

In ten minutes Jem found himself seated opposite me at the kitchen table. I had set out a glass of water with two aspirins, a cup of strong coffee, and a knife and fork. He drank the water and took the aspirins, but did not touch the coffee.

"Forgive me," he said, this time not referring to his attack on my maiden state. "It gives me heartburn worse than *l'amour*."

I withdrew the casserole from the oven, hoping its contents would not do the same. In lieu of potatoes I had made little half moons of toast and put a slice of peeled pear on top as decoration. I thought how docile and endearing Jem looked with his fork poised.

"Is it *very* painful?" I asked, chin on hands, "and is there *much* blood?"

The fork went down.

"Child, I cannot eat and discuss your virginity at the same time. Which do you want me to do?"

"Eat."

Obediently his head went down.

"You did not make this . . ."—he sniffed—"this exquisite Eastern confection yourself?"

"It's not a confection," I answered, offended. "It's mince."

"Madam," he pronounced after the third mouthful, this delicacy is to mince what silk is to string."

I laughed with pleasure. At least one part of the evening was going according to plan.

After he had finished eating, I offered him one of Richard's old cigars which I had found in the lounge. I parked him upstairs while I tidied up the kitchen. Kay would not question any of my doings so long as I did not leave anything messy for her to clear up.

Jem was ensconced on my mattress when I went up, leaning back behind a cloud of breaking smoke rings. He waved them away as I came in.

"Now," he said seriously, "come and sit by me and do not be afraid."

He made a kind of speech, telling me that yes, he was a rake but not a scoundrel. No fruit fell unwillingly to his hands. He sensed in me, he said, "a little well of sensuality, full of promise," and he said that whoever tapped that well would be honored—but must also be honorable. He made me feel in possession of something rare and precious. I broadened the subject with a joke.

"People are always telling me I am full of promise—potential is the word they use. It makes me feel uncomfortable."

"Ah, yes," he said musingly. "That was an accusation leveled at me once. It is a cruel one, at first flattering, finally threatening. It is hard to live up to. Potential, potential—potent shell. That is what I have become, a husk."

"Why do you say that?" I demanded.

With his beauty and his music and his poetry he seemed quite the opposite, rich and full of value.

"I am a fretful soul," he answered, "black and full of flaws. I want things I cannot even name."

There was a pause in which I moved closer.

"*I* want to see under your eye-patch."

"Hell's teeth," he said bitterly. "You would find me out in all things."

He turned his head away a second and when he turned back, the patch was gone. There was no burn scar, no glass monstrosity, but what there was I understood at once to be more painful to him than either of those would have been. His beauty, which rose above his pockmarks and his razor-nicked chin, was distorted by a squint.

"Thank you for showing me," I said, and trusting him now, stroked his arm. After a few minutes we lay down together and quiet as a child he fell asleep in my arms. The cigar, lying in a shell where I kept my hair-grips, glowed until my cupped hand snuffed it out.

Some time toward midnight I heard Kay come in. Even though I knew she would not disturb us, I must have stiffened for Jem stirred. I whispered, "Shh," in his ear. When her door closed and the last light went out I relaxed.

"My mother," I told him softly.

"And is your father downstairs?"

"No, he's in Scotland. Where's yours?"

"Ireland."

It was easy to ask things in the dark.

"How old are you?"

"Nearly twenty. You?"

"Fifteen."

His breath was warm on my face. His fingers found my cheekbone.

"Can I kiss you now?"

"Yes."

Right cheek, left cheek, forehead, lips. A benediction.

At six, standing in the cold drizzle on the front path of 309, Jem took a ragged silk scarf from his pocket, wiped it over his glasses and knotted it loosely round my neck. The bruises raised by his oyster mouth of the night before were tender, but he had not done anything to add to them in the night.

"Those marks of lust will fade, but the seal of amity I press upon you now will not."

With that he kissed my forehead one last time and was gone, a black-coated figure in the dawn, measuring the distance between lampposts with long, catlike strides.

I took Kay her tea at seven-thirty.

"What does 'amity' mean?"

"Something to do with friendship. Why do you want to know?"

"Somebody said it to me—a friend."

"Mr. Fox?"

"No."

I was irritated by her teasing tone and spoke without thinking. "Mr. Fox isn't a friend like that—he's a man."

It was only after the words were out that I understood the change that had come over my relationship with Jem, and when I looked up his word for it in the dictionary—"Amity: friendly relations between states bound by mutual causes"—my feelings were confirmed. Marking the difference between our sexes with tenderness, Jem and I would meet in the future as comrades. Our youthful searchings were too closely matched and my sexuality too unformed for him to take me any other way. And for my part, now that I had held him unmasked in my arms, empathy had replaced desire. I needed the mystery of distance for my body to be roused beyond my mind.

Accordingly, I chose as my first man a friendly lover as opposed to a lovely friend. I will never know how things might have worked out differently in years to come had I chosen the other way round.

The day before Christmas Eve, Kay was still trying to persuade me to join her and James at an aunt's in Yorkshire and I was still saying no. I liked the way James, home from his first term at boarding school, plunged the orderly dust of 309 into disarray by littering stairs, landing and hall with smelly piles of laundry and going through his rugger warm-up routine in the lounge. But even he, leaned on by Kay to put in a plea, could not change my mind. As far as I was concerned my aunt and uncle were strangers who went tight-lipped at the mention of Richard. James, more amenable, would lap up gifts and kindnesses without souring them with his own interpretations as I, unhappily, had done before. Besides I had my own plans.

They went off in the morning; James grinning and picking his nose, Kay waving anxiously and calling, "You will ring, won't you?"

"Yes, yes!"

I closed the front door and leaned against it, reveling in the thought of four days of empty 309, each one of which I would fill with my own music and moods. Best of all was the knowledge that it would be empty to come back to—if I came back. The first portrait session with Mr. Fox was that afternoon.

Out of comradely loyalty to Jem—my passionate attraction to him was already material for nostalgia—I made no plaits in my hair but let it hang free for Mr. Fox.

One of the first things he said was: "Would you mind putting your hair up somehow?"

As I had not brought any hairpins with me, I wound it over itself in a loose knot. "It's slipping," I said as he sat me on his chair in the music room and took my usual place himself, sketchpad on knee.

"Doesn't matter."

For the next hour the only sound was the soft scratching of lead on paper. I rested my gaze just above Mr. Fox's head, focus blurring on the nondescript pattern of the wallpaper. My thoughts, released by the stillness, roved languidly like the visitors in the Tate, pausing now and then when they found a pleasing image. After a while I was only distantly conscious of being drawn.

"Coffee?"

"Mmm."

"You can open your mouth, you know."

I laughed and said I liked the quiet.

"Yes—you're a funny little thing, aren't you?"

I did not answer. It was the first time he had said anything so personal. After coffee Mr. Fox suggested I sit in his studio for the next sketch. The studio was upstairs, and in the middle of it was a large white bed.

"Music?"

"Mmm."

A handful of slowly plucked lute strings fell into the quietness, then a man singing in a bell-clear Renaissance voice. Mr. Fox sketched, hidden behind an easel.

After half an hour the street lamps came on outside.

"Drat," he said.

"Does that mean you can't go on?"

"Well . . ." He put down his pencil and stood with arms folded, regarding the sketch he had propped against the back of a chair.

"What time do you have to be home?"

"Oh," I answered vaguely, looking at my toes, "no special time."

"Do you mind staying on a bit then while I set up some lights?"

"I don't mind at all."

Mr. Fox began by pulling the curtains and turning on the main light. I noticed with a slight shock as he did this that half a woman's figure was painted on the wall and the light-switch was her nipple. I had a vision of Mr. Fox's hands on my breasts and tried to imagine what it would feel like. I could not stop thinking about it and when he asked me to sit again—this time on the floor hugging my knees—I was more self-conscious than before.

"Move around until you feel comfortable," he said, selecting a fresh cassette. "The pose should feel natural, just as if you were having a little think to yourself."

I nodded stiffly. "I am."

The new music was Elizabethan court dances. In my mind, Mr. Fox was dressed in doublet and hose.

"I wish I was wearing a long dress," I blurted.

"It would be nice," he said absently. "I like girls in long dresses."

Damn, I thought. I wanted him to like *me*.

"What about a sheet?"

"Pardon?"

Mr. Fox's head appeared round the side of the easel.

"A sheet," I repeated. "I could wrap a sheet round me like a dress."

"What a good idea."

He found a sheet of thin, soft material like muslin. I did not know if he expected me to take my clothes off there and then.

"You might like to sort yourself out in the bathroom," he said, as though reading my mind.

I undressed looking at a mermaid he had painted in the bath. She had blue hair and a long green body winding all the way round the tub so that her fingers and the tip of her tail met at the taps. I imagined Mr. Fox lying in the bath with his head on her belly just where the skin became scales. The sheet was large and wound round twice, giving me a sort of tail too. I tucked it under my arms at the side, but when I reached up to centralize the knot in my hair it fell down, showing my breasts. I touched the pale pink softness of the nipples and was surprised when they pinched up into tight, uneven little buds. They normally only did that in the cold. Retucking the sheet, I shuffled carefully back into the studio and stood by the door, holding up my tail.

"Do I look silly?"

Mr. Fox paused in his arrangement of pencils and brushes.

"Actually, you look rather charming."

I colored with pleasure.

The background he had made was stark: large sheets of white paper on the floor, a screen of white behind.

"Put your bottom about there," he said, pointing to a space where some of the corners of the paper met. I was about to sink down, holding the sheet carefully round me, when he said, "Hang on. Stay just like that."

He left the room a moment and came back with a camera. I must have moved while he was setting it up because suddenly my hair fell right down.

"Oh!"

"It's all right, don't move. I'll fix it."

Mr. Fox's hand lightly steadying my skull as he combed my hair felt strange and intimate. His face was close and he was looking at me but it was as though he saw me from a long way away. Once, the comb touched my bare back and an involuntary shudder made the sheet slip lower. I knew if I took my arms away now it would fall down.

"Sorry, didn't mean to make you jump."

He went back behind the camera and took several photographs before saying I could sit down. Then he sketched. After ten minutes he stopped and ran a hand through his hair.

"It's no good."

He explained that the effect he was aiming for was one of curves and lines. The paper made the lines and my body was supposed to make the curves. But the sheet got in the way.

"It's like something fragile with soft contours—an egg, say—against a background contrastingly flat and angular. I see you like that. Very egglike.'' He looked at his watch. ''Never mind. Want to watch something on telly?''

I was disappointed that this picture had not gone well.

''What?''

''Old film. James Cagney''—he grinned suddenly—''old cars.''

He lent me a dressing gown and we sat side by side on the settee in the front room. Halfway through the film I went out to the kitchen to make us a snack.

''This is very nice of you, you know,'' said Mr. Fox, popping his head round the door on the way to the lavatory.

I hoped he would not be long or the omelette I had made would go leathery. It had stuck to the pan anyway and I had to serve it in bits. I gave him the best bits.

''It's a scromelette,'' I said. ''Cross between scrambled and ommed.''

''Great.''

He poured us each a glass of advocaat and wished me a Merry Christmas.

I snuggled deep into the settee beside him, my body in the warm dressing gown feeling silky and snug. When the film ended Mr. Fox got up and switched off the T V.

''Well, I suppose I ought to take you home.''

''I was just wondering,'' I said, inspecting a raised seam on the armrest beside me, ''if it would be better without the sheet.''

''Nude?''

Mr. Fox said the word just as if it were ''coffee?'' or ''music?'' I nodded and he went on.

''Actually that's what I had in mind when I thought of the set, but didn't like to ask.''

''I'll do my best.''

It had got colder upstairs and Mr. Fox brought in an electric heater. He put on some music and said ''Ready?''

On a chair the sheet lay crumpled where I had left it. The dressing-gown joined it now.

''Fine. Not too cold?''

I shook my head, purposely making the hair fall forward. My arms were shielding my upper body but it seemed to be my face I wanted to hide. My legs were straight and still; topped, from my view down, by a little ruff of goldy-brown curls. He took a photograph of my head and arms like that.

"Don't worry," he said. "I'm not going to take any pictures of your pubes."

I had not thought about it.

The next pose, sitting down with my limbs folded, was a long one. The woman on the cassette had a strong, fluid voice and soon my mind flowed with the story of her songs. There was one about two sisters, one dark, one fair. The dark girl was jealous of her younger sister and pushed her into the sea. Some shepherds found her body and made a harp from the breastbone which sang the tale of the crime so that the dark girl was haunted by it forever. I wondered if Marianne had ever wanted to kill me for usurping her place in Richard's heart. I would have if I had been her.

"You look miles away," said Mr. Fox, bringing me back. "I've about finished. Want to look?"

My buttocks felt square from the hardness of the floor and squinting over my shoulder I saw two matching red blobs. Embarrassed, I tried to rub them out with my hands before going round to Mr. Fox's side of the easel. The sketch he had done brought me up short.

"It's lovely," I said wonderingly. "But who is it?"

The face was nothing but the curve of a chin under a bell of hair.

"It's a young girl thinking a young girl's thoughts."

"So, it's not really me at all?"

"Well, *you're* a young girl. Aren't you?"

Pride a little thrown, I reached for the dressing gown. What he had said was interesting—a new perspective—but at the same time it robbed me of something. My reaction was lame.

"I'm not *that* young."

He laughed and yawned.

"So, what now? It's pretty late and I've got a piece of jewelry to finish before tomorrow. You can kip down here if you like and I'll run you home in the morning."

It was what I had been hoping he would say.

Mr. Fox went to finish the piece of jewelry downstairs and I climbed into the big white bed. After a few minutes in the dark, thinking, I got up and washed between my legs, being careful not to put soap inside as it stung. My eyes were shut but I was not asleep when Mr. Fox came in. I swore I would not jump when he touched me.

I heard his clothes fall to the floor, the clunk of his belt as it swung against a chair. Then he was beside me under the covers, cool and clean and smelling of toothpaste. I waited, yearning and dreading, but yearning more. So tense was every expectant inch of skin I thought the sheet must bristle.

But he did not touch me.

For the first three hours—the luminous dial of his watch clipped off the seconds less than a foot from my eyes—I lay ramrod stiff, unable to cancel hope. Then, after four o'clock, when I got up to go to the lavatory, the sap went out of me. He did not want me. I was blind, an idiot, had made a mess of everything. Thoughts darting about in angry confusion, I grasped at straw solutions in the dark. Jem had gone to Ireland for a while. I would go there tomorrow, find him, give him some whisky and make him do it out of comradeship. But my body betrayed me. Back in bed, to my horror, I started to cry. It was when I thought of the scromelette and how much I had enjoyed making it and watching James Cagney with Mr. Fox.

"Mr. Fox!" I said in a tiny, livid whisper, catching my lip. "What a bloody silly name!"

There was a creak from his side of the bed.

"My name is Sebastian," he said and, quietly rolling over, ran a hand from the crown of my head to my toes. And back again.

It was not too painful and there was not much blood. And all through the sweet, short sleep that followed I was aware of hugging the small torn tenderness inside me like a prize.

At nine-thirty on Christmas morning Sebastian—I had to remind myself not to call him Mr. Fox—brought me a mug of coffee in bed. He sat on the outside of the covers, blue eyes calm and kind.

"Feel all right?"

"Fine!" I said it so explosively that the skin on my coffee leaped out and hung over the brim. I felt very happy.

"Look," said Sebastian and he paused and fingered his moustache before going on. "I only did that because I thought you were expecting it."

Thought I was expecting it. The coffee skin started to slide down the side of the mug.

"I'm engaged to a girl in Stockholm."

Girl in Stockholm.

"But I want you to have this."

He placed a little nest of cottonwool on the pillow and parting it with those long cool fingers which had so carefully parted me, revealed a small polished stone. Stripes on it ran softly into one another, white to lavender, lilac to mauve.

"I'll set it in a ring for you if you like."

My hand set down the mug and closed over the stone. I thought of it at once as the Virgin Stone.

"No," I said. "I don't want a ring, but thank you." And for all that he had only done it because I was expecting it, added, "Thank you for everything."

6

The New Year brought a series of migrations. At the end of January Sebastian Fox told me that soon he would be going to Stockholm. It was not a great blow but I would miss the quiet afternoons I spent with him, the unhurried education of my body in his hands. Jem, who reappeared at the gray house after Christmas, thin and coughing from rough days in Ireland, announced that he must take himself and his sax to warmer climes or both would die. Armed with a battered copy of *Don Quixote* and Hemingwayesque visions of the Spanish Civil War, he set off for Madrid from Richmond station one afternoon. Our farewell was tender and he vowed to write. I told him to use the Scottish address because I could not see myself at 309 or the poly in the spring. Marianne came south and I took the overnight coach from Victoria to Inverness. Nobody was surprised and Richard was pleased. Lucy's Sweet Trolley lived again.

Much had been learned from one season in the hotel. I heard Richard say to guests: "Oh yes, in our first year we made an awful lot of mistakes." By that he meant Gordon and Gilbert and other staff disasters. It was people who were mistakes rather than ideas.

Staff accommodation was short and the waitresses bunked together in a building at the back of the hotel called the Bothy. From my room near Richard's—the night noises had grown less frequent since Edwina had taken on the job of chef as well as everything else—I could just hear the music and revelry which started up when dinner service was over. There were no Jems or Sebastians among the local youths I saw trooping up the Bothy steps after the bar closed, half bottles sticking out of their pockets, hair tokenly slicked down, but nevertheless I was drawn to them. And their maleness, pungent in the ruddy body warmth and animal odor of damp Arran wool, was more immediate than that of the well-turned-out guests in the dining room.

So I began to linger and chat with the waitresses, mostly university students from down south. One girl, Maxine, was particularly welcoming. She was the straw-blond daughter of an old ballerina flame of Richard's. But she only spoke to me when there were no men present, because when there were, she curled up in a short skirt against a cushion and gazed into inner space, trickling smoke mysteriously through a gap in her front teeth. She told me that on the whole she preferred older men—"wouldn't mind having a go at your old man"—but had recently got into waders and young fishermen. I was mildly taken aback by the mention of Richard as possible prey but found it intriguing too.

"I think you'd find he was too busy," I said.

She gave me a smoke-blurred woman-of-the-world look.

"Men are rarely too bithy for thex," she said with an oddly unchildish lisp. "Ith love that buggerth up their routine."

"What about women?" I asked, anxious not to let this mood of pearl-dropping go by without gleaning all I could.

"Thame thing, only they don't like to admit it."

It was years before I made any but the most abstract sense of her answer.

My visits to the Bothy were doomed on two counts. First, when Richard found out that I was hobnobbing with the staff and locals he made it clear that he disapproved. Second, it became increasingly obvious that by being the proprietor's daughter—as well as *only just* not a virgin (Maxine's pronouncement after hearing about my nonorgasmic defloration)—I was cramping the waitresses' style. It was natural for the staff of a small hotel to discuss the management and awkward when I, a possible spy in their midst, made them feel obliged to watch their words. As soon as I realized this I reverted to my former solitary ways and once again the most constant companions of my free time were the hills, the wind and the sea.

But I did not forget Richard's disapprobation and inwardly I railed against it. The new relationships I had experienced with men left a gap that love for him alone could not fill.

A card came from Jem in Spain: "ROOTLESS, BOOTLESS, FRUITLESS, STUMBLING THROUGH LORCA." There was no address. I put my current favorite book in my oilskin pocket (Dr. Desmond Morris's *The Human Zoo*), and did my stumbling on the hills. For all the success of the sweet trolley I felt as rootless, bootless and fruitless as Jem. Unanswered questions queued up at the back of my mind like fledglings anxious to fly.

Summer passed with the haze of heather fires, the bracken unfurling and fields crazy with thistles. Rain swelled the water in the hill lochs, and small trout rose in the reeds and flipped their bodies in brazen arcs through the air. Huge lilies, yolk-yellow and cream, sprung into being like mushrooms overnight. It was a fertile environment for a young girl thinking a young girl's thoughts to grow.

And on the crofts, the fruit of Richard's efforts burst through the wet black soil and filled trug after trug with abundant green mounds. His energy and enthusiasm seemed inexhaustible. Day after day he worked with both arms dug up to the elbows in the present but he never stopped thinking about the future. His plans for next year were extravagant; there would be a new staff house, a bakery, a darkroom, more cows, giant horticultural tunnels, quail . . . It was impossible not to be swept along in the fierce current of his dreams but some part of me held back. His world was so full, so diverse, it was overwhelming. And while I continued to create and see demolished the gâteaux and pastries which were my small contribution to it, I clung stubbornly to the idea of a world of my own.

Once, at a low ebb in the middle of the season, I had turned my back on the hotel and hitched 350 miles down the road south before loyalty caught up and I turned round. Richard's only comment was: "I should think so too" and we never discussed it again. Apart from guilt for threatening to leave him in the lurch, I felt ashamed of my own vagueness. Now that I was over official school-leaving age at last, the future awaited my own moulding, and the questions he did not ask I asked myself: Where was I going? What was the plan? There were still no satisfactory answers.

Because of this I agreed when Richard suggested that, instead of going south and starting something new at the end of the season, I should build on my one proven ability—dessert cookery—by taking a course in baking at a college in Inverness. Then I could run the new bakery he planned for next year. And if I did not choose to do that, at least I would have a recognized skill to make up for my lack of academic qualifications.

When autumn came and the hotel closed its doors, Richard hitched a horsebox full of pigs to the back of the Land-Rover and drove me to Inverness. Our goodbye was perfunctory because we expected to see each other again soon.

But it was over a year before we did.

I knew from the first day at the bakery course that it was not going to work. I was the only girl in a class of twenty-two boys, who as far as I could see were all miniature models of Gordon and Gilbert. They stole furtive looks at my legs from under lank swatches of hair and made obscene gestures with broom handles when they thought I could not see. The products we turned out—batallions of precisely matching, tasteless loaves—were things I would never cook for anybody and walking back to my digs past the River Ness, I tore them up and threw them to the gulls. I made my own brown rolls in a communal oven on the landing and ate them in bed with disks of hard goat cheese and pints of goat's milky coffee—my landlady bred goats and kept me generously supplied with their products.

I stopped attending the course at the end of the second week and spent my time mooching about the cold streets of Inverness, staring at the river and trying to decide what to do. I could not stay at the goat lady's much longer because sooner or later Richard would phone and I knew I would not be able to lie to him about giving up the course.

One morning, when I had walked up and down the same street five times and was considering a sixth, I saw an unusual figure emerging from a shop. He was dressed in long yellow robes of a chiffony material much too light for the weather and he was smiling into thin air. As he passed, the smile aimed itself into my eyes and he gave a sort of bow.

The shop from which he had come sold healthfood and I went in to have a look. Having established that their honey was twice the price of that in the supermarket, I was about to leave when I heard the women behind the counter discussing the stranger. They guessed he had come from a place out Kiltarlity way—"one of those commune things." I was curious. "Commune" was a word I had heard Jem use, making it sound exciting and revolutionary. (He was in fact referring to the Paris Commune of the 1790s but I did not know that.) I had also heard the word used positively by a young couple I had met during the summer who were hitchhiking round the Highlands. Having nothing better to do, I decided to investigate, and that afternoon I was on the road once more with my thumb wagging in the wind.

About sixteen miles outside Inverness, a truck with a cementmixer on the back dropped me at the end of an unsignposted lane. Weeds sprung thickly from a muddy ridge running down the middle and I crossed from side to side to avoid potholes filled with puddles. It was a still day, the air damp and clinging cold. I hoped these people had a fire. I was not sure what else I was looking for.

The place was a tumbledown farm. Rusty hub-caps, broken roof tiles and a trail of yellow cabbage leaves littered the approach. A youth with a pudding-basin haircut was staring at a row of gone-to-seed Brussels sprouts.

"Excuse me, is this the commune?"

A white, spotty face bobbed and blushed beneath the ridiculous hair. Looking at the sprouts he said, "It is the ashram of the Perfect Light Mission of Guru Kahan."

"Oh," I said, not sure where to go from here, "is he in?"

The youth clutched at his shirt and said, "He is in here. He is everywhere."

I started to ask another question but was interrupted by the arrival of the man in yellow chiffon. He came at the head of a troupe, some similarly dressed, others in jeans.

"Brother Giles!" he cried excitedly, "this is the sister I spoke of whose soul is already a plowed field. Welcome! Come into our Master's house, come into our hearts!"

His speech was accompanied by beams, head-bobbing and wringing hands.

"Thank you," I said, "but I did not know you were religious. I think I'll . . ." My words trailed away at the flurry of hand-waving and denials.

"Come!" said the yellow man, bowing a path toward the farmhouse. And because I was curious and because I was looking for something, I went.

The Kiltarlity sect of the Perfect Light Mission took me to its bosom. They led me to a bare room with a spreading damp stain on the ceiling and announced that they were going to give me *satsang*, the first stage of initiation which would be completed when I received the Knowledge at the hands of the Master himself. *Satsang* consisted of talk.

I was told that I had come because I was searching and the Perfect Light had shown me the way. Had they not all been in the same position once? Ah yes, they knew, they knew. Each one had been led here by the questions in his heart.

They spoke rapidly, in turn, for over an hour, praising their saviour, Guru Kahan, and their simple way of life. I felt so benumbed by the constant bombardment of words that I found myself nodding. And whenever I nodded, they nodded with me. It was as though there were ten strings attached to the damp ceiling, nine belonging to them, one to me. Everything that had been in my head before seemed to be driven out by the flood of words. When I laughed shakily in a second's pause and said I felt dizzy, they said that was the power of *satsang* and after "rice" they would give me some more. Too fuddled to resist, I nodded. And the nine heads nodded with me.

"Rice" came mounded in glutinous peaks in a plastic washing-up bowl. It was topped by a thin dribble of dhal. We held plates in our laps and dipped into the communal bowl. A lot of rice went on the floor.

As soon as the meal was over *satsang* began again. I was tired. I looked out of the window. It was dark. Where was the lavatory? What was the time? And then the singing began: "Shri Guru Kahan! Shri Guru Kahan! Our Master, our Lord, our Master, our Lord!" The meaningless couplets went on and on. My head was beginning to throb. I shut my eyes and immediately, without their eager faces beaming in, felt relieved.

"Look at us, Little Sister! For *satsang* the windows of the soul must be open."

"I'm sorry," I said, "I'm tired."

They waved their hands solicitously but went on yet again to praise the wonders of the Knowledge, which all of them, except Giles, had already received. He was just waiting for a gift from home to help toward his contribution. Contribution?

"Yes, as a sign that we are truly prepared to accept the guidance of the Perfect Light, we willingly give what we can."

The blessed Guru knew that many of his followers were humble so he accepted as little as £10. I looked at Giles's innocent, eager face and felt angry with myself for having allowed them to waste their *satsang* on me. They smiled and smiled out of eyes that were blinkered, shining with a light less divine than desperate. I lay down to sleep among them, unthreatened by their bodies ("we have no need of carnal pleasure"), but saddened and subdued. And in the half light of morning when I got up to go, I saw evidence of one type of passport to the Light. An arm, trailed out from a sleeping bag on the bare boards of the communal room, was covered with needle tracks.

I thought when I left—thanking some other god that they were too bleary at that hour to attempt *satsang*—that I had seen the last of the Children of the Perfect Light. But the next day Giles stopped me in the street in Inverness. He gave me a long brotherly greeting and asked if he could travel with me as I had mentioned I was going south. He was on his way to get the Knowledge.

I was preoccupied. A letter forwarded to my digs that day had set me on edge with excitement. It was from Dr. Desmond Morris, author and zoologist. After reading *The Human Zoo* I had written to him with vague hopes of a career working with primates. By now I had almost given up on a reply. But here it was, a fact in my pocket, complete with an introductory letter to a professor in London and the possibility of a job. And here was Giles, Child of the Perfect Light, on a mission of his own.

"Yes" I said, "you can travel with me, but on one condition—not a single word of *satsang*."

Hitching as a pair may be wise but it is far slower than traveling single-load. Giles's drooping presence felt like a severe encumbrance after two hours standing in a freezing wind without one car stopping, and eventually I resorted to the trick of hiding him behind a hillock so I appeared to be thumbing alone. A few drivers took exception to this, not believing the tale that Giles had been having a pee, but on the whole it worked and we arrived in London twenty-four hours later without mishap. Giles made a last attempt to lure me to the Mecca of Perfect Light but I shook my head, wished him luck and walked away. I wanted to find a Way—it was every young person's quest—but nothing would persuade me that Nirvana could be purchased tailormade for £10.

The good old 73 bus took me to Richmond and I walked over the bridge to 309 savoring the drab familiarity of the scene. Marianne and Kay made me welcome in their separate ways. There was no question of us all sitting down together; relationships in our family were strictly one to one. Marianne, who looked white and unhappy, brought me coffee in the studio and closed the door on Kay. Later Kay made tea which she and I took in the lounge. When these formalities were over I went upstairs, dumping my bag in the middle of the Big Room, and closed the door on them both. Allying myself more closely with Richard, I wanted to keep my life quite separate from theirs.

I found the number of the college mentioned in Dr. Morris's letter and telephoned for an appointment. The professor I spoke to suggested I should pop in for a chat one afternoon next week. My heart sank at the number of days in between but I felt lucky to be seen at all. While waiting, I wrote long, diarylike letters to nobody and spent a great deal of time in the local library finding out what I could about monkeys and men. My secret hope was that the interview might lead to something like an apprenticeship with someone engaged in behavioral research.

It did lead to something, and quickly, but it was rather different to anything I had imagined. I was given the job of Monkey Keeper at Fircross Zoo.

Halfway through the first month I wrote to Marianne:

Marianne:

Zoos are not much different to towns with lots of separate racial communities. Keepers float about between them like servants of Big Brother. The monkey house is small but some of the cages are bigger than the room I've been boarded out in. After the first couple of days I was left in sole charge, which was nerveracking, because the monkeys know the routine better than I do and if I do anything wrong they scream and glare and rattle the bars. There is one tiny spider monkey who pisses in people's eyes—lucky for me he chooses only men. I think most of them (the monkeys I mean) have gone odd in the head from captivity but I get on with them better than I do with the people.

All the staff have separate charges so we only overlap at mealtimes, all smelling of different animals. I never knew elephants smelled so strong. Those mealtimes are awful. My accent sticks out like a sore thumb—they're the sort who automatically think you're a snob if you say isn't instead of in't. The reptile man is the only one I like. I spend my lunch hour in the snakehouse standing like a tree with boas and pythons draped all over me while he cleans out the cages. It's a myth that they're slimy but they can certainly squeeze hard.

I don't know how long I am going to stick it out here. The ladies who run the place are definitely odd. They have headmistress faces, dress in kind of drag, and have Sumo the gorilla in for tea every day. That gorilla looks just how I feel—fed up.

The truth was I was ready to leave after the first week. The professor had warned me not to expect too much but I suppose I was still hoping there might be more to the job than an endless round of feeding and cleaning. If it had not been for the seed of a travel idea, which was growing steadily, I might have persevered a little longer, but I was impatient. Before the end of three months I wrote: "I've had it here. I'm going to save up enough for food and emergencies and aim to be off in the spring. Don't know where yet, but I'm going. And for quite a long time."

My saving prospects at the zoo were poor and I knew I could do better working freelance from 309. I tried out the idea on Kay over the phone.

"Of course," she said, "but are you sure you'll be able to find work? There's so much about unemployment on the news these days."

"Don't worry. I'll find work. You watch."

And while working out my notice at the zoo, I set to devising ways of making this assurance come true.

YOUNG, STRONG, WILLING AND ABLE

Young people with good references available immediately for any part-time domestic work. Gardening, entertaining help and babysitting also undertaken.

Advertisements to this effect appeared in shop windows all over Richmond and Twickenham and in every corner shop in between. The response was swift and almost overwhelming. After a week I had to dash round taking out all the notices to stop Kay's phone ringing.

Inevitably, I double-booked myself one day and asked Marianne if she would mind helping out. She had been ill again and was not yet well enough to take on a full-time job, but the prospect of just a few hours' work appealed. It was my best-paid job, a thrice-weekly cleaning routine in a luxurious bachelor flat opposite the skating shop where Jem had once wooed me with antique phrases in the rain. The owner of the flat was never there. He had had a set of keys cut for me and left my wages behind a clock in the lounge. I handed the keys to Marianne with a list of the jobs to be done, and gave her a number where I could be reached if she needed to ask anything.

I was in the middle of scrubbing out Mrs. Joanna Allerton's oven, up to the armpits in grease, when the phone rang. Mrs. J.A. was reading *House and Garden* in the sitting room. Her voice came floating through the hatch: "Lucy dear, I think it's for you—rather a bad line."

I lifted the kitchen extension gingerly between two dirty fingers.

"Marianne?"

There was an odd, muffled grunting noise on the other end of the line. Then a thick, whispered question.

"Can you come?"

There was nothing wrong with the line, it was Marianne's voice. Hurriedly, I transferred the receiver to the other ear so that the conversation was less audible to Mrs. J.A. and threw her a wide smile through the hatch to make sure she put down her extension.

"What's the matter? Have you broken something?"

There was a funny little laugh.

"I don't *think* so."

"Why do I have to come? I haven't finished here yet . . ."

That weird laugh again.

"You'd better come," she said thickly, and the phone went dead.

"Marianne?" I called foolishly down the dead line.

Mrs. J.A.'s ears must have been stretching.

"Everything all right, dear?"

I replaced the receiver.

"Well, no, actually. I'm afraid I'm going to have to leave early."

And I did, her bewildered voice pursuing me limply down the drive.

It was a fifteen-minute bus ride to the flat and there was often a half-hour gap between buses. I stuck out my thumb. There must have been something compelling in my attitude because the first car to come by stopped and the driver took me right to the door.

"You know why I stopped?" he grinned as I got out, already glancing anxiously up toward the flat.

"No idea."

"Because you have the sweetest blob of black on your nose. Want to come for a drink later?"

"Piss off," I said ungraciously, and smeared the blob of black up to my hairline.

On the landing of the second floor I heard singing. Soft, off-key, quavery: "I - e vow to thee my cou - untry all earthly things a - bove,/ Da da dar, de da de da da dar - the service of my love."

Marianne's favorite. She used to sing it over and over between bouts of sobbing when Richard first left 309. Her voice after tears had an agonizing frailty which drove my head under three pillows. But she had not been crying now.

I knelt before the door and spoke through the letter box.

"Marianne? Open the door."

The singing stopped. I called her name again. Could hear her listening in the pool of her own pause. I fastened my eyes to the narrow slit but could see nothing beyond a copy of *The Times*.

"For goodness sake, Marianne, let me in."

I was afraid someone would see me there, grimy and hissing. There was a lift shaft just across the hall and the front doors of two other flats.

"That you, duck?"

Our old greeting.

"Yes, listen, let me in."

The strange laugh I had heard over the phone grated through the thick door. It was small, distant, gently mocking.

"Can't," she said, "can't get up."

"Are you hurt? Marianne *please*, what is it?"

"Dlunk."

"What?"

"Dlunk."

She laughed again and this time it was more of a giggle. I caught on. It was a peculiar game with rules I had to learn as we went along. I stretched my fingers through the narrow slit and tried to push the paper aside. I could not reach it.

"Look," I said, beginning to feel angry because I was so helpless stuck out there, "you can get to the door, can't you?"

She answered like a little girl.

"Are you going to be horrid? I won't let you in if you're going to be horrid."

"I won't be horrid, I promise—just let me in."

There was a skidding sound and the keys struck the door on her side. Somebody got into the lift on the ground floor. Running my hand along the bottom of the door, I scrabbled for the keys. I could just feel them. The lift was one floor below, the doors opening and closing. With a violent effort, mashing the skin on my knuckles, I got the keys and was inside less than a second before the lift arrived. I sent a silent prayer that it was not the owner of the flat and did not move until the footsteps had gone. Marianne was lying on her back in the corridor, smiling. Thin hair striped her forehead and through it her big brown eyes shone and shone.

"What have you been up to?" I asked, eyes sweeping the flat.

"Up to," she murmured, beaming up at me.

The Hoover lay on its side in the kitchen. A spray can of polish sat beside the clock in the lounge. She had evidently tried.

"It's all the Hoover's fault," she said, pouting. "Dust coming out instead of going in. Tried to mend it but it wouldn't"—she found this extremely funny—"it wouldn't. So had a little drink."

"What drink?"

"There. Bit of each."

She pointed to the lounge and pulled herself after me like a baby along the floor. The drinks cabinet stood open and the tops were off every one of the twenty-or-so bottles.

"Didn't want man to notice," she slurred, propping herself against a chair to watch as I started mechanically to match lids to bottoms, "so had just a little gollop from each. Won't tell Kay, will you? Try that cherry brandy. S'lovely."

I looked at her to see if she was serious. She was. Smiling, encouraging, she was a total stranger.

My hands worked on. After I had gone through the lounge, dusting, straightening chairs, making it all just as usual, I carried on into the bedroom, then kitchen, bathroom, corridor. I used a dustpan and brush instead of the Hoover and left a note about needing a repair. And all the time this stranger followed me, shuffling, chatting amiably, crawling sometimes. When I saw the tracks her knees made through the carpet I told her to sit still. She sat like an obedient doll.

"Sorry, duck," she said once, and I stared at her. Did she know what she looked like with her white legs splayed like a cripple's under her rucked skirt and her hands, clumsy as paddles, pulling dimly at the twisted jersey over her chest?

"You won't tell, will you?"

"I won't tell."

And through some childish, perhaps misguided, sense of loyalty, I did not. But from that time on, when Kay told me Marianne had had one of her "giddy spells," after which she sometimes slept for as long as two days, my mind went curiously numb. The "giddy spells' had been going on since Marianne's last summer in Scotland. She was just eighteen.

I was sixteen when, true to my plan, I took to the road in the spring of 1972. I intended to start by crossing the Channel and then go in whatever general direction offered itself with the first ride. Left would mean France and the Middle East; right, Spain and North Africa. I had thirty pounds in my pocket. It seemed plenty.

And besides, I mused, as I twirled round at the first hitching spot, testing the weight of a rucksack christened Beverly, the sun would surely not cost much.

PART TWO

Bruise

7

Rolling, tumbling, heart pounding, spine whacked in the grit every time I rolled again. Tar on bruise-blotched legs and in my hair. Rolling with mouth shut, tires doing all the screaming as the white car wheeled and screeched away.

Beverly and I landed in a heap just over the unmade edge of the road. Fine dust scattered everywhere, making my brown skin matt, further staining already well-stained Beverly. After the giddiness went, I slowly brushed her down.

It was midafternoon. Below the road a shale slope stretched away under bright sun to acres of gravel wasteland. There was a building site in the distance—wire fences, red drums and rectangular slabs of cement. It was very quiet where I sat brushing Beverly, no cars coming along the tar-sticky road. The tire marks made an overlapping zigzag pattern, a singular left to right and back again among otherwise straight lines. I knew that if they came back I would throw myself down the slope rather than get in the car again.

After a while my hands stopped moving on the rucksack and I sat quite still. My face was hot and dry, the skin sore where one cheek had scraped in the dirt as I fell. I sat on, vacant, until the sound of a vehicle approaching threw me, unthinking, into action. Grabbing Beverly, I slung her under a narrow ledge where the road gave into the slope and flattened myself beside her. The rumble of the motor gathered as it rounded the bend where the white car had disappeared. It passed by booming, shaking the stones and my hands, and receded finally to a distant, impersonal drone. I dared then to lift my eyes and saw the fading back of a truck trailing twin streamers of dust. I stared after it a long time. It might have been going to Athens.

Slowly I clambered back on to the road. Stones disturbed by my feet bounded loudly down the slope, shale skittered. I remained motionless on hands and knees until the last stone stopped moving. The gravel bit into my palms. At last I stood up, one hand holding fast to Beverly's straps. As I bent to hoist her up, pain shot across the base of my spine, but I got her into position all right. Automatically, as they always did when Beverly was aboard, my feet began to walk.

The next car to come by was a silvery gray saloon. When it had almost passed and I had had a chance to see the driver's face, I jabbed out a thumb. He was not going to stop at first but a look in the rear-view mirror made him change his mind. I walked to where he had pulled up, opened the door and glared in. His head, thin on top, was ducked toward me, smiling. I glared harder.

"Athens?"

He nodded and made polite I-don't-speak-English noises.

"*Français?*"

"*Un peu.*"

As I got into the car I said loudly, in English, "If you try anything on I'll kill you. I've got a knife."

He shrugged helplessly to show he did not understand and leaned forward to help fasten my seatbelt. Flinching away, I did it myself. I did not look as we ran over the skid marks, past the shale slope and the distant red drums.

After a while he opened the glove compartment and took out a blue-spotted handkerchief.

"*Tenez. Essuyez votre visage.*"

I wiped. My cheek was tender but I rubbed hard. Blood came away with the grit and dust.

"*Attendez, je suis médecin. Etes-vous blessée ailleurs?*"

So he was a doctor. Was I wounded anywhere else? I hesitated.

"*Pas blessée, mais violée.*"

Violated. The word sounded theatrical.

"*Violée? Je ne comprends pas.*"

My French was becoming harder to find.

"*Un homme disait qu'il peut me conduire à Athènes. Mais il arrêtait la voiture sur un tout petit chemin et il m'a violée. Il voulait faire l'amour mais pas faire l'amour.*"

He wanted to make love but not make love. Did that make sense? The doctor nodded.

"*C'est bien ce que j'imaginais. Je vais vous emmener à l'hôpital.*"

"No—to the police."

He understood that but shook his head. Had I got the make and number of the car? No? Well then, he did not recommend it. As a girl hitching alone I did not stand a chance of being treated with any sympathy even if I was believed. It would be the man's word against mine and besides, he was probably miles away by now.

I shut up. If the man could not be caught at once, and preferably killed, I did not want to think about it any more. The thought of a physical examination was unbearable, so, against the doctor's will, I made him drop me as soon as we came to the main square in Athens. I knew that if we had not been speaking in French I would not have told him anything. The words I had used—*violé, faire l'amour*—seemed unconnected with the actual event, inhabiting a realm far removed from grit in the spine and gravel biting into palms.

Alone now with my body's private knowledge, my mind went numb. The aggression I had shown as I got into the doctor's car had evaporated. Without thought, without direction, I walked round and round Syntagma Square. As the pain across my lower back increased I began to limp, shifting the weight of Beverly from side to side. A long clump of sun-dried hair hung over one eye. After a while I did not bother to push it back any more.

It was late in the day now. Three times I had stepped over the shadow of a man reading a newspaper on some steps. Each time I came round the square again the shadow was longer. Seeing some young backpackers staring, I used a handful of hair to brush away tears which kept coming now. I wanted to brush away the stares. A man in a bright yellow open jeep stopped to talk to the young people, then drove on round the square. He slowed when he was level with me and hooted. I did not react, continuing my aimless, limping round. Cars behind blared for him to move on. He shouted at them angrily in Greek but shifted the jeep back into the main stream to go round again. This time when he came past he slowed almost to a halt and called out in English, "Wait please, I want to talk to you."

Again the blaring of the horns and his retort. The third time he came round, managing to bring the jeep closer, I started to yell, "Go away! Go away!"

Careless of hoots, he leaped out and sprinted to where I stood backed up against a telephone booth. He was short and dark, dressed neatly in cream trousers and a casual shirt. His shoes, on which I concentrated, were of pale, expensive leather. He wore glasses, but not dark, like that other man.

"Listen," he said, "I have been watching you. There is something wrong I think. I would like to help."

He was obviously in a hurry. The parked jeep was causing havoc.

"What do you mean help? I'm OK."

He scratched his head energetically.

"Listen," he said again, "you are not OK. I want to take you home to my wife. You will come?"

"Hah! Your wife!"

My head felt as though it were stuffed with clouds, and the alien words which came out of my mouth like bits torn off them.

"Come, what do you think? I want to go to bed with you? Look!"

He pointed to my reflection in the glass of the telephone booth. I saw a scrawny, wild-haired figure in shorts with scarred and filthy legs. Mechanically I pushed the hair off my face. There were streaks of dirt all over it, smudges of dried blood and tears.

"If you can't trust me, we will telephone my wife. You can talk to her."

He darted into the booth and picked up the receiver. Consternation creased his forehead and he worried at his short black hair with angry fingers. Pushing open the door of the booth, receiver still in hand, he shook it helplessly, a comic study in exasperation. I scowled.

"Come," he said, banging the useless phone back on the hook, "for a moment you must trust me. We go to find another phone."

He ran to the jeep, soothing irate drivers with large, calming gestures. Opening the passenger door he beckoned. Reluctantly, still scowling, I approached. He held out his arms for Beverly but I swung her round and clutched her to my chest. Awkwardly, I scrambled into the jeep like that. There was another phone booth on the other side of the square but it was occupied. Letting go of the wheel he waved his arms expressively.

"OK," he said, "we can go to a hotel."

Seeing my tight expression, he laughed.

"Not for bed, little silly one, for telephone!"

We left the square and he parked down a side street in front of a hotel. Telling me not to move, he ran in and spoke to the desk clerk. I watched as she lifted a telephone from behind the desk and he started talking into it. The conversation seemed to go on a long time and I lost interest, looking instead at a thin cat across the road. It was licking a back paw furiously, as though it would eat it. I had a headache and wanted a glass of water.

Then the man was beside the jeep and opening the door.

"Talk to her," he commanded. "Her name is Ursula—Uschi."

Still hanging on to Beverly I walked past him into the hotel. I held the phone to my ear but did not say anything. Then a hesitant voice, German-accented, spoke in my ear.

"Hello? My name is Ursula. I am the wife of Costas, who is with you. Please will you come to my house? You can have something to eat and a bath if you like."

Her English was formal, like a schoolgirl's. Costas made shooing gestures, round eyes encouraging behind his glasses. At last I said cautiously, "All right."

It seemed a long drive out to the suburb where they lived. Shadows of trees and lampposts sped by; a group of old women all in black; children playing catch with a pine cone outside white, flat-roofed houses. Costas pointed to where a small church stood on a hill. There were cypress trees planted close together in the graveyard.

"My place is near here."

The jeep climbed the hill and just on the other side, we stopped beside a block of flats. Costas let me out while he went to park and I stood holding Beverly, looking up at the flats. A young woman leaning over a balcony waved.

"There, that is Uschi," said Costas when he came back, and led the way up concrete stairs to the back entrance of the flat. Furious barking came from inside and Ursula's voice telling it to hush. When the door opened an excited Alsatian puppy bounded out.

"Down, Hector!" ordered Costas, and lovingly lifted him up.

I let go of Beverly to stroke the soft, deer-colored ears. Uschi—she said I must call her that—led me into the sitting room where the first thing I noticed was a bowl of strawberries on an elegant drinks cabinet. She disappeared for a minute and came back with a jug of iced water.

"Please," she said, "I think you are thirsty."

She had a face like a lovely pixie.

While I drank, Uschi bustled about, lips compressed in concentration. She heaped an assortment of clothes and toiletries on a table before me. There was a white blouse, a pair of dove-gray trousers, a bathrobe, soap and a comb. Glancing at my dust-caked tangle of hair she took the comb away and brought back one with larger teeth. She showed me the bathroom and where I could sleep if I would stay the night. She hoped very much I would. Looking in at the small spare room, I remarked more to myself than to her that it was a long time since I had slept indoors. Laughing delightedly, she said that if it would make me feel more comfortable I could sleep on the balcony with Hector. She would arrange a bed for me there.

I was a long time in the bathroom. Uschi had given me cottonwool, antiseptic and Elastoplast, and after I had washed my hair and thoroughly soaked my body—I could not bring myself to touch between my legs—I attended to all the minor cuts and scrapes. I had to cut the tar from my hair with scissors.

Back in the main room Uschi sat down with me and laid a hand very softly on my wrist. Her eyes, creased with concern, searched mine.

"Please, Eve'—that was the name I had given—"tell me, are you all right? There was a man, yes?"

I did not look at her but answered her questions.

"Yes, a man. But I am all right. Could I—have you got a pair of knickers I could borrow?"

Mine, torn, were still somewhere up a mountain above Cape Sounion. She jumped up, small fists clenched by her sides.

"Of course. How stupid I am."

They took me to eat at a place near the old port of Piraeus. We had *calamares*, followed by fresh fish with Greek salad. There was a bottle of chilled white wine but I had water instead.

Halfway through the main course I stopped eating. Costas and Uschi were talking together, laughing softly into each other's eyes. They had guessed, rightly, that I did not want to talk much. Watching them, liking them, I suddenly had a horrible vision of Uschi pinned in the same position as I had been, her pixie face distorted, hands scrabbling, body trying to snake itself into the ground. I looked away over the dark water. Light from paper lanterns in the restaurant shone on the surface in soft, crinkled beams.

We did not stay out late and Uschi made up my bed on the balcony as soon as we got back. She left me with a picture book of wild birds, another jug of water and some fruit in case I was hungry in the night.

At first I slept, comforted by the warm snufflings of the puppy and the familiar blanket of night air. When I woke it was with a jolt, heart pounding as it had when I was rolling in the grit on the road. I lay totally still, eyes wavering on the distant inner vision I did not want to see. It zoomed in closer and closer until I was right inside the scene, back on the hot road at Cape Sounion, waiting for the man in the diving-mask to take me to Athens.

It had taken the whole morning to climb up to the road from the tiny beach where I had been sleeping for the past week. I was hot and grubby and longed for a cool drink. The last of the water in Harold, my water bottle, was lukewarm and stale. I sat on Beverly, squinting up at the sun. We had agreed to meet at midday.

I had only seen the man twice before, both times when he had been snorkeling and surfaced in our bay. He seemed uninteresting: a white, middle-aged body bulging over a pair of black and yellow swimming trunks. He never took off his diving-mask. It was kind of him, though, to offer to take me to Athens. The Texan thought it a good idea too. In fact he wanted to come. But I knew if he did, I would never get rid of him in Athens. That was where he had latched on to me before. We had both been standing in a queue, waiting to board a boat to Haifa when we were told that it was already full; we could use our tickets for the next one in nine days' time. I had spent nearly the last of my money on the ticket, so there was nothing for it but to muddle through the next nine days, find a beach and eke out the spaghetti I had bought in Brindisi. Luckily I had a full jar of honey, too. The Texan, a thin, Jesus-bearded student, was in the same position and suggested we pool our resources. It had seemed a sensible idea but after a few days I found his company tedious. And all he had to contribute to the food kitty was one jar of Special Crunchy Kretschmer Wheatgerm. After the first day, when we scraped together enough between us for a loaf and some *feta*, we lived on spaghetti cooked in seawater with honey as a sauce and wheat-germ in lieu of parmesan.

On the beach the sun had been welcome, a brilliant white diffusion in a tall, blue sky. At any moment when the quartz-bright tinge of heat became too much I could plunge into the sea. Here, at the top of the cliff, heat and brilliance merged in a chalky glare from which there was no escape. I gazed for a while at the blank spot in the road which the car would fill when it came, then turned and watched small, fidgeting patterns of light on distant waves. When at last the white car drew up, I was miles away in a heat-hazy dream.

The driver's window was wound down. He put out his head and smiled. His eyes, behind smoothly curved dark glasses, were invisible.

"I'm glad you've come," I said, climbing in beside him, "It was getting very hot waiting there."

The comment was wasted as we had no common language beyond a few words in French and German. "Athens" and "midday" had been easy enough to get across but conversation as we drove along was another matter. I wanted to know roughly what time we would arrive in Athens and tried framing the question several different ways. His shielded eyes stayed on the road but he nodded and shook his head to show he was trying to understand.

"Athens," I kept repeating. "When? *Quand? A quelle heure?*"

He indicated the road ahead.

"Sounion," he said. "After, Athens. *Café trinken* in Sounion."

Evidently there were one or two words he knew in English. Catching his meaning I said, "Ooh yah!"

The thought of a cup of strong Greek coffee was very welcome. It did not matter if it took us a little out of our way.

I settled back to enjoy the ride, fluttering a hand in the breeze that came through the window. Before long the small, pillared temple of Sounion came into view, perched on a promontory overlooking sea blistered with light. We stopped at a tiny café, its three Formica-topped tables spindly beside the splendour of ancient columns. We were served by a silent old woman who brought, along with the coffee and glasses of water, some thick yellow fingers of sponge. I ate one and the Greek two. Out of habit I wrapped the remaining one in a paper napkin and slipped it into one of Beverly's side pockets. The Greek smiled. He was smoking a cigarette. Laughing, I refused when he offered one to me. I was sure not many Greek girls of sixteen smoked.

Back on the road, heading now the right way for Athens, we passed the spot where I had climbed up from the beach. I waved—as a small joke to myself—goodbye to another one of my many homes under the sky. I thought I might spend tonight on the Acropolis where I had stayed before. It was beautiful up there alone under the columns and the moon.

The car rolled on, the hot road stretching ahead like a panting gray tongue. I imagined that somehow if we drove far enough we would eventually disappear beyond that tongue, swallowed by the heat.

The Greek interrupted my thoughts by passing me something. It was a plastic wallet containing photographs of a plump woman and two little boys.

"*Mein Frau,*" he said proudly, "*und meiner Kinder.*"

I made suitably admiring noises. I was looking forward to reaching Athens; this man was not interesting company.

Then, out of the blue, he announced; "We swim."

"Swim?" I was puzzled.

"*Oui*, yah, swim."

"But Athens, *nous allons à Athènes* . . ."

"Yah, yah. Swim, swim"—he made swimming motions—"after, Athens."

"Swim where?" I asked. We had left the coast road.

He waved an arm inland toward the mountains.

"*Klein* swim. Good, nice."

I frowned out of the window, wondering if I should get out now and try for a more direct lift. But there were no other cars about and besides, it would seem ungrateful. He had bought me coffee, after all, and would get me to Athens eventually. There was no reason why he should not have a swim *en route*.

A mile or so further on he turned off the main road and headed uphill along a meandering single track.

"Is it far?" I wanted to know.

He smiled and his dark glasses caught the sunlight.

"No far."

The road we were climbing was steep and, as we went on, became rough. Large stones caught on the exhaust and made the car jerk; the tarmac, patchy at first, soon ended altogether. We came to a fork where a still smaller track joined the one we were on. Some warning bell told me that if he took that track there would be trouble. I looked carefully at his face. The smile was still there, the masked eyes the same black blank. There was no human habitation in sight now. Lower down we had passed a farm. An idiot boy had cooed as we drove by, thick droplets of sweat shining on a white, distorted face. Up here at the crossroads there was nothing but yellow-gray boulder-strewn land falling away on all sides. The sun seemed to clamp on to the roof of the white car. He took the small track.

The car lurched through sand and rubble. The Greek was concentrating now, leaning forward and steering carefully to avoid rocks and potholes. As we came to the brow of a hill he straightened up and pointed to the scene below.

"Swim."

He wiped sweat off his face with the back of a large hand. Moisture glistened on a few black hairs below the knuckles. Below us was a lake, kidney-shaped, with a scattering of rocks at one end. It might have been a reservoir. He stopped, lumbering the car off the edge of the track, where it settled in a low cloud of dust, one wheel crushing a tussock of dried grass. I wound the window up partway against the dust.

"You swim," I said clearly. "I will wait here."

His eye-blank face turned toward me, broad mouth open with a half-smile expressing noncomprehension. I repeated what I had said, with gestures. He shook his head, grinning.

"Two swim," he said slowly, "me, you."

As he said the last words he demonstrated by pointing first to himself, then to me. His finger was on a level with my chest. Still pointing, it came closer and poked experimentally. Through the thin cotton of my sleeveless top he touched my breast. I flinched and froze, the perspiration on my thighs suddenly cold. Then my hand flew to the handle of the car door. It would not open. I tried to wind down the window to get at the catch on the outside but accidentally wound it up instead. He sat back facing me and laughed, his big red mouth wide.

"OK," I said, trying to play, pretending the touch had been a joke. "Let's swim. Let's swim now."

He laughed again and casually reached over a long arm. With the ends of his fingers he took hold of my left breast and squeezed it three times as if he were squeezing a motor horn. I tried to push him away. He shook his head, grinning, and I felt his free hand land heavily on my neck, the thumb curling round to the throat. He swatted my hands away and the thumb played softly up and down.

"Naughty," he said through his grin. "No swim now."

His other hand returned to my breasts. Every time I made a move to strike him away the grip on my neck tightened. He tweaked and twisted the nipples through the thin cloth and then pushed one shoulder-strap down. Taking the edge of the cloth in the very tips of his fingers, he peeled it slowly away until one frightened brown breast lay exposed. As he jabbed a thick, inquisitive finger into the tender auriole, I made a frantic move to pull the hand from my neck.

"Naughty," he said again, this time louder. Letting go of my neck for an instant, he grasped both wrists firmly and pulled my hands down by my sides, indicating that this was where they should stay.

"No!" I cried, voice wavering, lost like the puff of dust from the car tires over the brow of the hill. "No!"

One hand closed over the lower half of my face, thrusting my head over the back of the seat. I tugged at the heavy, sweat-sticky palm and heard his gleeful laugh again.

"Oh naughty, naughty!"

While I struggled, he reached lazily into the back seat and lifted a long package on to his lap. It was his scuba gun. The metal tip of the spear caught bright asterisks of light through the plastic wrapping.

He removed the hand from my neck and wagged a finger under my nose.

"Naughty Fräulein."

I sat rigid, back pressed into the hot plastic of the seat, thighs sliding with sweat. The smile still in place, but slacker now, he unwrapped the gun, keeping the curved rectangles of his blanked-out eyes on me all the time. He shifted his legs apart and unzipped his fly. Then, very carefully, he placed the tip of the spear gun just above my heart. With the other hand he pointed to himself and pressed my chin down to make sure I was looking. His mouth was completely slack now.

His fingers parted the opening of his fly and dug out the heavy roll of flesh. It lay against one trousered thigh like a thick white slug. His fingers pulled at it but it remained limp. His hand came back to me.

Aware all the time of the pricking spearpoint over my heart, I could not move. I watched helplessly as he undid my shorts and tried to tug them down. Hampered by holding the gun, he motioned impatiently for me to do it. Slowly my hands found the waistband of my shorts and stayed there, not moving. He shouted and made feints with the spear but it was no good, I was paralyzed.

Sweat poured off him now. He flung open the door on his side and yanked me outside, landing me hard on my knees beside the car. He stood above me, the white slug dangling outside his trousers. I tried to stand up but he caught my hair and twisted my face up to look at him. He hit me on the cheeks and nose with the limp white thing. Then, bending over, legs straddled, he pulled my head back so that it almost touched the ground. I was still kneeling, so that my back was painfully arched and my pelvis thrust up to him. With short, angry jerks my shorts were dragged down and suddenly the whole world was great thick fingers digging into me. A noise like a bursting bubble of blood came from my throat. Pulling my legs down now and flinging the shorts away, he wedged one of my feet behind the front tire of the car, pushing the other outwards. I felt the tendons of my groin pull like wires. My hands leaped down to protect but he grunted angrily and grabbed the spear gun he had left in the car. Touching the broad arrowhead to my throat, he bent over and tore the flimsy cotton of my knickers to get them off. He gabbled at me in Greek and, standing with one foot grinding into my thigh to hold me wide, lowered the gun meaningfully. He took hold of himself with the other hand and, making harsh panting noises, pumped himself up and down. I turned my head and closed my eyes, hands digging into the sand; spine, shoulders, buttocks burrowing to get away.

Then the sweat and weight of him was everywhere and his fingers were pressing me open; thick fingers pushing and stretching, forcing a path unheeding as my whole being tried to close itself to him. I cried out loud as the white slug shoved in. Three times he thrust before he was fully inside and with each stab my body convulsed, tried wildly to expel. But he was deep as a buried fist now, punching again and again on the same bruise. On, on it went and the sun was still shining and the earth would not give way. He got hold of my face and twisted it round to look at him.

"Laugh!" he ordered savagely. "Laugh!"

The stretching inside deepened into a dark red flower of pain. Something small and hard was grinding into my chest.

"Laugh!" he shouted again, shaking my face. Then he gave a short double jump and flopped on to me, a damp dead-weight. There was wetness flooding inside and a new smell mingling with dust and fear. I looked up to where the sky beyond his sweat sodden head stretched wide blue twinkling eyes over the sand and rubble and the lake, or reservoir.

Then I laughed.

He raised his head to look at me. Crushing the falter from my voice I laughed again. Slowly, his wet mouth slid into the old grin. It had all been a game then. It was still a game now.

"Good," he said, starting to get up, "good."

The spear gun was at my side. I did not touch it. The vision of it pointing into me had been in my head all the time. He must forget it now, pretend that it had been part of the game too. Leaning against the car, trousers already zipped, he took a pack of cigarettes and a metal lighter from his breast-pocket. So that was what had been grinding into my chest. I reached for my shorts and put them on before standing. Then, walking up to him, I held out my hand for a cigarette. I laughed again to cover my shaking as he lit it. He laughed too and making "one" signs made me understand that he was asking if this was my first cigarette. I nodded, wondering what to do with the bolus of smoke in my mouth. When I opened my lips it trickled out messily and I huffed to push it away. The Greek gestured to the scuffled patch on the ground where my body had lain and indicated "not first." I shook my head. My laugh was a bleat as I took another puff of the cigarette. Barnes, paintings, photographs and Renaissance music shimmered among the rubble for a moment.

Bored now, he looked at his watch.

"We go."

He let me into the car and I kept my eyes averted as he slung the gun in the back. It was not easy turning on the rough ground and he muttered irritably in Greek. But when we were back on the larger track he began to laugh again and make what I assumed were jokes in his strange mixture of languages. I did not understand the words but laughed where it seemed appropriate. To cover the trembling of my legs I hoisted Beverly on to my lap and scrabbled in one of her pockets for a comb. I found a scarf instead and wiped at the sweat on my neck. We passed the farm with the idiot boy. He was still there, lolling like a broken puppet against the fence. He cooed again as we drove by. Beneath its distortion his face was gentle and wondering. Part of me wanted to leap out and scream in the dust at his feet.

When we reached the main road the Greek seemed to go into a world of his own, humming and tapping out bits of rhythm on the steering wheel. I could not look at those thick fingers. Once he said loudly, "Laugh!" as he had done when I was under him. I laughed and his gleeful chuckle joined in. Under Beverly my legs shook and shook.

The road wound on and the sun winked off the car's white bonnet. Sometimes I could see the sea, sometimes just endless banks of high, yellow stone. We came finally to a garage next to a dump for old cars. The Greek pulled in. Leaning out of his window—both front windows were wound right down now—he shouted across to where a group of workmen sat in the shade smoking and reading magazines.

One of the men got up and strolled over. He was middle-aged with a creased complexion and dry, squinting eyes. All the men wore dusty blue overalls. This one had on a flat blue cap as well. He bent close as the driver continued speaking and I saw his eyes come over to me. Then he made a wide beckoning gesture with his arm and the four other men began to move. They folded their magazines and one stubbed out his cigarette in the dirt, grinding it flat with the toe of a workboot.

Then they were all in the car, squashed together in the back seat, voices loud, the smell of sweat-stained bodies strong. The tires crunched on the gravel as the driver swung the car back on to the road. As he drove along his voice was merry and his hands waved airily toward the mountains. Towards the little road.

My hands on Beverly began to twitch uncontrollably. I could feel the attention of the men in the back on me as the driver held forth, describing something, laughing between phrases. The car went faster, swinging round curves in the glinting road. The sea was gone now. There was tall stone on one side, acres of gravel wasteland on the other. Tightly, tightly, I gripped Beverly, one elbow resting on the hot frame of the open window. There was a blind bend in the road ahead, the ground falling away sharply to one side. The car had to slow.

One hand left the rucksack and I hung it casually over the side of the door. As we drew near the bend the driver hooted and at the same moment my fingers found the outside catch. With all my strength I jerked it up and flung my weight against the door, bending up my knees. There was a rushing vision of gray, streaking road and wild voices in the car.

Then the rolling, tumbling, heart pounding, spine-whacked-in-the-grit every time I rolled again; tires screeching like a crazed seagull, and the white car was gone.

8

The stars came gradually back into focus above Costas and Ursula's balcony. I noticed small, irregular mounds along a drainpipe. Swallows' nests. I counted them three times, each time getting a different result, before I slept.

Costas had already gone to work by the time I got up. Uschi said that she too must go out but would be back at midday. I was to help myself to anything I liked from the kitchen, "do play some records," and was there anything I needed from the shops? I shook my head, smiling, and in a minute she was gone, a gay scarf tied over her chignoned hair.

She had left me a magnificent breakfast—including the strawberries I had had my eye on, even in yesterday's dazed state. After washing the dishes I decided to turn out Beverly. It would be the first time I had unpacked her properly since leaving England three months ago. I put on a record of South American flute music and stood listening to it for a moment in a wide rectangle of sunlight slanting through the balcony doors. Hector, chin on paws as he watched my every move, wagged his tail.

With her main part empty I attacked Beverly's pockets. In the front was my scarf and the comb I had not been able to find yesterday. My purse was there too, ancient and held together with an elastic band. It contained a boat ticket, a franc and five centimes, two Italian lire and a few drachmas. In a special recess inside was a one pound note. In the left-hand pocket was a tiny velvet bag of sewing bits—I was forever repairing Beverly and my shorts—and my all-purpose red-handled knife. The righthand pocket usually held only two items: a coil of string and a matchbox with a butterfly painted on the lid. I kept the matchbox in my hand as I took out a third item.

Until now my mood had been light, busy, the music easy in the background, sun shining in. But as I held the napkin-wrapped object my hands began to shake. It was the thick finger of yellow spongecake

I had taken from the café where the Greek bought me coffee under the Cape Sounion gods. Unwrapping it and screwing up the napkin I hurled it through the balcony doors. Hector was up like a shot, ears pricked, gauche puppy body leaping. His teeth snapped and it was gone. He sat down panting, crumby mouth agape, hoping for more.

Sitting down beside him in the sun, I opened the butterfly box. Inside, buried in a nest of cottonwool, was the Virgin Stone. I ran my fingers over its delicate, egglike smoothness, traced the white-mauve-lilac-lavender stripes. The music had stopped and my mind was reverting to the misery of the day before.

Then—it might have been minutes, might have been hours later—I felt Hector's damp snout nudging under my arm. I gave him a hug and he darted long, doggy licks at my face. By the time Uschi got back Beverly was packed, Harold filled with water, and I was ready to go.

Uschi did not understand and neither, really, did I. My boat did not leave until tomorrow, I could have stayed another night. But something was telling me I must get back on the haphazard track of my own world before what happened yesterday took over and made me incapable of facing that world again. If I allowed Uschi and Costas to go on lulling me with their kindness any longer, the jolt back to my chosen brand of reality would be that much harder to bear.

As Uschi made a cool drink for us, a slight line of perplexity marked her pixie brow. I knew I could not explain, so I lied. I said I had friends to meet in Athens, people who were also going on the boat. Her face cleared. Of course, I had my own plans; it was selfish of her to have imagined I would be free to spend the weekend with them. But I would stop for lunch first, wouldn't I? She would walk me to the bus stop afterward. I smiled, wanting to please her, and secretly hoped the odd change in my purse would cover the fare into town.

Hector came with us to the bus stop, bouncing along beside Uschi on the white pavement and stopping at every lamppost and tree. When the bus came, Uschi jumped in before me and paid the driver my fare. Kissing me goodbye on both cheeks, she said, "Eve, should I tell your parents? Do they know where you are?"

I shook my head and assured her that I was all right now. Just as the bus began to trundle away, there was a great shouting and barking. Uschi was running alongside banging on the window with her small hands. The driver stopped and wiped the sweat from his face good-humoredly as she handed in a carrier-bag. It was passed down the bus from hand to hand. As we moved off again I turned to wave. Uschi was smiling and waving and Hector was wagging his tail.

*   *   *

The bus lumbered unhurriedly past the church, the flat white houses and the groups of children playing. The last person to pass on Uschi's bag was a wrinkled old man with a bright smile showing toothless gums pink as a baby's. His eyes twinkled as he saw me peek into the bag. Uschi must have dashed round her kitchen at the last minute. There was pumpernickel, *feta*, three packets of biscuits and a grapefruit. The old man smiled again and bobbed his head up and down like a turkey as I held up one of the packets for him to admire.

By the time we reached the city it was late afternoon. I got out at the far side of Syntagma Square and headed straight toward Parthenon hill, back turned on the scene of yesterday's lost circlings.

As I made my way through the maze of small streets at the edge of town my pace evened out. Properly packed, Beverly was an easy, even load and my feet moved comfortably into their old stride. The pain across my back was almost gone. I came to a drinking fountain and stopped to take a long pull from Harold, topping him up afterward. There was a white child's moon in the sky already. I looked forward to when it began to shine and I was lying in my sleeping bag watching the stars form their clear, faraway patterns.

I found my sleeping place on the far side of the hill, a broad trough beneath a bank of stone. Before settling down I changed into my old shorts and ate a piece of the white, watery *feta* and some chocolate biscuits. A last band of sun haze flattened slowly into a brief gold-silver line and the bulging white columns of the temple turned black. I must have been wearier than I thought because my eyes were closed before I had a chance to trace the patterns of the stars.

Hours later, it seemed, sleep and darkness were pierced by a great beam of light. It swept like white rain across my eyes. For a moment I lay motionless with shock. Fear doubled my heartbeat.

Then it came again, a huge, dazzling eye sweeping right over where I lay. In a second I was on my feet and stuffing everything into Beverly. In my haste I dropped a packet of biscuits and when the light came round again, that was all it found. I was crouching out of reach on the darkest part of the slope. Looking up, I saw similar beams moving all over the Acropolis and then there was sound as well. Slow, majestic music. Suddenly I realized what it was all about. It was not a police raid, not a visitation of the gods. I had been caught out on the night of the *Son et Lumière*.

Keeping well outside the sweep of the beams I slithered down the slope. The descent was long and dusty. Finally I emerged, worried and dishevelled, on a side road leading to the city. Reluctantly, not knowing where else to go, I followed it until I reached Syntagma Square.

It was a warm night and there were plenty of people about. Music came from the tavernas and the *souvlakia* stands were busy. There was a crowd of young people sitting outside a bar. Quietly, I slipped in among them.

I had been sitting there for some time, wondering where to go next, when a big girl with short blond hair turned to me. She wanted to know the way to the youth hostel. Her voice was a little slurred.

"I have to go there and pick up some gear," she said. "I'm going to an all-night party." Under the slur her accent was Australian. Sniffing the possibility of shelter for the night, I offered to show her the way.

"Great!"

We set off along the crowded pavement. She was large all over and walked with heavy rolling stride. Her name was Fred.

"Hey!" she said, "this is really nice of you. Do you want to come to the party?"

"Well . . ." I hesitated. "I'd like to but I'm all dirty."

Fred gave a donkey's bray of laughter.

"You don't have to bother about that, it isn't a *smart* party."

She was right about that.

When we had picked up her backpack at the hostel, we followed directions she had on a piece of paper. A signpost in blue and white told us we had arrived at the street where the party was meant to be. We checked with the Greek word scrawled on the paper and stood looking at the sign. It was the same, no doubt about it, but there was no street and no sign of a party. On either side of the unlit road ahead were the flattened remains of demolished houses. Only one or two low sections of wall still stood. Fred scratched her head and said, "This is crazy!"

"Hold on," I laid a hand on her arm. "Listen."

Very faintly, coming from the far end of the nonexistent street was the sound of a guitar. Three long broken chords followed one another, then silence. Then another three chords. Every time the chords began, Fred and I moved forward. When they stopped, we stopped. All at once there was a shrill, yipping laugh ending on a long trill.

Fred's voice twanged loudly into the dark.

"Where *are* you guys? Is this the party?"

For a moment her words echoed limply. Then we heard whispering. Fred gripped my arm.

"Hey, they're here! Let's go! Let's go to the party!"

As she swung me jubilantly toward the sound, a gangling specter loomed out of the dark. For a moment I thought it was the Texan off the beach at Cape Sounion. It had the same endless stringbean legs and huge feet in ethnic sandals.

"Fred!" it cried, "you made it!"

We were taken behind a section of half-demolished wall. Crumbled stone steps led down into what had once been the basement of a house. There was a strong smell of brick dust and fried food. Light came from three tall candles in bottles on top of a packing crate. Beside them were other bottles filled with red and white Greek wine. Two young men sat by the crate on seats made out of bricks and a third lay full length on the floor, his hand clutching an empty tumbler. From shadows on the other side of the room came the guitar music, playing softly now. A large tumbler of wine was thrust into my hand.

As my eyes adjusted to the light I saw that aside from the crate and one chair there were two iron-framed beds in the room, one balanced drunkenly on three legs and strewn with backpacks, empty retsina bottles and the remains of a paper-wrapped meal. The gawky youth—who I had secretly christened Stringbean—swept an arm round apologetically.

"Sorry all the tucker's gone, ladies. There's a heap of retsina though, and Jock here"—he indicated the prone figure with a chummy kick—"brought along some ouzo. We've been putting it in the wine to liven it up a little. Here, try some."

A quantity of clear, strong-smelling liquor was poured into my tumbler. Fred knocked hers back.

"Phew! That's great!"

Tipping back the tumbler as she had done, I took a good mouthful. It was sweet, oily and acid all at the same time and brought back memories of aniseed balls and the school bus stop.

"Something for the music man," came a voice from the corner.

"Sure," exclaimed Stringbean. "Let me introduce our host, Jorges."

He filled a tumbler and taking one of the candles, crossed to where Jorges sat. The sputtering light revealed a small, dark figure sitting crosslegged with a large guitar on his knees. Huge wide-apart eyes like twin moons shone from under a mop of short, heavy ringlets fat as fir cones. A grin from almost negroid lips displayed superb teeth and a little catlike tongue. Jorges struck an introductory chord on the guitar.

"I greet you," he said grandly. "I will play for you."

And he did, closing his eyes, and leaning his head against the wall. The palms of his hands were pinky brown like a monkey's and his shins under the big guitar were lean and full of knots. The candle was left by him as Stringbean returned to the rest of the party.

Fred was clamoring for a game. The man on the floor had been propped against the wall and there were cheers as he began to revive. He was ordered to stay awake and I was ordered to shell some peanuts, which Stringbean said were needed for the game. He poured a whole lot down on to the crate in front of me, and I set to work cracking the shells with my teeth. I was not sure where to put the kernels and, as if in answer, a large green beret sailed into my lap from Jorges' direction.

"Put them in there, little Queen," he called over the music.

The rules of the game seemed simple enough. Taking it in turns, we would each demonstrate some action in dumb show which the others then had to copy. If they failed to do it properly the penalty was to drink a tumbler of wine. Fred insisted on going first. She shook my arm, scattering peanuts.

"You OK, you? I've forgotten your name. Just watch me."

Lumbering to her feet she stood beside the crate, massive in the candlelight. She bent her carthorse knees, thrust out her arms in the shape of a giant caliper and leaped into the air. It was not clear what her feet did but she assured us that they "changed" at least twice. The boys followed and I heard a bubbly giggle pop out of me as their hairy legs struggled to repeat the changements. Jorges did not join in but went on quietly providing an accompaniment. When my turn came I thought I did rather well but there were cries of: "Your arms were wrong, your arms were wrong!"

I had held them above my head as I had been taught at dancing class. I got halfway through my penalty wine and lowered my tumbler. There were furious cries. The rules said you had to drink it all in one go and if you failed, the penalty was to have ten peanuts thrown at you which you had to catch in your mouth. I leaped about feeling idiotic but at the same time determined. I laughed, snarled, hiccoughed, biting on hands, nuts, air. Then I drank another tumbler of wine.

Recollections of how the game proceeded are vague. The happy, silly faces in the candlelight were flushed, the voices loud. I remember at one point tying my legs in a knot, an action nobody could repeat except Jorges, who came to join us then. He not only knotted his legs but stood on his head at the same time, skull cushioned by his extraordinary hair. I studied with rapt attention the vision of him grinning upside-down. I was not sure whether it was he or I who was the wrong way up. I threw a peanut and it bounced off his foreign little bump of navel. The brown skin creased and shook as he righted himself, laughing at the same time. He crouched beside me, shoveling peanuts into his wide mouth and occasionally popping one into mine. My mouth would not always shut when I meant it to and sometimes the peanuts fell out.

"You all right, little Queen?" he asked.

"Fine," I said emphatically," but I mustn't miss the boat tomorrow."

"Where are you going?"

"Going on the boat, with Beverly."

A thought struck: "Where is Beverly?" I felt around with my hands and encountered Jorges' knee.

"Sorry. Oh, there she is."

Beverly was leaning up against a bedframe.

I smiled at Jorges and said confidingly, "You know, Jorges, I only came to this party because of the *Son et Lumière*."

I described it to him, waving my arms in the air to show the sweep of the arc-light beams. He shook his head and grinned and grinned.

"You were out there all by yourself?"

"No," I said, "with Beverly."

There was an upheaval on the other side of the crate. Fred and one of the others were attempting to lift the man who had fallen unconscious again. A candle and one of the wine bottles, now empty, crashed to the floor. Jorges started to sweep up the broken glass with a piece of paper.

Thinking I might help him, I got to my feet. The room slid round and round and up and down. It was not unpleasant but I wished it would stop. I made an almighty effort and it wound to a halt, only to start sliding the other way. Fred's form wavered before me and I felt my head whack into some part of her big soft body as I fell.

"You know what?" I heard her say, slurred and warm, "I reckon this kid's about fifteen years old."

"I'm bloody not!" I retorted and slid into cozy oblivion, the shocks of the last few days blissfully, if only temporarily, expunged.

Like a ponderous daddy-long-legs the morning light climbed over my eyelids, but it did not react when I tried to swat it away. My mind groped, as it always did on waking, for the bones of the current plan.

Israel via Crete and Turkey, that was it. On a boat. Today. Slowly awakening physical sensation pulled me back to the immediate. There was dust itching inside my nostrils and my throat was dry as a husk. A peanut husk. It clicked. That ridiculous party.

Whose were those basso profundo snores so close by? Warily I opened one eye. And blinked. Bone and blubber like a beached whale, Fred lay sprawled across the three-legged bed. The snores were hers. From beneath her protruded an assortment of arms and legs and heads. Stringbean's head rested on one huge thigh, his thin fuzz of hair catching the sunlight that streamed down the stone steps. Brick dust rolled in the air. There was no sign of Jorges.

I looked at my own bedding arrangements. Hogging the whole of the only other bed alone, I was resting on a large striped poncho and my legs were modestly covered with a towel. Beverly was nowhere to be seen. Alarmed, I sat up and stared round the room. I hung over the side of the bed, searching, and remained hanging there. Jorges was underneath.

He lay straight as a ramrod on the stone floor, his head pillowed by his guitar. Looped across his feet were two straps, one belonging to Beverly and the other to a red backpack. But it was his eyes that riveted me. Without any doubt he was asleep, but his eyes were open. In their great wide-apart sockets they were rolled right up so that only the whites showed. With his negroid lips fleered back from his teeth and the curved bladed knife I saw resting under one hand, he looked like some devilish djinn. Just then his eyes closed for a moment and re-opened, irises in place. He blinked at my face hanging down.

"Hi, little Queen. Did you sleep OK?"

"Very well, thank you. Jorges, tell me, was I very drunk last night?"

"In my opinion, which I would not hold to be of any great value, you were about as half-assed as anyone I've ever seen. I guess you're not accustomed to drinking retsina and ouzo."

"That's true."

"What time does your boat go?"

"Five o'clock."

"Do you like cherries?"

"Yes."

"Would you like to go with me to Ethiopia?"

"I don't know."

The others showed no signs of stirring. I got up and splashed water from Harold over my face.

"By the way," said Jorges, emerging from the dust, "I want you to meet a friend of mine"—he pointed to the red backpack—"Max." I introduced him to Beverly and Harold and for once gave my real name, but he gave me a new one. "Ivan," he said, "I think I'll call you Ivan."

I spent the day with Jorges and Max on the Acropolis. Under the great white furrowed columns we sat in the sun and ate fat black cherries. Jorges seemed always to be smiling, the whites of his eyes and his perfect teeth shining. I showed him the bag Uschi had given me and watched as he sliced the grapefruit in two with his curved knife, using the tip delicately to free the segments.

"You coming to Ethiopia, then?"

"I'm going to Israel to work on one of those kibbutz places. I've run out of money."

He considered, looking up at the sky and twisting the few dark hairs on his chin.

"Lemme see. Israel's kind of on the way. I could drop by and see if you'd changed your mind."

"Mmn," I said, not really believing him.

In the afternoon we dozed, Max and Beverly beside us, back to back against a column in the shade.

We said goodbye in Syntagma Square, Jorges executing a strange little bow, slender brown legs held straight together, shoulders stiff. Then he shook back his fir cone ringlets, smiled wide and departed. Beverly and I made our way down to the port alone once more.

9

The boat was overcrowded. I took up a firm position with my back against a great white-painted funnel and did not budge until we were past Crete. During the night I had plenty of time to regret my exclusivity. I had parked myself against the foghorn.

"Phwhaaaaaaaaaargh!"

Silence for a moment. Just enough time for the hair to lie flat on my head after the first shock. Then again: "Phwhaaaaaaaaargh!"

I lost count of how many times this happened. After a while the raw, gormless idiocy of the sound became familiar, welcome even. When morning came I was hardly well slept but felt strangely refreshed, as though everything in me had been thoroughly shaken up and then clicked quietly back into place. For breakfast I took a swig from Harold, and cracked another packet of Uschi's biscuits. I thought of Jorges and practiced his djinn's grin. I did not imagine I would see him again.

Crete passed; the ferry ploughed on toward Rhodes. Abandoning the foghorn for a while, I made my way forward, and commandeered a giant coil of rope. A warm breeze blew wrinkles over the sea's fine skin and I drowsed, watching the skyline through slitted eyes and noting in the distance islands like lopped fangs appearing whenever the ferry rose on the highest point of a wave.

Without brooding on what had happened, I was aware that in a short space of time I had been the object of not one, but two extremes of human behavior: the first remarkable for its ugliness, the second for its beauty. And resilient as my sixteen-year-old body and psyche were, the example of rare selflessness shown by Costas and Uschi occurring almost immediately after that contrastingly horrible event seemed in a way to cancel it out. It had to. I could not live with the memory of the rape, so, consciously or otherwise, I decided to live without it. It had not happened. It did not exist.

I was unaware then of how deep the bruise had gone; how there are some things the body, if not the mind, can never forget.

At noon stark outlines of long hills and abrupt cliffs came into view; colors of hot earth, dust-yellow to terracotta, stippled with the misty gray of olive trees and the coarse green of salt-bitten scrub. We passed cliff faces with curved horizontal striations white as bleached bone and tall slabs of rust-orange stone scored with vertical lines neat as cross-section diagrams.

But my first hours in Turkey were colored black. Stinking, viscous, clinging black.

It was hot, and welcoming the chance of an all-over wash I walked round to the far side of the tiny harbor where we moored and plunged feet first into the dark, choppy water. I landed heavily, straight on a squid.

Slime from a jet-shot stream rose in bubbles like farts in a bath and my feet churned deliriously. I flailed, gasping, and face squeezed lemon-tight, heedless of grazes, pulled myself clear. There was laughter. Men with narrow heads and elegant ankles curled their lips; pantalooned women hid titters behind bauble-tinkling scarves. I grabbed Beverly and scrambled clumsily over pitted shelves of rock to find another bay away from mocking eyes.

The bay I found was beautiful. Thyme grew wild in prickly abundance at the feet of carob trees and bands of wet weed, translucent and rubbery, gave off a sweet tang banishing the last of the ink-sac fumes.

I trod with clean, newly dusted feet among the fallen carobs and rustling herbs and stood for a long time watching a busy task force of ants striving with all their puny strength to maneuver the large, husklike carcass of a cricket. I wanted to know where they were taking it and when they got it there, what happened next. I never found out, for my dreamy observations were shattered by an all too familiar sound.

"Phwhaaaaaaaaaargh!"

Like an old ewe gone hoarse calling for its lamb, the foghorn blared again, measuring the distance between me and it, the distance between a sea lane and the land. And for all that I might halloo and scramble, for all that I might dart and gibber and wave my arms, the ferry plowed on aloof, first past, then gradually away, away, averted portholes winking in the sun.

I dashed at a rock-hopping run all the way back to the harbor. Beside the bollard where the ferry had been tied a glinty-toothed Turk stood picking warts on the palm of his hand. He flicked a sideways glance at me as I approached. It was a look I had seen before, casual, impenetrably foreign, registering only the fact that I was female. I changed direction, heading toward the harbor buildings. A group of children, silent and watchful as little gargoyles, stared after me.

The harbor office was a three-sided shack. Inside, a desk curved under the weight of a pair of uniformed legs. Their owner lounged back on a tipped chair, eyes half closed. Three other men were bent over a board game at a makeshift table. Lizardlike, the eyes of the uniformed man gazed through me. I dreaded the moment when the look would change and become that alien, bed-flesh-appraising stare. They would all look at me like that as soon as I spoke. Unable to face it, I walked on. The next boat was due in a week.

It was evening by the time I got back to the carob tree bay. I climbed onto a shelf of rock I had noticed before which jutted over the water just beyond the reach of the waves and curved into an anonymous roll of shadow against the cliff. Rolling out my sleeping bag as a mattress I lay down, knife held tightly in my left hand. It was good to feel the big heart of the sea beating close by.

I might have stayed the whole week in the bay had it not been for the little girl who arrived on the second day. I was up in the scrub plundering the branches of a wild fig tree when I heard voices and saw a boat round the rocks into the bay. It stopped long enough to allow a small, bundled-up figure to jump ashore. Then the old man in the rowing seat pulled away. The small figure dragged its bundles into the shade of my rock shelf.

From my concealed eyrie I had a clear view of the beach. After a little while the child emerged from the shade and stood inspecting the rocks below the water. One small toffee-brown hand twitched impatiently on a long stick.

Squatting suddenly, she dived the stick into the water and prodded fiercely. There was a light grunt of satisfaction as her hand, covered with a cloth, swooped down to catch whatever she had poked free. A small pyramid of black prickly objects grew at her side. Sea urchins. When she had decided there were enough, she drew the four corners of the cloth into a hobo parcel and carried it, swinging, to where the rest of her things lay. She made a small fire and round the edge of it arranged four or five thin aubergines. The urchins sat on top, right in the flame.

One of my legs was cramped and I stirred, inadvertently sending a small avalanche of scree down the slope. The child's head swiveled on her neck like an owl's and she looked straight up at me, hands frozen in the act of peeling an aubergine. As I stood up slowly she leapt to her feet grabbing all her bundles.

"Don't go away," I called.

But she had started to run.

She fled left and right, staggering to where the rocks began at both ends of the bay. Plum-colored rags trailed from her, scarves and charred urchins scattered in her wake. She nearly fell under her load.

"Wait, don't run away!"

At last she stopped, panting through a gaping mouth, backed up and shrinking against the ledge where Beverly lay. Her arms clutched her possessions, eyes darting to the items which had fallen. I approached slowly and reached behind her for Beverly. As my arms went up the child cringed, hissing like a cat. Kneeling, I opened Beverly's front pocket and brought out a raisin bun, gift of one of the ferry's galley stewards. I offered it on an open palm as though to an animal. While her eyes, unblinking, stayed fixed on mine, one hand crept forward. In a flash the bun had disappeared among the ragged folds of her dress. Her pupils, unwavering, were huge.

I tapped my chest and said, "Lucy. My name is Lucy." Then I pointed at her, making a question of my eyebrows. Unwillingly her hand retrieved the bun.

"Elucy," she murmured and offered it back.

"No, no!" I laughed, trying again with the name. She relaxed a little and hunkered down, placing the largest bundle beside her. I saw now with a shock that it was alive. No wonder it had been a struggle for her to run. Seeing me looking at the bundle, her face assumed a grown-up, world-weary expression. With a brisk movement she flipped back the piece of cloth covering its head. I caught my breath.

It was a tiny thing, a baby, and its features were almost invisible under an oozing crust of sores. Its mouth hung open but no sound came out. Inside the voluminous wrapping some part of it moved and the little girl replaced the shading cloth and sat back hugging her knees.

By now she had lost much of her fear. While I collected the scattered urchins, she poked up the ruined fire. We sat down side by side and from time to time one of us added a stick to the flames. When I went out into the sun to gather more wood she tut-tutted like a granny and loosened one of the baby's rags, indicating I should wear it on my head. Recoiling, I fetched my own scarf but when I put it on she frowned. It was incorrectly tied. I knelt for her to do it and the feel of her sure little fingers busily knotting and smoothing was very sweet. I gave her the last bun out of Beverly and in exchange she peeled me a roast aubergine. The baby lay between us, mute, unstirring, as if it might already be dead.

When the old man came to fetch the children, I went with them. The little girl spoke to him, eyes darting to me, and he nodded once, pulled a ribbon of phlegm from his throat with two fingers and rowed us out of the bay.

The journey was dreamlike and slow. The sea, deep turquoise with long indigo shadows as the afternoon smudged to evening, was very still. Only dark wave stains on white rocks revealed a sighing movement deep down. Heavy drops like silver oil ran off the old man's oars.

I was wondering if there was still far to go when the little girl gave a wriggle and waved toward a cluster of lights on the shore.

"Ooch Als," she said. This was her village.

The glances that came my way at first were sharp; dark eyes raking from behind wheezing hurricane lamps, faces covered and turned away. But everywhere I went the little girl came too, shrill, exclaiming, chasing a shy welcome from the goaty-smelling shadows. Beverly was taken from me and placed on a cot in a hut whose roof showed every star in the sky. The baby was settled in the same room, bundled and dumb, and the little girl stroked a mat on the floor to show that this was where she slept.

Outside there were fires, and people were gathering on a rickety jetty. I was led to the cooking area where a lamp was held up proudly to show five barnacled shellfish tethered to a post. When jabbed with a stick they marched without moving. Their shells were mud brown and studded with blistered eruptions, reminding me of the baby's face. Further on I was shown a lamb, newly killed, hanging upside-down, and a bucket of fish cool under salt and weeds. In a corner a woman with cheeks as hairy as pig's ears patted ovals of dough between her hands. When I rubbed my stomach she ducked and bounced madly, hairy jowls flapping.

We sat late on the jetty, food appearing in slow relays. The men were served first. Women moved softly outside the light and children sat crosslegged on the wooden floor, scraps from their fingers falling between the planks straight into the mouths of tiny fish which glimmered in the water below. The fresh lamb seemed barely touched by the flame, tasting of smoke and mild, milky blood. The bread was spongy and warm, ballast against the fiery chiles that were the only vegetable. My tea was scented with half a stem of mint.

When I went to bed three small faces propped on hands watched me from a cot opposite. Their eyes and fingernails, more pinpoints of light among the stars, were the last things I saw before I slept.

Ooch Als. It meant Three Mouths, and I learned next day why the village had this name. Climbing at dawn to the crumbled honeycomb of a former citadel, I saw the sunrise gild the nipples of matching hills on two islets no more than half a mile from the shore. Channels on either side and one between the islets made three distinct approaches to the village from the sea: three mouths.

Turning round to explore further inland, I saw that I was not alone. Daylight gave mass to the outlines of shrouded figures lying on the cracked and potholed stage of an amphitheater. One by one they stirred and sat up, hooded profiles like crows amid the rubble, centuries late for pickings from the last show. They hawked and spat and when they saw me, smiled. Stumbling sleepily past to get their first glass of tea in the village below, they pressed sprigs of thyme and carob pods into my hands.

I thought of letting the next ferry pass, for I liked Ooch Als. But the people were poor and I was an extra mouth they did not need. From the walls of the ruin I saw through the skimpy stick and leaf canopies of their homes and felt the coarse, precarious texture of their lives, a universe away from the standards of a child brought up in Richmond-upon-Thames. Standing by a wall draped with hanging gourds, breathing in air heady with the fermentation of trampled figs, I felt the incongruity of my own presence. Being a fly on the wall was a luxury these people would never know.

Twice I went out in the fishing boat and saw green-stained tombs hewn into the hills, and shorelines dotted with fat little sarcophagi. Ooch Als had its own minarets and a taped muezzin whose dust-wrecked voice scraped into the still hours like a nail on a blackboard. Once I looked over the side of the boat and saw the walls and corridors of a sunken city. Or was it that the water had risen? Ooch Als had known other patterns of sea and land.

I did not have to ask for a lift when the day came to return to the harbor. The women gathered on the jetty to see me off in the fishing boat and the little girl pushed her way to the front bundled up as on the first day. I still had not learned her name but knew now that the sick baby was her brother. The mother was dead, a fact conveyed through a chillingly dispassionate pantomime of death in labor. I was waiting for the little girl to join me in the boat when, without warning, she leaned forward, opened Beverly and popped the baby inside. Her hands pulled the drawstrings neatly. There was silence as they all watched to see what I would do.

At first I tried to make a joke of it, removing the baby with a creaky laugh and holding it out to the little girl. Expressionlessly, she took it from me and put it straight back, retying the strings. With gestures to breasts, heart and arms she made it clear that I was to be its new mother. Was this what she had hoped all along? The baby's face-covering had slipped and between swollen flesh and scabs flies were trying to squeeze under its eyelids. Unthinkingly, I brushed them away and at once there was a satisfied muttering among the women. Clumsily my fingers grappled with the knotted string and I lifted the small, silent body again and held it out to each of them in turn.

"I can't," I said hopelessly, "I can't . . ."

For hours, it seemed, they just watched. Then at last my anguish was acknowledged and an old woman took the baby from my arms. But the little girl cried out angrily and ground her fists into her eyes. Even so, as the old man made to cast off she stepped into the boat. I had let her down but was still her special charge.

I watched the coast all the way back to the harbor but saw nothing. All I could think of was the baby. At the carob tree bay the little girl shot me a glance but would not look again when I tried to talk. I knew that even if she could understand my words, nothing I could say would alter the fact that by refusing to shoulder the burden of the baby I had rejected them all. Their life and their problems were no business of mine. I found myself wishing that the baby had been dead, not dying, then I could have whisked it away and buried it under a stone.

The ferry was there, waiting to take me to another world. Just before the gangplank was raised, I ran down to where the little girl stood, pinched and alien, with a group of harbor children. I took her hand and placed in it the Virgin Stone. Her fingers closed over it and, expressionlessly, she pulled from her sleeve a gauze headsquare. It was new and white with flat gold disks sewn round the hem.

The ferry was about to leave, someone was shouting. Wrenching my old scarf off I knelt down, patting my head. The child understood at once and, tut-tutting like the little virgin grandmother she already was, deftly tied on the new scarf.

"Tish'koor," I said—thank you—the only Turkish word I knew.

"Elucy," she responded gravely, sum total of her English.

"Phwhaaaaaaaaargh!" A final, stateless wail.

And I was away.

10

At the port of Haifa I was given a choice of kibbutzim. I asked myself what I wanted besides a roof over my head and food.

"Are there any near water?"

In Scotland I had had the sea; in Richmond, the river. If I was going to stay here a while, I would like to reestablish links with that safe, nonhuman thread in my life.

"Galilee," was the quick answer and I was put on a bus for Tiberias.

For a week I worked in the kibbutz kitchens swabbing floors and scrubbing out huge pots stained green with avocado. Alongside me, brown Swedish arms stacked crates of yogurt, Australian accents twanged in syncopation with pinging cutlery, and sinuous Swiss thighs canoodled with hairy Canadian knees behind the fridge door. After work, mosquito screens were fastened in the communal cabins, guitars came out and American voices led the way in sing-songs that went on almost until it was time for the field workers to change into a fresh pair of shorts for the day. "Good vibes" were everywhere; high spirits, fun times, the Beach Boys, John Lennon and *The Way of Zen*. I hovered awkwardly on the periphery, unable to pick up on the good vibes, and when a soldier came down from a *moshav* on the Golan Heights in search of volunteers, I went. The memory I refused to acknowledge was like an invisible barrier, cutting me off from my carefree cosmopolitan peers.

Ramat Hagolan, the Golan Heights. There was no road up to *moshav* Ramot in those days, just a broad ribbon of sandy dirt crisscrossed by the tracks of canvas-covered army trucks and small, beetley tanks. Plowing upwards through the dust, we stopped twice to pick up soldiers, one with a motorbike which was tossed into the truck and sat between me and him like a desk.

"You speak Hebrew?" he asked, in Hebrew. I recognized the phrase and shook my head. He switched to English.

"Stay long enough and you will learn." He had a brown, handsome face and spiky black hair made matt by the dust. I had no idea if I would stay one week or one year.

"Is that your boyfriend?" asked the soldier, pointing to another volunteer.

"No."

"Then maybe you will stay forever. Some of us are looking for wives!"

There was laughter and I found myself smiling too.

"Ramot," he said, poking aside a canvas flap with his gun so I could see out, "is a good place."

On a hill ahead stood a cluster of red-painted triangles like pieces of Toblerone. Each one was a solid little house with an area of sand in front raked clean and clothes flapping on washing-lines in the yards. There were pot plants in the windows and a family of kittens played in the sun. The only things that gave away the vulnerable position of the *moshav* were the machine-gun placements at intervals beyond the washing-lines, and instead of hedges, low walls of sandbags around each house.

A girl soldier waved as the truck came in.

"Shalom! Shalom!"

This was Ayelet, who would show me around.

"Where are you from? What is your name?"

The questions I had been asked so many times since leaving Richmond.

"Ivan," I said, sticking to the name Jorges had given me, "from Scotland."

"Well, Ivan, welcome to Ramot. We hope you will stay a long time."

And I would have, if Cape Sounion had not gone before.

Day began at 3:30 A.M. when Uri, the foreman, padded across from his room at the top of our Toblerone house and shook my big toe. Lights would pop on all over the *moshav*, blocking out the gray cut-out forms of guards who shifted softly at their posts all night, silhouettes of guns pricking up over their shoulders like extra limbs. Sometimes, Ayelet told me, she smuggled one of the kittens on guard duty and kept it in her pocket to warm her hands when the night was cold.

At 3:45 A.M. the field workers assembled in the communal kitchen. We helped ourselves to strong black coffee from Thermos jugs and chipped sticky fistfuls of halva off a giant block in the fridge. At four

our transport was ready. Ten bodies fitted into the trailer and the other five ranged themselves on the tractor: two perched on each massive mudguard and one behind the driver on the tow bar. Everyone held tight to something and the sleepy bodies bounced and thudded into one another as we lurched over the rough half mile to the fields. Galilee was quiet, a great gray lake lit in one place only by a thin rippled shaft from the moon. The hills of Ramat Hagolan crowded a blurred skyline, hiding the border not far away.

My first job was to help with irrigation. Lines of black hose pipe, punctured at strategic intervals, wound through the sloping fields like veins. Stooping and straightening, soft-limbed puppets in the granular light, we lifted and repositioned the pipes, sandaled toes clogging with mud which would dry and crumble off soon after the sun rose. With the first breath of heat, kibbutznik hats popped out over brown faces like colorful pods, and strong-smelling insect repellent was passed along the lines. Uri, always smiling, directed operations without ever seeming to give an order. His short, compact figure moved about dispensing tenderness and enthusiasm to one and all. "Come!" he would say persuasively when my hoe slipped inaccurately among roots and weeds, and the same "Come!" to a watermelon as he gently turned it so that its pale whale's belly greened evenly in the sun. At nine o'clock, with the first sweat of the day running down our backs, we downed tools and headed back to the *moshav* for breakfast. The small area of cultivation, growing daily, stood out like a green flag against the ocher and gray-blue of sand and sea.

Breakfast was a feast. Plates were filled and emptied and filled again. Health glistened from eyes and lips and in the laughter that bounded round the room. I sat with Ayelet and did not care that I could not understand all the jokes. I understood the language of hard work, hard play, determination and pride—it was the same language Richard spoke.

The second half of the morning was the most demanding, sweating away in the fields until the blissful moment when Uri cried "OK!," and we all scrambled aboard the tractor to be dropped in a laughing, dust-blinded body right in the sea of Galilee. We played catch with one of the heavy round watermelons until somebody dropped it, whereupon it was pounced on and split. Earth-cracked hands clutched bottle-green rinds and lollipop-red juice dribbled down laughing chins.

"One day," said Uri, waving a hand to encompass the whole of Ramat Hagolan, "all this land is going to be green."

I believed him.

"And there will be many houses at Ramot and many children."

And hopefully, I added silently, no need for guards.

The knowledge that this fledgling community was launching itself in the face of constant threat left a deep impression. It made the struggles of my own world—truancy, family divisions, searching for causes— seem like idle self-indulgences, things for which these people would have no time. Here the issues were simple and profound: the land that was defended with blood was cherished with both hoe and soul.

But for all that I was drawn to the spirit of the *moshav* and swept up in the hard work and hard play, I could not ignore the messages of my own body. My period was nine weeks late.

Tel Aviv: dry heat, broad streets, girls with proud bodies, boys with proud eyes. I started my search on Ben Yehuda but knew as I wandered with Beverly past bright American-style cafés and the store fronts with famous names—Levi, Helena Rubinstein—that I would not find what I needed here. What was Hebrew for gynecologist anyway? And who could I ask?

Two months on the *moshav* had rounded out the hollows left by Greece and Turkey. I was tanned, skin and hair glowing, a picture of health. But my glowing legs dragged because inside I saw a dark shape slowly bloating like a tick in my womb. Ayelet thought I had gone quiet because it was "that time." She had given me a packet of sanitary towels. Uri had put an arm round me and tickled my feet to make me smile. But I could not smile and I could not tell anyone, so I left.

A good-looking soldier eating a pastry outside a café patted a chair for me to join him. When I shook my head he smiled anyway. I had never met men so friendly in their flirting as the *szabres*. Don't look at me, I thought. I do not want to see or be seen until this stain is removed.

I left Ben Yehuda for smaller streets and in a chemist's asked where I might find a doctor. The dispenser, an old man with white hair fluffed round his head in a halo, said kindly, "There are many doctors in this city. What is the trouble?"

I looked without seeing at his cabinets. *I was raped. I think I am pregnant.* No.

"I have a headache."

He gave me two aspirin—free—and two more wrapped in a piece of paper to take away.

"Stay out of the sun," he said.

All afternoon I searched, and at last I found a white plaque on the wall bordering a garden full of flowering cacti. Dr. C. B. Wiedkowitz, Gynecologist. I hid Beverly under a cactus and followed white arrows round to a door. A speaking-grille crackled when I rang and a man's voice said, "Ken?"

"Excuse me, are you a doctor? I'm sorry, I don't speak Hebrew."

"I am the doctor, yes, but it is not my hours. Come back after six o'clock and you can make an appointment."

The speaker crackled off. An appointment. God. That could mean a week. Even the hour until six o'clock seemed too much.

Half a dozen houses on there was another white plaque, another name full of W's and Z's. A woman in a white coat answered the door. She looked me up and down out of heavily bagged eyes, said "Vait" shortly, and disappeared.

It was hot on the doorstep and the sky, jigsawed by television aerials, seemed a very long way away. There were red flowers with black tongues drooping over the wall where Beverly was hidden. The woman came back.

"The doctor is busy. You are sick or vot?"

"Not sick, I . . . I . . . I . . ."

"A baby or vot?"

"That's it. I'm afraid I . . ."

"All right he vill see you. Vait zere."

She was like something out of a bad film.

There were three chairs in the waiting-room. No magazines. Feet clomped upstairs and there was a loud masculine sigh. My thighs felt sticky on the plastic-covered chair, reminding me of the white car. I wished I had a long skirt, a sack to cover me to the ground. The woman's face appeared.

"Zis vay."

The doctor's back was to me as I entered the surgery: broad, white-coated, sleeves rolled tightly over dumpy forearms. He was drying his hands on a towel.

"So," he said, tossing the towel in a crumple on the drainingboard, "you think you are pregnant, yes?"

"Yes."

He had round, rimless glasses which distorted the shape of his eyes. Wiry tufts of hair stood out around a bald crown. When he spoke again I saw that his teeth, set deep in a thin, mobile mouth, were evenly gray.

"You are what age?"

"Sixteen."

"Nationality?"

"British."

"Remove your lower garments and sit on that chair."

The chair was large, like a dentist's, mounted on a solid metal swivel. Seat, back and arms were upholstered in green leather. The doctor tore a piece of paper off a white roll and spread it on the seat before I sat down. Then he lowered the back so that I was lying almost flat.

"When was your last period?"

He made tut-tutting sounds when I told him, plump palms turning and pressing on my belly.

"You have had sickness?"

"I do feel sick sometimes."

There was a rattling noise as he wheeled some sort of apparatus in front of the chair.

"Put your feet here."

The apparatus was a tubular frame with two wide-apart stirrups on chains. The doctor, fingers looking like vacuum-packed meat in a transparent glove, waited, hand raised, while I inserted first one foot then the other into the stirrups. My knees flopped apart in the air and I concentrated on a spider's web of cracks beside the light fitting.

"Breathe deeply. This does not hurt."

Nailless fingers slid in. Soft slugs. A hand on my belly pushed down.

"Breathe!"

I gulped and my eyes rolled off the light fitting on to his bald crown where brown irregular moles merged together like amoeba. The hand slid out.

"Hmm hmm, well, something, I think."

What? *Was I?*

"We will do a urine test. Step down."

The chains on the stirrups danced as I withdrew my feet.

"Come for the result day after tomorrow. Goodbye."

And within minutes I was on the doorstep again, looking at the red flowers with black tongues.

At six I went back to Dr. Wiedkowitz, and when I explained what I had come about he agreed to see me straight away. I could not wait until the day after tomorrow.

His surgery was larger than the other, the gloves he wore thicker, but the chair was the same. He fired questions in a flat tone.

"Do you think you have venereal disease?"

I had not thought of that.

"I don't know."

"Have you ever had an abortion?"

A-baw-tion. He made it sound very boring.

"No. I've never been pregnant."

He was doing things with instruments on a trolley.

"You mean never until now."

Oh God. I winced as cold metal touched my vagina and a long, rounded snout pushed in. There was a winding sound and the snout expanded into a thick cylinder. I pressed my fists to my eyes, saw a black tick, petals and tongues.

"Keep still."

He went away for a minute, leaving the metal thing inside. It hung, dragging down at the opening, pressing up near the womb. When he came back he straightened it and put some other surgical instrument inside.

"I am taking a smear to test for infection. Might be problems, you know."

This ceiling was magnolia and did not have cracks.

"Problems?" I said to it.

"Well, it depends"—he was busy now with pincers and cotton wool—"if you have disease and you go on with the pregnancy, might be problems. That's all."

This business about disease flapped across my mind meaninglessly like a bat in fog.

"Why should I have disease?"

His answer was swift.

"Why shouldn't you?" He gave a grim little chuckle. "If you can catch a baby you can catch disease! I don't think you are married, no?"

There was no need for an answer. The thick cylinder came out from between my legs with a sucking sound.

"You can get dressed now."

While I pulled on my shorts—back to him—I said "Do you do . . . abortions, here?"

He had stripped off the gloves and was washing his hands. Tel Aviv had become for me a white-coated figure washing its hands.

"So the father does not want to marry you, heh?" It was as though he were talking to himself. "Yes, well, these things happen quite a lot nowadays and sometimes we can help and sometimes we cannot. It depends."

Everything, I thought, depends. He went on chatting to himself at the basin.

"It is a pity you did not come earlier. It is not so easy at this stage."

But can you do it? I did not say it aloud.

". . . And time, you know, is not cheap. But of course you want it to be safe. Sure, I could promise you that. Quick, too."

"When?"

"It would have to be before next week," he said, because he was going away. Then he mentioned a sum. It was in lire. Hundreds. It did not matter to me whether it was one hundred or five. I had none.

"So come back and let me know."

As he showed me out he pointed to the white plaque.

"By the way, that is not my name."

I walked back toward Ben Yehuda and the bright American-style cafés. As I passed the spot where the smiling soldier had been I realized that my back, my arms were empty. Beverly was still under a cactus. I went back to fetch her and knew that was the last time I would enter that garden.

Evening in Yafo: Jaffa, where the oranges get their stamp. People came up here for the view in the daytime, sat in cars at the top of the cliff and watched the sea beyond ancient walls. The walls looked golden and the water sparkling clean from here. In the daytime, that was. It was all glimmer and blackness now, slits and rectangles of light marking the streets lower down. I should go back down, try harder. I was only half drunk and it had failed, so far.

There were groups of young people around, generous with bottles of Maccabee beer. But beer was no good. All the old wives' tales spoke of the hard stuff. Gin and hot baths, shocks, falls, thumps in the gut. Israelis did not seem to go in for gin but there was brandy in the bars. Cheap stuff in straight bottles. Half a bottle should be enough.

But I got a whole one. Walked in and swiped it off the bar. In Beverly in a flash and me gone. A fat woman in a polka-dotted pinnie waddled out to serve the footsteps she had heard too late. Me plastered like a slap of bird dirt against the window of a shop two doors away. Beverly another lumpy outline beside a pile of litter bags. I drank before I ran.

Beside a river, I don't know where. Kneeling, retching, under a big fat moon. Song coming out of a window: something about another big fat moon and "you won't regret it."

Don't be sick.

Benches in the moonlight under trees. An Arab body on one, shrouded like at Ooch Als. Asleep or dead, been there years. I am not afraid.

Break this bottle and twist it through the leather of his skin if he says one word. Black tick going to break away in red petals, *please* . . .

Oh God, give me arms around.

Oh God, make the black tick let go.

Leaning against the trunk of a tree. Smell of shit. Moonlight over the Arab's bare feet, cracked like elephant hide. Will it make a noise when it happens, suction breaking or a crunchy rip like Velcro? Laugh! Laugh!

Oh God, help me find the Greek. Stake him out on the same ground. Choke his thick fish mouth with the burst belly of the black tick. Grind his dark glasses into his eyes. And laugh, laugh, laugh as the boneless white slug shrivels in the sun.

Sliding down. Clipped grass on the bank cool as a drink. A wrist through Beverly's straps, hand on Harold. Sliding more. Trying-to-stay-open eyelids crimping off the moon like pinking shears. To unpeel, aeons later, on the stapled mesh of a litter basket and a sunlit close-up of a green stem tickling my nose.

I got up and walked. There are streets on the edges of towns that go on for miles. My head weighed and bobbed like an extra Beverly, a nugget of nausea knocking around to one side. But I was hungry. If I could pinch a bottle of brandy I could do the same with a loaf of bread. Nearer into town there would be bakeries.

Nearer into town there was a sack of kittens in the road. Two were spilled out, flattened to bloody gloves. A third, covered by the sack, still moved. A car rolled by, oblivious, droning. More cars came. I stood on the curb and watched as though five miles outside the scene. Then the kitten mewed. It was not a piteous sound but a small, strident announcement: *I am alive.* A head appeared, blind, swaying, four wobbling legs and a damp striped tail like an erect rudder pointing straight to the sky. The cry again, pale, tiny mouth opening wide and yelling yah-boo-sucks and here-I-am at the world. I ran out in front of the next car and scooped it up. Hoots and swearing. I swore back and so did the kitten. It settled in my bush-jacket pocket and every time it squawled I said shut up and every time I said shut up it squawled. I loved it for that go-to-hell sound.

We walked. Daytime on the big streets where the cafés had bread on outside tables, nighttime in the shadow of half-made buildings by the grubby sea. On the third day I got the address of a clinic where you could sell blood. It was far, right the other side of town, and on the way I tried a dozen times to give the kitten away because I could not feed it and it was getting too lively for my pocket. At the clinic they said, "You can't bring that animal in here."

I looked for a place to leave it. When I set it down in a corner it tottered, blaring its small announcement of life, straight toward the road, toward dogs, cars and mashing feet. My life and the black tick's and the kitten's all seemed bound in the same nightmare vision. Moving within that vision I retraced my steps to the tourist part of town, booked into a hotel which did not ask for identification and stroked the kitten on the bed until it fell asleep, purring for the first and last time in its life. With the small red frying pan I carried in Beverly, I cracked its skull and then held it in a sink full of water for ten minutes, staring through my own eyes in the mirror. I wrapped the wet body in a scarf—the white one with gold disks the little girl had given me in Turkey—and put it in my pocket. I believed that even if I had to wait nine months I would do the same with the legacy of the Greek.

Two hours later, with four words, my whole perception of the future changed.

"You are not pregnant."

After selling my blood, I had found a place similar to a welfare clinic. I was not supposed to be there as I was not an Israeli citizen but a woman in the long gyny queue, whose child I held while she went to the lavatory, gave me her card. I think the doctor knew I was not Shoshana Ezra but he was kind.

"Why have my periods stopped then?"

He let me down from the straddle chair.

"It sometimes happens—traveling, a change of climate, some tension perhaps."

It sounded so sensible, the amiable voice of reason dissolving the black-tick-glass-in-the-eyes dream.

I was heading out of the clinic, mind already flying ahead to the range of next possible moves, when a woman's voice, tight with exasperation, made me look round.

"Ee-un, Ee-*un*! Come 'ere when I tell you!"

Breaking into Hebrew she pushed her way through the crowd of waiting women.

"*Slicha, slicha*, excuse me."

She was dank-haired with flabby arms and a bad complexion, but her figure was handsome and beneath the dank hair, her features strong.

"Ee-*un*!"

The cause of her annoyance was a golden-haired child of about two. He had toddled out of the queue and was quietly peeing under a chair. As she shoved her way toward him her number was called and in a panic she scooped up the child and slapped him so that he began to wail. As she passed me, snarling at him to "stop that row," I held out my arms.

"Bless you," she said, *"todah rabah."*

Thrusting him at me she fought her way back to the front of the queue. The golden-haired Ian hung limply over my shoulder. Gradually his wails dropped to a gurgle and he dozed.

The woman's name, I learned, was Glynis Weitz. Over coffee, which she insisted on buying me after her appointment, she told the full story of her married life.

"We was both workin' in Selfridges, see. He was in men's shoes and I was in 'aberdashery. He used to pass by me every mornin' and give me this lovely smile and then he'd blush and go all funny. I thought he was ever so nice. All the other blokes were just ordinary nudge-nudge, you know."

She stirred more sugar into her coffee and went on.

"Anyway, one day I get moved up to 'osiery and he gets to pass my counter three times a day. I knew he was Jewish, and I'd never been out with a foreign bloke before, but I was dyin' for him to ask me. Gawd, though! I had to wait until the Christmas party before he got up the nerve."

Ian dropped the bagel he had been tearing at and began to whimper.

"Don't you start," said Glynis, swiping crumbs off his front, "just when I'm feelin' relaxed for the first time in ages." She turned back to me.

"So, well, we start going out. You know, the pictures and tea and that, and before I know what's happenin' he asks me to marry him. I dunno, it sounded excitin', movin' to Israel and that."

She pronounced Israel, Iss-ray-ew.

"I even went Jewish and everythin'—took ages!—and we'd talk about what it was goin' to be like, livin' in Iss-ray-ew. And it *was* all right at the start. You know, everythin' different. But, oh my Gawd, these last two years! Stuck in the flat with the baby, no one to talk me own language to. I'm just about goin' round the bend!"

She finished her coffee with a gulp and looked at the clock on the wall. Moshe was supposed to be collecting her from the clinic.

"I suppose I'd better get back. He'll only be sittin' there with a face long as a coffin. Hey, you couldn't come back for a meal, could you? Save me from another 'orrible dreary evenin' with that long face?''

I said I would love to come and wheeled the pushchair back to the clinic for her.

Moshe was there, the long face unmistakable. It drooped like a wilted flower on a level with dozens of massive, milling female hips. He had saved a chair for Glynis. Her mouth gabbled at him angrily.

"Saved a chair for me? Whatever for? Do you think I want to 'ang around this place after I've been 'ere all afternoon? Anyway, we've got someone comin' 'ome to tea. This is Ann.''

Moshe propelled his long form forward and held out a hand. His eyes, wet and full above sharp cheekbones, were pained.

"I'm so glad you can come," he said formally.

The Weitzes lived in a sand and tenement suburb forty minutes from the center of Tel Aviv, and for the next month I lived with them. It was Moshe who, after a violent and apparently unprovoked tirade from Glynis that first evening, took me quietly to one side and asked if I could stay. Glynis, he explained, was going through "a bad patch" and a bit of company would "do her the world of good." He uttered these stock phrases so hopefully and with such a plea in his sad eyes I could not refuse. And from a selfish point of view the prospect of free board and lodgings was attractive. I could use the flat as a base while looking for a paying position and it would also provide a limbo in which to recover my equilibrium after the little madness of the last few days. The doctor who had lied in order to secure an abortion fee, the drunken retching and the kitten were all part of that madness. Gone now, a curtain across the mind.

But a limbo exists only in the imagination. From the moment of waking each morning to the cry of *"Avateea! Avateea!"* from the watermelon seller who trundled his barrow past outside, to the sigh of relief I breathed each night when poor Glynis's overwrought snarls were muffled by the slamming of her bedroom door, I was involved, physically and emotionally, in the world of the Weitz family.

Sometimes, as I wheeled Ian's squeaking pushchair to and fro on hot suburban streets, I thought how I could have returned to the *moshav* and become involved in that world instead. But there was trouble on the Golan Heights, and one night I woke up soaked in sweat from a nightmare of Ayelet lying mashed at her sentry post like the kittens in the road and all the other *moshavniks* crawling around on their knees crying: *"I am alive! I am alive!"* I closed my eyes to that vision as I had to the reality of Cape Sounion. Another curtain across the mind.

And then Moshe returned very late from work one evening and reported with a blank face that over seventy innocent people had been killed when two Japanese with machine guns opened fire in the middle of the airport. Glynis, who was always ready to hold forth on the disadvantages of living in "this bloody country," started to make a scene. For once Moshe turned an indifferent back on her and that night slept in my usual place in the sitting room while I, unhappily, shared with Glynis. Next day I went into town to put up some of my Young, Strong, Willing and Able adverts. I gave the contact address as the post office as I did not want Glynis to know I was going to abandon her soon.

Returning from that trip to town an incident occurred which showed that beneath a second superficial recovery from the Greek episode lay a mass of dangerously volatile feeling. The curtains I was pulling across my mind must sooner or later be torn down.

I was leaning up against a wall in the central bus station, waiting for a connection to the Weitzes suburb. I had already been there an hour and the heat and squalor of the place made every waiting second swell. A man with a urine stain down his trousers leered at me. I looked away. Loud cries and the smell of fried chickpeas were thick on the air.

In a neighboring queue there was a convulsive surge forward as their bus arrived and a dithering old man was knocked down. A woman stepped on his headdress, printing the mark of her heel in the cloth. There were cigarette butts clinging to the sleeves of his *djelebiya* when he sat up, mouth working, after the bus and the charging feet had gone.

A solid rail, the width of one person from the wall, was designed to channel those waiting into an ordinary line. As I and two dozen others spied our bus nosing its way toward us, the line bunched up into a bulging worm of humanity. Sweat from alien legs oiled my own and the mesh cap of a wig in front bumped my chin. All around lips were clamped and eyes distant. Then two calm, deliberate hands and a third pressing presence molded themselves to my hips.

I could not see the man but I could smell him, feel his breath like a sweating palm on my neck. My universe became a wig and two knowing hands. And amid the heat and pulse of that bulging human worm I became a stranger, as calm and methodical as those two hot hands, but cold.

In the carrier-bag I was holding was a notebook, an orange and my small, red-handled knife. Calmly, as the man's hands worked round, on my skin now, under the edge of my shorts, I reached into the bag and worked the serrated blade out of its homemade sheath. The handle tucked snugly into my palm and it was just a matter of waiting now until his hands came round to the front. I knew they would.

The bus, the hands and the third pressing presence nosed on.

Crushed against the wigged woman in front, I could not see. I would have to strike by feel. As the hands made a pouch over my groin and the breath slopped like soup behind my ear, I ran a hand over the back of the topmost hand. All the veins on it, like little pulsing animals, were raised. The man was working hard to finish before the bus, drawing in now, sucked his chance away. Memory of thick Greek fingers, harpoon tip pointing; soft, helpless lips pleading to expel.

The bus doors opened with the opening of the veins. There was a scream, a double jerking, fear smell and blood gushing, as the man ground back against bodies that would not give like the sand that had not given under my burrowing spine.

Small, terrified triumph as I felt the knife drop neatly back into the bag beside notebook and orange. My head turned as the queue, split now, absorbed another scream and a hand lashed under my chin. My scream now and blood from his hand lacing my throat. The woman with the wig raised a raucous female call-to-arms. The man, jaw shaking, clutched hand leaking, struggled to dive under the rail. His ducked head was beaten, women scrabbling in their shopping-bags for vegetable truncheons, while other hands guided me up the steps of the bus and voices, jabbing fingers and a ticket machine punched the air. The bus doors closed as he, lips curled back in panic, gained the other side of the rail and fled. A boy with curly hair in blue trousers who would never touch up a girl in a bus queue again.

Quietly, under cover of the bag on my lap, I fitted the knife back into its sheath. And the curtains, a little tattered now, drew back across my mind.

"So how you doing, little Queen?"

Jorges. And Max, the red backpack. We were in a train on the way to Jerusalem. I beamed at his moony, foreign face as at a white knight. He had found me, tracked me down somehow and we were going to eat cherries together again. I told him I was fine, just fine, because that was the way he made me feel. He sat crosslegged beside me in the carriage and peeled an orange with his big curved knife. His dark body rocked to the rhythm of the train and our knees bumped companionably. Through the segments of orange he sang:

I've been through the desert on a horse with no name,
It was good to be out of the rain.
In the desert you can't remember your name
Coz there ain't no one for to give you no pain . . . la . . . la . . .

It was an easy, clip-clopping rhythm and I liked the words.

"Let's go there," I said, "into the desert."

"OK," he said, heavy ringlets nodding, "but I want you to let me buy you a dress in Jerusalem first. Because honey, one of these days those zazzy little shorts are going to get you into trouble."

He dozed against the window after singing the desert song through again and I went on humming it, as the Weitzes, the massacre at Lod airport and the miniature horrors of the bus station receded further with each rocking bend in the tracks.

We passed flat fields of grapefruit and low brown rivers lined with bright weeds and humped with creamy dollops of scum. Everything, the golden weeds, the fruit, the scum, sparkled in the sun. Then all at once we were in the midst of hills blue with bracken and there were terraces of olives and flat-leaved cacti slumped over wire fences like saddlebags.

". . . 'I've been through the desert on a horse with no name . . .' "

Jorges woke up in time to join in the last two verses and see the first white houses of Jerusalem glisten on tanned hills.

We put up in the Arab quarter in a room with one bed and eleven bodies and Jorges lay under the bed—me on it—with knife drawn, arms through Max and Beverly's straps and eyes rolled up, just as he had in Athens, my gentle djinn. He bought me the most beautiful dress in the market, hand-embroidered on black velvet with huge trumpet sleeves. We stocked up Max and Beverly with dates, halva and flat cakes of Arab bread and took the road south to the Gulf of Aquaba. One night at Eilat, the southernmost point of the Negev—and in those days little more than a Coke kiosk and four salt-water showers—then we moved into the Sinai where, deep in the wadis and in the laps of the dusty pink hills, we learned what "in the desert" really means.

It was there, when sand had clogged my hair into a crazy Struwwelpeter thatch, dug its way under every toenail and filled laughlines I never knew I had, that I revisited the careless days of traveling before Cape Sounion. In the dunes of Nuweiba I conjured for Jorges nights of tramping the rainy autoroutes of France, days of lazing with the lizards in Pompei. And watching the moon rise over the Gulf, paring itself like a white peach from the skin of the sea, I spoke of how I had skipped naked on Corfu. How, scrambling for half a day, I had come upon a cove in the shape of a perfect horseshoe and danced, laughing for the sheer pleasure of being alive, until every inch of virgin sand had been churned.

"I felt like a goddess!"

"How do you know you're not?" grinned Jorges.

I liked the way he said that kind of thing and, in the desert, the idea seemed no more fantastic than the reality around us: raw bones of rock stacked face upon face, fading to pastel ghosts under the eyelid of a whitely sliding sun. I would wake up, a foot away from him on our double sunken mattress of sand—Jorges said that if you scraped away the warm surface-layer snakes were less likely to come—and not know whether it was summer or autumn or sunset or dawn. And not care.

Jorges told me that he was dodging the draft, running from a second stint in Vietnam. He showed me an angry strawberry-colored stain around his groin, which had to do with days spent up trees in sweats of heat and fear. "It was awful," he said once, breaking off from stroking my back, something he liked to do for hours. He seemed to know without being told that I did not want him to go further than that. Somewhere beyond the pink hills, Vietnam, Sounion and Richmond Bridge existed. But it was hard to believe, in the desert.

At a waterhole in the heart of a maze of wadis we met a bedouin called Ayash. He was leading two camels, one of them lame. Jorges, who did not smoke, produced a pack of cigarettes and we sat with Ayash while he smoked three. I could not stop looking at his eyes which shone out from under his white headdress like a beautiful woman's, rimmed with kohl. I showed how much I liked the effect and Ayash immediately offered to paint my own. We must come with him into the next wadi and meet his brothers.

Jorges and I rode on Ayash's good camel; the lame one carried Max and Beverly; Ayash, the cigarettes. First sight of the Bedouin camp was from above: white and gray figures in the dusk, squatting beside puddles on the cracked wadi floor or lying full length beside dung and palmleaf fires. Camels stood in twos or threes, long legs knobbled like jointed reeds. A young girl watching goats on the wadi bank drew her sleeve across her face as we passed, peeking shyly from the side. A group of boys ran to greet Ayash, rimmed eyes swooping up at us, brown hands vying to be the highest on the camel's rope. Beneath long *djelebiyas* small feet fluttered like birds. After protesting with a belly rumble our camel knelt and we were led away to sit by the biggest fire.

An old man lay sideways in the sand to blow up sparks and made tea in a tiny dented kettle. When it had boiled he lifted the lid, using his sleeve as an oven glove, and threw in four handfuls of sugar. It poured like syrup and glided sweetly over the tongue after the acrid invasion of hashish. I, who did not take sugar and did not smoke dope, did both—in the desert.

We ate roasted sheep's ribs and soft bread baked in the ashes. My eyes were painted four times until they wept with kohl. I fell asleep with the moon dilating in my brain and in my ears the chant of Jorges teaching the Bedouin the desert song: " 'In the desert, you can't re-member your name/Coz there ain't no one for to give you no pain . . . la . . . la.' "

Two nights later, when Jorges and I were alone again, I awoke to a pain like a red-hot needle in my chin. The same place where four years ago a cut from a wrought-iron gate had throbbed. I must have yelled for we both sat up at the same time and saw the culprit scrabbling away drunkenly over the sand. A scorpion.

"My God, Ivan, did it get you?"

Our voices—we—seemed insignificant in the massive silence of the Sinai.

"Yes," I said, pointing to the pain, "here."

"My God, Ivan!" he gasped again, and dived.

He bit me so hard I screamed. Broad negroid lips welded themselves to my jaw and sucked and sucked until I felt the blood was being vacuumed from my toes. The stars swung round and round as Jorges, releasing me, turned away to spit.

"Shee-it!" he exclaimed weakly. "Anybody ever tell you you need looking after?"

I have no doubt that Jorges would have looked after me all the way through Ethiopia and beyond, but it was not to be. Perhaps I knew even then that I was destined to go on a different kind of journey, alone.

PART THREE

Dangerous Bends

11

It began on Richmond Bridge. I had made it, hitching without a penny through Greece, Yugoslavia, Austria and Germany, but on Richmond Bridge, I broke down and cried.

Kay was at 309, nothing changed. Marianne, between bouts of sickness, was away on a nursing course. James was at school. When I telephoned Richard he sounded pleased that I was back and asked what the plan was now. I said I did not know and the conversation trailed off. Nothing had changed.

For the next few months I was based in Richmond. I worked in a fish and chip shop during the day and cleaned out a grocery store at night. In between I went for long walks, avoiding sleep as much as possible because when I slept, I dreamed. And when I dreamed, although nothing would have made me admit it, I remembered.

The sleeplessness built up and soon I took to lying down on the ground during my walks and dozing. I found secret places all over the area: churchyards, deserted golf courses, people's back gardens. And nobody ever found me until the day I was so tired—tired of avoiding the past and no longer having any vision of the future—that I lay down right by the side of a motorway. When I woke up that time, I found myself in a mental hospital.

I had thought it would be like the place the Child Guidance people had sent me to after I ran away from school, but it was not. There I had had a room to myself and most of the other inmates were families. We had meals together and meetings. Nobody was really mad.

In this place the heat disturbed me straight away, a heavy, airless fug which sapped the body and slackened the mind. I went round opening all the windows, none of which would go up more than six inches in case people tried to jump out. The whitecoats watched to see that I did not suddenly go wild and put a fist through. I never meant to, but their watching made me think about it.

I had a diary, a big one with room to draw pictures as well as write. I kept it with a fountain pen in a carrier-bag but was always having to change the bag because the pen made a hole in it and fell out. It was lucky the red-handled knife had not fallen out in Tel Aviv. I could not write during the day because there was no privacy, so the diary came out in the evening and I wrote in bed. Anger would boil in me if the night nurse switched off the light when I was in the middle of a sentence. I asked to be allowed to have one of the individual side rooms and my doctor agreed.

"So you write, do you?"

"Yes."

"Would you like to show me what you write?"

"No."

"Do you write about people?"

"Sometimes."

"Do you write about me?"

"No."

"Oh."

But it was worse in the side room. There was a window in the door, a judas. At night when the staff made their rounds the light, a high naked bulb in the ceiling, would snap on without warning and an eye appear at the window. Once this made me so angry, I dragged the wardrobe into the middle of the room, climbed on top and unscrewed the bulb. I was moved back to the main ward.

I spent a lot of time wandering about the grounds where there were beautiful imported trees. Some of the other inmates, confined to wards, would ask me to fetch things from the canteen.

"Get me a packet of fags, love, just ten. Anything'll do."

"Kitkat and a box of Smarties—"I'll swap 'em with me tablets."
(Cackle.)

The canteen was in the middle of the grounds. To get there, I walked along the main drive where there was a big notice to visitors saying CAUTION, DANGEROUS BENDS. There were a couple of old men always patrolling the drive. They moved with identical shuffles and one of them sucked constantly on an unlit cigarette. When their paths crossed, one always touched a nonexistent cap. The other ignored him.

Some people hung around the canteen all day. There was one woman, very fat, with bright orange lipstick painted on like a clown's mouth and hair dyed boot-polish black. She sat to one side of the canteen steps, legs apart under a short mauve skirt, asking everybody who passed for a cigarette. Once I saw an old man offer her two but he kept them just out of reach, bargaining. When I came back out on to the steps I nearly tripped over them. He was on top of her and she was smiling to herself, holding the cigarettes in one hand. One fat leg with a rheumatism bandage on the knee slapped against the step, up and down. Two whitecoats pulled them apart and she screeched because one of the cigarettes got broken.

In those days I wrote in my diary:

> *Everybody here lives in their own world and they all believe that the world they live in is real and that there is only one real world and it is theirs. I suppose it is like that on the outside too. Sometimes I think reality is just a word.*

More often I just jotted down things people did or snippets of conversation.

> *Overheard Stan talking to one of the other men about a new woman who came in today. She is a nun but in here they have taken away her habit and she has to wear a striped dressing gown like everybody else.*
>
> *Stan's friend said, ''Wouldn't mind defrocking her myself.''*
>
> *''Nah,'' said Stan, who is thin and rubs his hands together all the time, ''boobies on her like a coupla poached eggs, you can tell.''*
>
> *Fat Michael, who often repeats the ends of other people's sentences, was there.*
>
> *''Poach deggs,'' he kept saying, ''poach deggs.''*

The nun went twice a week for ECT. When she came back there were sticky patches in her hair where the pads had been and it took her a long time to recognize people again.

> *Judy asked to borrow my green dress today. She said her boyfriend was coming to take her out for a drink. Somebody gave her some makeup and she appeared at supper with the dress hiked into a miniskirt halfway up her thighs. There was blue slapped anyhow over her eyes and great dobs of orange foundation on her cheeks. She had tied her hair into flaxen bunches like a little girl. She is about forty-five. She cried when her boyfriend did not turn up.*

Botswana Steve has been put in the worst locked ward again. He said he had a flight booked back to his country on the fourteenth of this month. When he was told he had another six months to go he went berserk. It took six whitecoats to hold him down while they gave him an injection. I asked one of the Charge nurses if what he told me about himself is true. It is. In South Africa he was imprisoned as a political agitator of some sort. In the prison he was beaten up and his testicles were crushed with a hammer. When he was released he came to England, but he was caught drunk-driving one night and attacked the policeman who tried to arrest him. They put him in Broadmoor for two years where he had a breakdown, which is why he is here now. He is a half-caste with a beautiful speaking voice and permanently bloodshot eyes.

I used to smuggle in bottles of beer for Steve. He said it was the only thing he had to look forward to. I had a long Afghan coat with the pockets worn through and I could hold two bottles in each hand without being detected. All that came to an end one evening when I went joyriding with a new boy.

The meals were trundled round to the wards on trolleys pulled by battery-operated trucks. When there were no trolleys on the back, these trucks could go quite fast. They were kept in a shed behind the kitchens, hooked up to chargers. The shed gates were padlocked but the new boy and I could just squeeze underneath. Expertly, he detached the wires from the charging apparatus and tested the thin planks of the gates to find the weakest point.

"Jump on," he said, and I was reminded of a boy on a motorbike saying the same thing to me when I was twelve. Again, I jumped on. The boy turned the key—he had stolen one earlier from a porter's pocket—and drove the little truck at the gates like a battering ram. It went straight through, yard-long splinters flying everywhere. I was amazed that we were not caught on the way out, but there was no one on the drive except Larry the religious maniac who was addressing heaven in his pajamas. I waved as we flew past and his gentle, startled face broke into a huge smile.

"Mary, Mary, mother of Jesus, you are so beautiful!"

We drove out of the main gate and on to the road. I had the money for Steve's beer in one hand; with the other I clung to the back of the driving seat like on the tractor at the *moshav*. I was standing on the platform where the trolleys were usually hitched, wearing a big black hat as disguise. A car passed at speed, its engine sounding loud beside the low whine of the truck. I noticed out of the corner of my eye that it was a white car and held on more tightly as we swung off the road down an alley. I had a dread of falling off to land in that rolling, tumbling, heart-pounding memory.

There was a pub just across the road as we came out of the alley. Behind it was a yard full of rubbish and cardboard boxes. The boy pulled apart some of the boxes to cover the truck. In the pub he bought me rum and blackcurrant and I bought Steve's beer. The place seemed to be full of faces split in grins. There was a woman with a front tooth missing and a dirty nest of bouffant hair. Hectic veins mapped big cheeks which forced her eyes out of sight every time she laughed. It was easy to see which of the customers came from the bin.

I tapped the boy's elbow after only a few minutes to let him know I was ready to go. Out in the yard he uncovered the truck and handed me a bottle of cider he planned to drink back in the ward after suppertime curfew. I crouched on the platform, cider gripped between my knees, beer wedged behind the seat.

In the alley again he tested the truck at maximum speed and, as we turned back into the road leading up to the hospital gates, told me to hold tight and jump when he gave the word. In the distance white-coated figures milled about near the gates. Four of them were getting into a car. One shouted. They had spotted us. A group of middle-aged patients from an open ward, all dolled up for the evening, cheered as we went by. The boy did not slow down on the main road. The white-coats, expecting us to swerve, positioned the car ready for pursuit. I ducked down, glad of my hat disguise.

When we were just twenty-five yards or so from the gates and still going at top speed, the whitecoats realized we were not going to turn. Pouring themselves out of the car and yelling to their colleagues who stood by the porter's lodge, they spread themselves into a line across the drive. Shooting by, I caught a glimpse of the porter's eyes alive with excitement as he picked his teeth distractedly with a match. The boy drove straight on as though the line of whitecoats did not exist. They waved their arms and hallooed. In a second we were on top of them, the line cracked in the middle and the whitecoats fell back like skittles into the hedges on either side.

There was a ramp in the drive ahead and the CAUTION, DAN-GEROUS BENDS sign. As we lurched over the ramp the cider leaped from between my knees and bounded off the truck, smashing foam and glass in our wake.

"OK, get ready!" the boy shouted.

Where the hedge ended, there was a stretch of lawn. We were on it now and racing full tilt at a round flowerbed. I could hear above the truck's whine the jog-jog-jog of whitecoats in pursuit along the drive. I hated the businesslike clomp of their boots.

"Jump!" yelled the boy and as the truck careered through a forest of rose bushes he leaped clear, on his feet and running as soon as landed, pale-shirted back flecked with earth.

I did not jump but stayed clinging to the back of the driverless truck as it plunged on, back on the grass now and belting toward a thick wall of bushes behind one of the wards. A picture of wrought-iron spirals and elegant fleurs-de-lis flicked across my mind like a slide, and before the snub nose of the truck slammed into a trunk in the heart of the bushes I had flung myself clear and was worming away flat to the earth, beer and the long Afghan coat abandoned.

There was music coming from the ward, a scratched record playing "Jumping Jack Flash." The weekly Social was on. Pulling off my hat, I used it to brush the dirt from my dress, then buried it under a clod of earth. The coat, as it was shared by a number of inmates, would not give me away.

By the time I got inside, the music had changed. "My Boy Lollipop" was jerking out loud and clear. Most of the patients sat on chairs round the edge of the room smoking and drinking orange squash from paper cups. Judy was there in her flaxen bangs. Her eyes lit up when she saw me and she brandished a bag of Dolly Mixture. I chewed some quickly to mask the rum on my breath.

"Let's dance," I said suddenly to an elderly man sitting next to her. He shambled on to the floor between the few individually jigging bodies and courteously extended a hand. At that moment there was a commotion at the door, voices of whitecoats firing excitedly in Chinese. Keeping my back to the door I accepted the proffered hand and was immediately steered into a rigid ballroom-dancing-school waltz. Staring fixedly over the man's shoulder I saw an old woman with a black eye and six handbags give me a wink and a thumbs up. As the eyes of the men at the door searched the room, I absorbed myself completely in the dance, heart thudding more rapidly than the staccato "giddy up" of the girl on the record, feet moving in staid accordance with my partner's slow-slow-quick-quick-slow. After a few moments the Chinese voices faded and in my gratitude I saw the end of the record through with the gentle waltzing man and curtseyed when he bowed. Then Judy and I cleared the floor as we danced a wild can-can to "Honky-Tonk Women." Everybody clapped.

But Steve never got his beer and a week later he hung himself. It was fat Michael who told me.

" 'ung isself," he kept repeating. "Yes, 'ung isself from the lavatory chain."

That was shortly before Addie came.

I knew at once that Addie and I would have much—or a great deal of poignant nothing—to say to each other. Because of his height and a strange combination of clumsiness and grace, I christened him at once the Heron. He had a diary too, in which he scribbled at length in a violent hand. He only wrote on the right-hand pages and worked from back to front of spiral-backed notebooks bought by the dozen.

For days neither of us said a word. He spent hours lying on his bed staring at the ceiling, but the whitecoats told him to get up and go into the dayroom, where male and female patients mixed. There we circled one another like cautious animals, acutely, excruciatingly aware of each other's presence and constantly avoiding a collision of eyes. We took to sitting close by, faces carefully averted. Then one day his large, bony hand strayed to the broad edging of my sleeve.

"That suits you," he said quietly and I jumped as though shot. There was a long silence. Then he observed, "You always cover your body completely."

"Yes."

I could feel myself blushing and wished his hand would come back to my sleeve. It did not. About a week later, when we had been sitting near each other all afternoon and he was making a mask out of summer burrs picked up in the grounds, I touched his foot. Days afterward he said, "I liked it when you touched my foot."

That was how we were.

The hospital world around us—we called it the bin—seemed to recede on to another plane, distant and incidental like the backdrop of a ribald scene on the stage of a serious play. Obscenities could be shrieked, people could writhe in fits, women smash lavatory bowls and men shit on the floor: none of it touched us. The delicate structure we wove around ourselves was resilient. In our private shell, where the subtleties of communication were conveyed with few words and fewer touches, we were able to block out the crudities of other people's worlds.

Addie never asks why I am here. It is one of the reasons I am drawn to him, part of our unspoken pact. I like the way he moves so carefully and feel his self- and body-consciousness like my own. Everything he wears calls to be touched and yet he holds himself aloof as I do all the time. His heavy, knobbly hands poke out from the ends of his sweaters like clubs. There are holes in all his sleeves where he pushes his thumbs through. All my sweaters have holes over my belly button where I trace round and round with my forefinger when I am alone and thinking of nothing.

For a week or so pale, beautiful Imogen was included in our hushed world. She drank real coffee from a Thermos all day, sucking it in with hissing, desperate sips between lungfuls of smoke. Her face was like a bruised white valentine, a mobile abstract heart. She wore men's clothes, pullovers with sleeves she could hide in, and died all muddled up in her long black hair, Tchaikovsky booming from big sponge earphones. When they found her, the "1812" was just a thin, busy bleat on the air, the earphones having slipped off. I hardly knew her but the image of her face, alive and dead, stayed with me a long time. One of the battery trucks came to tow her away.

Beyond the hospital and the quiet twilit rim of the world I shared with Addie, I did not look. The bin was for me a limbo in which it was easy to believe the future was out of my hands. And when I was not with Addie, its inmates provided an endless source of distraction from thoughts I wanted to avoid. Like why I was there. My diary kept up a running commentary on goings on in the ward, but did not say much about me.

This place is all long corridors, red and white as a raw lamb chop. Beds laid out in blue-gray rows, a body here and there making a blue-gray lump. In the morning the lumps shift to the dayroom where they sag in plastic-covered chairs by the always, always too hot radiators.

Black Liza woke me with her ravings this morning. She saw me blink and came running, waving her handbag at the end of frantic arms, tubes and tissues falling everywhere, a lipstick rolling in a long oval grabbed, I noticed, by that big lump Jean. Black Liza talked so fast I couldn't hear the words. She'd got something special in the bottom of her handbag. "It talks," she gabbled, "talking talking." She emptied the bag on my bed and grabbed the talking thing.

There was a rhythmic vibration as the whitecoats came jogging in time.

It was the telephone receiver, yanked wires trailing. She pulled my head under her pink-sweatered bosom and jammed the phone against my ear. "What's it saying? What's it saying?"

The jog-jog-jog came nearer. Curses and wailing as Black Liza and the telephone were taken away.

There are two or three on this ward who treat this place as a kind of holiday camp with free meals, free pills, free telly and pocket money from the State. They suck up to volunteer visitors knowing that because they are on the inside and their victims are from the outside, they will get sympathy whether they deserve it or not. There is one woman who cadges gifts of chocolate and cigarettes, hoards them up in her wardrobe, and has a business going with the inmates of the locked wards. The men suck up to the Charge nurses by a show of diligence over the ward chores. Their satisfied little world-weary sighs as they put their feet up and roll the 'nth cigarette of the morning are sickening. If I had been Hitler I would have tried to wipe out this lot, not the Jews, but some of them put on such a professional act it is hard to distinguish them from those who are really trying, those who have hope and an aim.

I could not escape my own criticism. In my own eyes, rape or no rape, I was a failure. I was not sure that in the holocaust I would mete out to those others I considered to be malingering, I deserved to survive. Whatever the reasons for my being in hospital, I was ashamed that I had not found some other way to cope.

By now I was expert in the art of using the hospital. An old file dating back to the days of truancy and connecting my name with such terms as "maladjusted," served as a sort of multiple reentry visa. But still I could not just announce that I wanted to come in. I had to produce evidence that I *needed* to, something forceful enough to bypass the usual waiting list yet not so violent as to get me locked up indefinitely.

One weekday afternoon, having walked for hours along the Thames with no particular aim, I found myself within easy reach of a large shopping center. I did not know where I was going to sleep that night—not 309 again with Kay's anxious, noncomprehending eyes— and this worried me. I knew before I left the towpath and mounted the steps to the town that I was going to do something which would take the worry out of my hands.

The streets were busy, milling with shoppers and office workers hurrying on their lunchtime rounds. I held open the door of a department store for a well-dressed woman and two others took advantage of my portership to push through. I followed, entering a bright, luxurious atmosphere designed to divert the weary shopper. Today, with a little assistance from me, they would be well entertained.

I lingered for a while on the household goods and china floor. There were tables laid up to display dinner services, apricot-colored napkins folded into tongued cones, stylish placemats with elegant hunting scenes. In my mind I rearranged the settings, banishing the formality and making them warm and colorful as I would want for a family of my own. I passed on into the clothes section, taking my time, finding sudden value in the last quarter of an hour of freedom. Before the mirror of a hatstand I tried on a wide-brimmed Garbo showpiece, tipping it down at the front so that only one middle-distance-gazing eye could be seen. Then I swapped it for a big Russian fur, drooping my mouth to look suitably proud and mysterious, and after that a Faye Dunaway beret, worn at a ludicrous slant. I liked hats for the clues they gave as to who I could be.

On the escalator to the restaurant floor, past lampshade and light fittings and long rolls of carpet, I stood behind two women discussing shopping problems. They were on their way to get their hair done but would stop for coffee first and "a little something wicked to go with it." I thought coffee a good idea too. My little something wicked would come afterward.

The coffee shop was situated to one side of the main restaurant, surrounded by a low white rail. It looked out over the rest of the floor which housed the store's lavish display of lounge and bedroom furniture. It was a busy time and most of the tables were full. The women from the escalator joined the counter queue ahead of me and filled their trays with quiche and tinned fruit gâteau. The "kwitch" reminded me of Sebastian Fox, married in Sweden now. I bought my coffee and headed quickly for the one vacant table near the front. I needed to be near the front. There were dirty plates cluttering the table and I smiled at the overalled waitress who came to clear them away. She did not respond and gave the surface a perfunctory swipe, red fingers wielding a damp cloth. Memory of Kay. My head felt full of irrelevant little snippets of the past, each one pointlessly clear, as irritating as advertising jingles repeating themselves uninvited.

I watched the traffic at the counter. Talk ebbed and flowed all round. It seemed to me as if the words were unimportant; it was the nods, the affirmations which mattered. Each separate table was like a cog in a wheel of ritual reassurance. When one removed the mind a short distance, the voices were reduced to a few simple patterns of sound: animals signaling. I was back to being a fly on the wall again. When the coffee was finished my gaze wandered to the wider spaces of the room and rested on the rich drapery of an ornamental fourposter. There were modern bunk beds in bright colors, long walkways of thick carpet, a yellow velvet divan.

With me I had a bag containing comb, purse, toothbrush and a library book with the address of the hospital clearly marked inside. I stood up and politely interrupted two women at the next table.

"Excuse me, would you mind looking after my bag a moment?"

After a slight pause there were nods. I laid the bag on a chair, bending as I did so to slip off my shoes. Then I stood up straight and took a deep breath.

One, two, three. . . . Hup! Over the rail. Long diving somersaults down the nearest length of piles. Up on to feet with the last roll and three skips to the springboard of the yellow divan. Big leap and I'm on the Rest Assured mattresses, row of three. Spring! Spring! Spring! To land thunk among the jolly bunks and chintzy singles. Whumph! Air farting out as I hit a deep pink kingsize, satin bedspread all in a whirl. Short run up to a designer number, whoops-a-daisy it's on wheels— skid slide crump into a fat settee.

P-rring! The bell. They're quick. Got to make it to the fourposter before they catch me. Come on run, short cut, dash toward the coffee crowd, brave it, brave it, oh look at their faces rolling back in a messy wave. Crash! A dropped tray. Yippee! Steady now for a big jump on to the final, the most inviting, row. Deep, satisfying springs, breaths. . . . Damn! They're coming at me from the other end. So what! They're going to get me anyway but not before I've had a bounce on that fourposter. . . .

We reached it at the same time. They came at me over the bed, one at the side and one at the end. Blue, this time, instead of whitecoats. At the last moment I dived under the valance to slide out unexpectedly the other side, dust up my nose and hands clinging trustingly to a pair of serge ankles. I kept my head down, mouth shut and went limp. Upside-down, dangling from their arms, I saw the pink satin bedspread crumpled like a bruised camellia.

What followed was always the same. a familiar treadmill of formalities, the wheels of administration turning up Madame Tussaud copies of police, social workers and locum psychiatrists. I knew the reception routine at the bin by heart: clothes removed, taken away and replaced by the candy-striped dressing gown, always too broad, always too short; forms filled in, nurses crackling around. Then waiting for the physical on hard, paper-covered couches in bare, cracked-ceilinged rooms. I hated those ceilings and those paper-covered couches, reminders of black ticks and red flowers in Tel Aviv—that other little madness I refused to connect with this.

A confrontation with a senior clinician did not occur until some days after admission when I would join a row of inmates in a draughty corridor examining the linoleum and red and white lamb-chop walls.

There was one doctor I rather liked. He was short and round with a perennial yellowish tan and a plump face like a kindly gnome. He had quick blue eyes which darted up sharply now and then from the notes he was jotting. Unlike other doctors I had seen, he seemed genuinely interested in signs that I had an active, if muddled, mind and he treated me like an adult, using technical expressions as though he assumed I would understand. I found this flattering and on one occasion when he used a term new to me did not like to admit it. We were discussing a phase of compulsive eating I was going through. I told him I had a thing about éclairs.

Dr: "You know in some cases this type of obsession disguises a desire for fellatio."

I was cagey.

"Really? Do you think that might be so with me?"

Dr: "I don't know. Is fellatio something you enjoy?"

I was out of my depth but kept my eyes fixed steadily on his.

"Mmmm . . . *quite*, but I think I still prefer éclairs."

When I looked up the word later—finding it only with difficulty— I was astounded. Nothing in my past had taught me about such things.

I was good at diverting myself, and others, from the deeper causes of my "maladjustment." The curtains I had drawn across my mind to shut out Cape Sounion and Tel Aviv acted both as a protection against the violence of my own feelings and a barrier preventing other people coming anywhere near the center of the problem. It never occurred to me to describe the white car episode to the doctor. Instead I threw out a trail of red herrings, behaving sometimes in a wild, extroverted manner and then withdrawing for days into a depressed shell. Being in the bin gave me a license for lunacy and I used it to the full.

My use and abuse of the hospital system might have gone on in-definitely had it not been for a crisis one autumn weekend. It was a Saturday, Addie was on leave and I was at a low ebb and a loose end.

I had spent the afternoon wandering in a grove of trees. In the twisted intertwining of the branches I saw all the complexity of unwordable feelings spelled out. That the strong, smooth limbs of the trees should fold themselves into agonized knots, splitting, bleeding and developing strange growths, seemed synonymous to me of my own condition. I was half infatuated with, half horrified by, both the trees and myself.

Beyond the trees, in a meadow out of bounds to patients, I came upon Daphne, a great clumsy horse of a woman who did nothing but sit slumped in a chair all day, weeping and spilling tea. She did not see me coming and I crouched down in the long grass and watched. This was a different Daphne.

She had lost her slippers and her large feet, steadily trampling down the grass in a circle, were streaked with earth. She was humming to herself, her throat occasionally vibrating like a bird's so that the hum became a gurgling croon. Her eyes behind clear-rimmed glasses were girlish and happy. I had never seen her smile before.

After a while her feet stopped moving and she wriggled her shoulders out of her dressing gown and let it drop to the ground. She stepped into the middle of the circle, back toward me, and the split down the back of the white gown showed her big innocent bottom wobbling. Her iron-gray head was thrown back, a lock of straggled hair waving in the breeze. The humming croon became a song and her heavy legs began to move rhythmically, knees lifting up and down. Her hand found the collar of the nightgown and she lifted it from her body, the ties at the back falling apart as she pulled. Naked, she moved with new confidence, singing louder, and as the beat of her dance quickened she raised blotched and flabby arms to the sky, her old breasts shook and her sagging belly flopped against her loins. In ecstasy the middle-aged thighs trembled and the veined calves glistened like bright columns brushed by the damp grass. A leaf was stuck between her toes. She was beautiful.

"Gawd! Come an' 'ave a look at this—the old twat's starkers!"

The porter's voice chopped into the still air like a shovel, crunching and clanging against Daphne's song. I ducked my head and kept quiet. Daphne did not seem to hear.

The porter's companion was a male nurse. From somewhere they found another, and the three of them strode purposefully into the field. Not until they were right upon her did Daphne understand that her moment of beauty was at an end. She went on singing and dancing, feet to the earth, face to the sky. When the hand of the senior nurse grabbed her shoulder she turned round and gave one low cry, eyes astonished behind glasses knocked askew. Efficiently they trapped her paralyzed arms and bundled the dressing gown around her. One of them had a cigarette in his mouth. All three moved quickly in case she should suddenly resist. But Daphne did not resist. They carried her limp, like a thick roll of carpet, and as they passed my hiding place I saw tears slide silently out of her eyes.

Upset and disinclined to return to the ward, I wandered out of the grounds.

Before long a man in a car stopped and gave me a lift into the nearest town. This was not unusual. There were always hopeful cruisers in the area. Before I had grown wise to their hopes, I had allowed one to park in the corner of a pub car-park where he nervously tried to kiss me. My reactions had been rapid and, as in the bus queue in Tel Aviv, disproportionately brutal. I bit him viciously and gave him a hard punch under the eye. After this I made use of the cruisers for lifts whenever I wanted, quashing familiarity before they got further than the opening gambit by quoting their car numbers at them and threatening to turn them over to the police. Surrounded as I was by extremes of human behavior, neither the men themselves nor my habit of using them as a convenient chauffeur service seemed peculiar at the time.

In town a lonely boy attached himself to me. He was also from the bin but unlike me, officially on leave. We strolled together and he told me about the unhappy hour he had spent visiting his mother.

"She's never been the same since me dad left."

I said I knew what he meant.

As we passed a restaurant he commented that he was hungry. He had been meaning to go into a café but had felt too shy alone. I offered to go in with him and he said that would be great.

We sat in the window of a continental steak house and the boy chomped his way through a large mixed grill. I was not hungry but had a salad to keep him company. When he had his pudding I ordered a liqueur.

Halfway through a mouthful of chocolate cake and cream, the boy's jaws suddenly stopped working. Leaning across the table, too panic-stricken to swallow, his words came thickly through a mass of crumbs.

"I 'aven't got any money. I forgot I give it to me mum. She said I wasn't fit to look after it meself."

His well-smeared lower lip shook. Whether it was the effect of the green liqueur or the way he said "I give it to me mum," I don't know: I laughed. I did not have nearly enough money to cover the bill. We were going to have to do a bunk.

"Oh God," I said, and laughed again.

The boy looked scared when I told him. I explained that the alternative was to give ourselves up and maybe have to go to the police station.

"No!" he said, "me mum'd kill me. I'm scared!"

"Well, stop *looking* scared," I snapped, and smiling at the waiter, ordered two brandies. The boy swallowed his in gulps as I outlined what we were going to do. By the time he had reached the bottom of his glass and had mine as well he was nodding enthusiastically. I made him repeat his lines and before he had time for second thoughts told him to get up and say them straight away. He pushed his chair back and lumbered to his feet, beginning faultlessly.

"Sorry about this. I won't be a moment. I'm just going to . . ."

He dried up and stood there gormlessly with crumbs on his chin.

"Yes, of course," I said, "your cigarettes. There are bound to be some in the cinema down the road."

I jerked my head meaningfully and he walked to the door, opened it, and was gone.

I saw the waiter look my way. It was there, a hint of suspicion round the eyes. Feeling reckless, stuck on the merry-go-round of a situation I had not planned, I ordered another brandy. It came and I drank. Immediately the taste brought back night in Yafo and dead kittens. My cheeks were hot. I began to feel more fierce than afraid, thoughts tumbling through my head like small serrated-edged knives. By the time the drink was finished I was wild, ready for anything; ready to run, fight, laugh, cry, rage.

I stood up while the waiter had his back turned and made for the door. I was out before they saw me but in a second there were two of them at my heels. Reflected in dark shop windows I saw short red jackets flying out from white shirt fronts, shiny black shoes pounding. Pounding inside and outside my head. Alcohol and adrenaline lent speed but not direction to my feet and in the doorway of a shoe shop I was caught. The grabbing hands and excited faces maddened me and it took both of them to pin me face down on the pavement as they shouted for a passer-by to call the police.

The stranger they hailed did not run to call the police. He bent down and looked into my face. I looked back, dumb, and heard him say calmly, "If she has not, as you say, paid the bill, I will pay. There is no need to call the police."

Now that he was standing, I could only see his trouser cuffs. He had a kind voice. But they would not have it. I must not be allowed to get away with it, it was the principle of the thing. The kind voice was shouted down, jostled away by others, and I got away with nothing, for when at last I was passed from the hands of the police to the heavy gang on duty that night in the bin, I no longer had any self-control. I twisted away from the hands they laid on me and refused to speak. I was snarling and crying at the same time. When I understood that they were going to give me an injection I exploded. I did not kick or lash out for there was one on each limb, but I writhed and bucked with all the strength in my being. And I screamed all the way down the throat of the void as I felt the needle go in.

12

On the fourth day, after the worst of the sickness was over, I felt a featherlight presence near my bed. Peering out of a slim periscope made of the sheet, I saw through blurred eyes a tall apparition waver and divide. As I struggled to concentrate, the figure became one again, still swimming and rippling but recognizable. A gray-sweatered arm with a thumb pushed through the sleeve was bent round a black box; a canvas bag stuffed with dog-eared notebooks hung over a bony shoulder. Addie. How he had managed to creep undetected up the back stairs to the far end of the female dormitory I will never know, but there he was, cautiously settling his long heron form on the perch of the bed. A wheeled screen and a locker closed us off from the rest of the ward.

"Are you awake?"

His low, slow voice was clear. I nodded the periscope.

"I've brought some music. Do you want to hear?"

I did not move. His strange club fingers pressed knobs on the black box.

"Play," I murmured, and the word in my drugged mind was huge and endless in meaning. He inched the box under the bedclothes and I sucked it into my submarine.

At first nothing but the whirr of winding tape. Then, as though accidentally spilled over from some distant land where all was gentle order, came couplets of soft chords like a cat slowly kneading a rug by a fire. Lulling, but at the same time subtly insistent, the chords were overlaid by a melody of single notes taking me outside the window of the hearth scene to where calm water shone toward the end of day and wound into streams whose winking passage over moss and stones was a joyous hymn to life. It went on to conjure in my mind blue sky through a pattern of twigs when I was twelve; sun-warmed heather in the Highlands; the glow of the moon on pink desert hills.

"Good, isn't it?" said Addie quietly when the tape wound back to a whirr.

"Yes," I said, groggy but sure and meaning far more than just the music, "Yes, yes, yes."

Coming at that time, when I was little more than an oblivion-bent lump of misery, that gentle music—it was in fact Satie's "Trois Gymnopédies"—served as a reminder of all the simplest and most beautiful things I had ever seen. And it spoke of new things too. There were tendernesses there which made my body long to stray first with the sounds, uncurling from its denying ball, and then beyond, to open and grow, to give as well as receive, create as well as respond.

The music and the feelings it aroused were poetic and sentimental but neither sound nor feelings were frail. Those beauties existed. They were as real as darkness and pain, and as powerful. It seemed to me that I had a choice of ways to go and I must choose now. Looking and yearning, dreaming images from a hospital bed was not enough. It was time to get up, get out and say *yes* to life once more.

Experiencing a moment of profound personal realization is one thing. Acting on it is another.

During the months spent at 309, working and going for endless, aimless walks like a zombie, there were occasional moments of clarity in which I knew I must do something to break the frightening downward slide of my mind. In one of those moments I applied for membership of a club called Winners. The blurb said that the club existed for "exceptionally bright" people who wanted to "mix, learn and grow" with their own kind. "Bright" was about the last thing I felt at the time but I needed something to convince myself that I was not as dim and incompetent as I seemed and membership of Winners was restricted to those who could pass a test.

Without telling anyone what I was doing—this was between me and me—I took a day off from the chip shop, washed my hair and caught a bus up to the West End. I arrived early, in time for a look at the other candidates. Whatever I had been expecting, I was disappointed. With the exception of one plump youth with a foolish grin, there was no one under forty. Dark jackets showed up uniformly sagging shoulders well dredged with dandruff. There were no other females sitting the paper that day. No one said a word while we waited and I, already marked apart by age and sex, felt too awkward to be the first to break silence.

However, when the test began, the others became irrelevant. I threw myself into it with a verve I had forgotten I had and finished twenty minutes before the final bell, feeling stretched and exhilarated. I sat idly until five minutes before the end when I thought I would have a last look at a question I had found too hard. I turned to the place and froze. No wonder I had finished before anyone else; two of the pages were folded together at the top, stuck. I had missed them out.

Feeling idiotic, I put up my hand to explain. The invigilator's response was acid.

"Young lady, you have come here to apply for membership of a club which requires of its members, among other things, exceptional intelligence. You cannot expect me to sympathize with such a stupid mistake."

My mouth dropped open and then shut fast. Ignoring him and the plump youth, who giggled, I ripped the pages apart and worked through them like fire. When the bell rang I had not finished but was nearly there. I handed in my paper with the others and treated the invigilator to my stoniest glare. Infuriatingly, he smiled. When the results came through several weeks later I was tempted to go and wave my membership card under his nasty nose.

But then the bad dreams and the memories became too much, and it was not until I had been three months in the mental hospital that I made my first moves as a member of the club for Winners.

I had received several copies of the club magazine which listed activities available to members and I decided to make my début at a major gathering based in town and lasting a whole weekend. The gathering, for which I obtained special leave after two weeks confined to grounds following the injection, began with a party. It would be my first party—not counting the session with Fred and Co. in Athens—since the lie-down-and-grope affairs I had dallied with amidst all else that was happening at St. Paul's. I took the opportunity to wear the beautiful dress Jorges had bought me in Jerusalem.

The main activities of the weekend were held in a large hall. I was daunted by its size and the hundreds of confident-looking, smartly dressed people milling through its doors. Most of them seemed to know each other and the hall resounded with squawks and growls of greeting. My loose hair, worn sandals and exotic robe felt out of place and I considered escaping before the party got under way. But I had not reckoned on the sociability of the lone academic female. A pair of broad, powdered, middle-aged shoulders bore down on me.

"Hello dear, whose little sister are you?"

I bridled. Sister, and little. It was assumed I was a tagalong. It had said in the party blurb that members were allowed to bring guests. I moved to a snacks table and scooped up a handful of crisps, crunching them before replying.

"Actually, I'm here on my own."

Her eyes lit up behind donnish spectacles. She looked a little like Daphne with a perm.

"You mean you're one of us? But your pin, dear, where's your pin?"

I noticed then that everyone else had a small pink and white label pinned to their chests. Delighted to have an errand, the large lady dashed away to find me one. I was immediately approached by a smiling young man in a white rollneck sweater who asked if he could bring me a glass of wine. While he was fetching it another youth, with an eager, friendly face, started chatting amusingly. I giggled and chatted back. Suddenly it all felt easy and fun. The Daphne lady must have spread the word that I was new blood because a number of people came to say hello. My ego grew fresh buds every time someone squinted to decipher the name on my pin.

A Winners club jamboree is an unlikely occasion for a young girl to discover her social wings. There was no music, no dancing and the majority of people were much older and not essentially given to frivolity. But it worked for me. From a curled-up ball on a hospital bed emerged a happy butterfly insouciantly fluttering her wings in all directions. By the end of the evening I had made three dates, none of them of great individual significance but all adding to the proof positive that I was ready and able to start living again. I parried questions about "what I did" with a fresh answer every time. I flirted, sparkled, giggled, glowed.

Then the next day something happened which knocked all the small pleasures of party games into a cocked hat. I fell under the spell of a man.

On the second afternoon of the gathering there were a number of events one could attend. There was a lecture, a self-hypnosis class, a discussion group on "Winners in Business" and a tour of a printing works. I found out that the lecture had something to do with people and potentials and decided to give it a try. My "dates" were opting for hypnosis and the tour.

Adrian Massell came as a shock. From the moment he walked on to the platform I was hypnotized. And it was not just his unusually green eyes and tall, confident form that captivated me, it was what he said. Here was a man I could listen to for days, someone who had much to say and who said it brilliantly. His words, swiftly chosen, firmly uttered, clipped away all the trimmings of an argument. With a light step and a quick, bright smile, he forged a path straight into the heart of my mind. He was positive without being fanatical, clever without flaunting his wit as a weapon, a man not only creating his own music but dancing to the tune. He shone, he burned, a strong, flame-headed, laughing-eyed god; arriving at precisely the point in my life when I most needed one.

And I was by no means the only one enchanted that afternoon. After the lecture a bevy of eager acolytes rushed to congratulate him, newly made admirers hanging shyly at the edge of the crowd. I remained seated, watching him handle their questions and praise, his mind operating like a dancer performing a faultless impromptu routine. Then I rose quietly and left. Outside the hall one of my dates was waiting. Damn. I wanted to be alone to think about Massell.

It was a while before I saw him again but the seed of the future had been sown. I learned that he was to hold a series of lectures in the New Year and telephoned to ask for a place on the course. He answered the phone himself, giving me the chance to print again on my mind that strong, sure voice. He could not put a face to my name as I had not introduced myself at the gathering but he was pleased to enroll me for the lectures.

I could hardly wait, believing that, through him, my whole life was going to find a new and positive direction.

13

Addie and I left hospital at around the same time. Our contact after that was sporadic, the empathy between us making meetings irresistible but stiflingly intense. I spent some days and nights at his mother's house and saw the cavern of a room where his journey from adolescent solipsism to a state of virtual catatonia had begun. The rest of the house was conventional and his gamine, vivacious mother imbued it with strident normality, but upstairs in the closed sanctum of Addie's room, the outside world ceased to exist.

I had not yet read Cocteau's *Les Enfants Terribles* or Huysmans' *Au Rebours*. Nor had I looked at the lives of Van Gogh, Rimbaud or a dozen other doomed and brilliant heroes. If I had, perhaps the atmosphere of Addie's room might not have seemed so unique.

Torn red velvets and creamy satins draped bed and walls, muffling and enclosing the occupant like a womb. Within that womb, ranged on bowed shelves beneath a permanently shuttered window and pinned with six-inch nails to the walls, were objects of timeless and macabre appeal. There were skulls of birds and snake's jaws; domed boxes like temples holding hair and blood-colored stones; complex umbilical knots hacked from trees; pillboxes, razors and a sinister row of surgical blades.

On a sloping table in a corner jagged half-bricks weighed down hectic columns of notebooks. Yarrow stalks, charcoal, paintbrushes and bones were jammed into jars like sheaves of straw on end. Propped on the floor was a stalagmite of mirror so spotted and green the reflection it gave of Addie's haunted eyes was not so clear as the penciled self-portraits which rose in a ragged diagonal to the top of the wall, interspersed with prints of Munch's "The Scream" and Da Vinci's bisected man. The mask of summer burrs made in the bin hung like a shrunken head on a nail and, beside the bed, sculptures taken from molds of Addie's feet and hands held butts between the toes and ash in the palms.

In that narrow bed Addie lay like a cross between sleeping Endymion and liver-torn Prometheus, with me beside him not quite touching anywhere. It was sensitivity, not sensuality, that held the highest sway in our world. Nevertheless the meat we fed our minds on was strong. Head propped against a never-changed pillow, smoking needle-thin cigarettes and taking deep draughts from a mug of old, cold coffee, Addie read long extracts, in a low, mesmeric voice, from Nietzsche.

I listened, eyes closed, and before long that thin black book with the bone-yellow pages found its way into my shoulder-bag and accompanied me everywhere. On the tops of jolting buses I swallowed great tracts of Zarathustra's railings, often so absorbed I failed to alight at the right stop and ended up wandering bemused in Staines or Hounslow wondering what had happened to the funambulist and the serpent and the cave.

With the exception of my private future link with Massell and his contrastingly ordered world, there was a great deal of wandering and wondering and pondering and blundering in those days after the hospital. Finally those wanderings led to Mole's End.

It began with a rendezvous by the river with Julian, a friend from Addie's past. It was clear straight away that he suffered from none of the mawkish self-consciousness that we did. The first thing he did when he saw our two self-effacing forms approaching was, quite literally, jump for joy. He gave a deep, melodious whoop and sprang into the air like an exuberant Cossack. His costume, made entirely by hand, consisted of white sherpa boots over capacious breeches and a magnificent minstrel's jacket of almond green. Dark hair swarmed down his back and he had a long soft beard divided into three tapering plaits. The middle plait quivered expressively as he embraced Addie, his smile broad and glistening as a river in the sun.

The moment of ebullient greeting over, there was a pause in which I felt acutely the differences in our physical presence. When I was with Addie, my butterfly wings were closed in sympathy with his own. I moved at his pace which in those days was hesitant and slow. Julian was a startling contrast, a boy/man overflowing with *joie de vivre*. His wide-open eyes gleamed with health and body heat vibrated from him in an aura three feet deep. Beside him, Addie's ascetically fleshless form seemed more than ever like a stricken heron. I, aware by now of the chameleon flexibility of my own persona, took a step back from them both.

We sat by the wintry Thames, Addie smoking, hunched in duffel coat and half a dozen scarves, Julian apparently oblivious to the cold, drinking in and puffing out great lungfuls of vaporous river air and speaking in ardent, never-completed spasms of phrase which gradually died under the delicate steamroller of Addie's deliberate pronouncements.

"I wish we had a fire," I blurted suddenly, "a great big blazing fire to feed."

"Mmmmmn," breathed Julian in pulsing concurrence. And then, round-eyed as though amazed at the simplicity of the solution, he cried, "Mole's End!"

I raised a quizzical eyebrow at Addie.

"It's a cottage," he said, "about half a day's hitch from here. I think you'd like it."

And we decided there and then to go. I would hitch on ahead and as Julian, pressing my hands in temporary farewell, said, "light a candle in the window."

Sixty miles down the M4, following the boys' instructions, I crossed a bridge marked with a No Entry sign and found myself on a country road.

As I moved further away from the motorway, the hush of gently rising winter fields settled round my ears like a large, cool, unassuming hand. Remnants of magenta leaves clung to spiky hedgerows. Soft ridges of mud stood up in clodded curves where a tractor had turned in the road, and round a corner where a rabbit lay flat-ironed on the verge picture-book smoke rose from a red-bricked house on a hill.

A muddy van with chinks of road showing through the floor took me to the village of Renton. Here, children with cheeks the color of crab apples pressed white noses against the window of a cake shop and a string of race horses with jockeys like frozen scarecrows unwound down the street. I walked on to a fork in the road where one sign showed clearly the way to Wetherbourn and another pointed mysteriously straight into the ground. On it was written Belleston Warren. Julian's directions, couched in a series of lopped, descriptive bursts, had been obscure from this point on.

"There's this long straight . . . you'll see the barrows . . . clump of trees on a hill . . ."

Addie had tried to be more precise.

"You head toward Belleston Lisle, Lucy."

Again Julian broke in confusingly.

"Of course there's Belleston Bagpuize . . ."

"Belleston what?"

"Bagpuize, Bagpuize, Bagpuize!" His glistening mouth bounced and dandled the word.

"But do I want to go there?"

"To Belleston Bagpipes? Whatever for?"

I gave up. I would find the cottage somehow. And lo, as I set off along the fork away from Wetherbourn, there was the long straight dot dot dot, the barrows and the clump of trees on a hill.

Hills in broad slopes and billows rose and fell like muted green waves. A straggling circle of crows flapped clumsily between one slow swell and the next, raw cries splintering the silence, ragged bodies stippling the sky. That long straight stretch of road passed over a high tract of the Ridgeway and plunged, after a tidy four-way crossing, down the steep, humpbacked scarp of Blowing Stone Hill. Dark trees alongside the road became with the fading light one continuous columnar screen, seeming to lean inwards, forming a tunnel.

At the bottom of the hill a sign pointed the way to Belleston Lisle and a smell of cold cattle rose to meet me. Further on there was a village pub and opposite, a tiny cottage extension marked Post Office.

A squint SHUT sign on a piece of string told me that business was over for the day but I saw a figure moving behind a thin curtain and heard the gravelly clatter of a till. When I tapped on the door a woman's face appeared suddenly in a triangle of light where she had pulled back the curtain. One cheek bulged with something she was chewing and a bright eye goggled from beneath a wave of heavy brown hair. I smiled apologetically and the bolts were drawn back.

"Ye-es, what can I do for you?" A comfortable country lilt matched her cushiony figure and bird-sharp eyes.

"I wonder if you could tell me the way to a cottage called Mole's End?"

"Oh, going to Mole's End, are you?" She looked me up and down with interest. "Well, you can't miss it."

She pointed over my head to where the road led out of the village and gave simple directions. I thanked her and was about to go when, stepping back and shifting whatever she was chewing to the other cheek, she said, "Is there anything you'll be wanting to take down? I've a pint of milk here . . ."

I saw now that the Post Office also served as the village shop. There were rows of old-fashioned sweet jars, bottles of soft drink, a block of yellow cheese and some bacon under a plastic dome.

"Well, perhaps some milk. That's very kind."

She bustled behind the counter making a long business of finding the milk and as I hunted for change she said slyly, "You're not that Orpheus's sister, are you?"

"Orpheus?"

"Well, that's what folk call him"—she grinned girlishly—"going round the fields with that flute and them baggy trousies."

I laughed. She must mean Julian.

"Be staying down there a day or two, will you?"

"I expect so."

Again I was ready to go but before parting with the milk she looked me straight in the eye across the counter.

"You'd best use strong thread to sew up them baggy trousies—and it won't be before time!"

The grumbling affection in her voice was unmistakable.

The moon was rising as I launched into the last straight lap, softly lighting the wooded corner of a field where Mole's End lay. There were no other houses nearby and my eyes remained fixed on the little building as I walked, taking in its quiet square face, the twin sets of windows on either side of a porched front door. The cold had settled in hard now and I pushed on with a final burst of speed to get there quickly, light a fire, and set a candle in the window.

The key, on a long piece of linen tape, was old and bent and it took several tries to open the front door. The narrow entrance way, walled on either side, was for a moment pitch black. Ash and potato dust added themselves to a general scent of butt water and herbs. My hand went out and encountered something stiff which crackled, an ancient oilskin. Beyond, a window threw a broad lozenge of outside's dim visibility on to a square of tiles, to the left of which I could just make out the stepping diagonal of what appeared to be a gigantic set of pan pipes on the wall. A window seat held a squat crock of spiky ferns whose shadows rose like clawing hands to a low, bulging ceiling. To the right was the main living area and after a quick glance at a spiral of triangular wooden stairs leading up into total black, I concentrated my exploration here; the first task being to discover a source of light.

On the mantel beam above the gray gape of a fireplace, my hands found a metal candle holder with a box of matches at its rim. Damp had penetrated Mole's End's walls and five matches died before the candle would light. Then, faintly lit by the yellow flame, shapes came into view that over years would become as familiar as the knuckles of

Addie's fingers and the warmth of Julian's breath. I found another candle to set before the largest window, a star to guide my boys.

Despite the damp, the fire I made took well and the hush which made the cold seem more intense was banished by the spit and scuffle of fast paper flame igniting twigs which in turn licked the belly of a damp log dry until a sudden burst of bright fire curled round and gripped it like a burning hand. I found water in jars beneath a church pew and filled a huge soot-blackened kettle which hung over the fire from three meat hooks dangling on chains.

In a trug on the floor were potatoes and onions and I made foil parcels of them to bake, enjoying the simplicity of little choice, few decisions. I was pottering contentedly with a candle, about to explore upstairs, when I heard singing outside.

It could only be Addie and Julian, one voice deep, flat and scowling, the other murmuring and round, innocent as a King's College choirboy. What detracted from the charm of the duet was the fact that each was singing a different song. Addie's voice tortured the lower rungs of a lyrical modern ballad and Julian fluted angelically through an *Agnus Dei*. The combined effect was bizarre, two dogs howling to separate moons. I was laughing as I ran to open the door.

Julian clowned as they came up the path, playing the bumpkin and doffing an imaginary cap.

"Ah, good lady, might there be room by your hearth for two strangers this cold night? We have traveled far and are wearied by our load . . ."

Addie's wry voice chopped into the flow.

"Wearied by our load is right. One guy refused to give us a lift when Julian told him that the sack was full of human hair."

A large sack was dumped in the porch.

"For the garden," said Julian proudly, "or a pillow for you, my dear?"

Then, uncharacteristically, Addie burst out laughing.

"Talking of hair, Lucy, have you seen yourself?"

I put my hand up to my head and it came away gloved with cobwebs. We all laughed. It was a fine feeling to be so careless of appearance after the painful self-consciousness of recent months; to be a thousand miles away from the shrinking ghost on the hospital bed and the bright superficial doll at the club party. Here, isolated in the trough of a Berkshire vale, there were no standards to conform to or deny other than our own. There was no established order for Addie to rail against and nothing for me to run from except myself.

As the two of us stepped into the cottage, leaving Julian outside a moment bidding an elaborate good night to the moon, I wondered how we would cope with the freedom to be ourselves in this quiet base in no man's land.

Once all three of us were inside, the contrasts in the boys' characters cluttered the place immediately with two distinct atmospheres. With the lavish endorsement of Julian's praise the small domestic moves I had made erupted into an extravagant paradigm of all that is homely and warm. The modest fire I had built became, with Julian kneeling before it and lovingly turning the foil parcels in his hands, a glowing heart for the room. Chairs were drawn up and rosemary-scented sheets draped to air, while bricks were heated to warm the beds. From the recesses of a long kitbag Julian produced a single enormous cooking apple. Holding it in both hands as I bent near he begged, "You do it—you'll do it so beautifully."

I took it and rolled its cool bumpiness against my cheek. He watched, pleasure flowing from him in gusty murmurs. From across the square hall I could hear Addie repeating in a sinister echo: *"Do it beautifully,"* his voice loaded with the voluptuous innuendo of Hedda Gabler enjoining her lover to kill himself. Julian took no notice. While I wrapped the apple and made a place for it in the fire, he set an Aladdin lamp on the table and began carefully to trim it.

Addie sidled into the pool of light like a long black moth.

"What about a drink, Julian?"

Julian leaped up, conjuring from nowhere three mottled tumblers made of horn and a bottle of mysterious pinky-orange liquid.

"What is it?" asked Addie, flexing large nostrils over the rim of his horn.

"Rosehip," cried Julian enthusiastically, "pure rosehip."

"Oh God," said Addie, but took an obliging sip.

Julian swallowed his in huge gulps and bounded out of the door murmuring about turning on the water.

"Got any coffee?" Addie called after him.

"Dandelion roots," came back a cry, "whole bowl of them under the pew."

"Oh God," said Addie again, starting to roll a cigarette, "no booze, no caffeine. What a setup."

While Julian was outside, Addie lapsed for a moment into his old hesitant self-consciousness. I left my seat and quietly fed the fire.

"That suits you," said Addie from behind his smoke, and I recalled the first time he had said that and wished it had been here instead of where it was.

"But look!" he demanded, suddenly fierce, and lifting his gangling length positioned himself before a pair of giant organ bellows to one side of the fire. He fiddled with a metal pipe under the logs and began to pump.

In the space of seconds the fire was transformed from a homely glow to a demoniacal blaze, violent orange forks of flame leaping up the chimney, wild sparks flying out on to the hearth like glittering eyes. The sounds it made were like some panting bird-beast at bay, gasps and roars and the hysterical beating of wings. Even when it was obvious that the flames were feeding on their own blasting intensity Addie went on, making the crazed red tongues speak for his own directionless fire. When Julian came in, arms laden with logs, Addie grabbed them all and hurled them on to the blaze, pumping the bellows again but this time misdirecting the air so that ash flew about madly, dusting the hearth and kettle silvery-gray.

Half laughing, half in anguish, Julian scrabbled the burning parcels from the heat, reprimanding Addie like a naughty child.

"Oh Addie," mocked Addie, flouncing away, "wicked Addie."

And he disappeared with a candle into the room across the hall and struck wild bursts of Rachmaninov from an ancient piano there.

While Julian was gentling the fire, I collected up the sheets, shaking off their hot dusting of ash. There were two doubles and a single sewn into a coffin-shaped tube. My candle threw a yellow semicircle of light on each triangular stair as I moved upwards and lit up a spider straddling its mummified prize in a web under the bannister. A new, sweet smell met me at the top of the stairs and casting the light around I found its source—a small army of late autumn apples spread on the floorboards in rows.

Through a curtained doorway lay one bedroom with a low bed covered in a black plastic sheet. I lifted the edge and there was a muffled scrabbling followed by a soft plop on the floor and then silence. Mice. I was about to duck under the curtain again, hoping to find the other bedroom not so occupied, when I caught sight of a high shelf made of a single curved plank, the bark still on it. Ranged from end to end were books of all shapes and sizes. One end seemed to be all children's books: fairy tales, *The Water Babies* and anthologies of morality verse in old editions. I lifted one of these down and it felt both heavy and frail with age. Inside there were startlingly vivid pictures of "The boy

who would not eat his soup'' and ''Basil who was eaten by bears.''
Further along there were novels and books of short stories. I looked at
the author's names: Sholokov, Fournier, Silone, Voltaire. Paperbacks
were stacked at the end: Camus, Hesse, Hemingway, Sassoon, and,
although I did not know it then, downstairs there were works of Che-
khov, Anouilh, Plato and Donne. During the weeks I was to spend
alone at Mole's End I caught up on a lot of the hours I had missed at
school.

Beyond a corridor with a single bed under a window lay the master
bedroom. Apart from a painted wooden chest, a huge, high bed was
its only feature. An uncurtained window looked directly over coolly
moonlit fields. This bed was also draped in black plastic but there was
no evidence of occupants when I lifted it clear. Dried lavender and
thyme were strewn over a striped horsehair mattress all of lumps and
dips impressive as a mountain range. When I approached the chest,
where Julian had told me the blankets were, my foot met the edge of
a hatch on the floor. Curiously, I lifted it and was greeted with a burst
of light from the fire below. This was Julian's central heating system.
At that moment his upturned face appeared in the gap.

''Onions coming along beautiful, Ma'am,'' he announced, and handed
up three heated bricks wrapped in socks.

After making up the big bed I took the sewn-up single sheet into the
small corridor room and laid it on the bed there, wondering whether
it would be used by Julian or me. I knew in advance that one half of
the big bed would be Addie's—unless he decided to sleep with the
mice. I slipped in a brick to warm each place before joining the boys
downstairs.

By now Addie had exhausted the more violent pieces from his rep-
ertoire on the piano and was producing a diverting version of the ''Trois
Gymnopédies'' from a homemade organ. Those shadowy pan pipes I
had seen on the wall were attached to a keyboard. The higher register
was perfectly pitched but some of the lower notes sounded like loud
raspberries. Solemnly, lovingly, Addie thrilled and farted through that
piece which not so long ago had reminded me of the beauties which
made life seem worth embracing again. On the music stand, in place
of a score, he had propped a picture of Salomé dancing with John the
Baptist's head dripping on a plate. I found a triangle on a shelf and
joined in with serious tings.

At suppertime Julian sat on the hearth dividing the vegetable parcels
onto irregular blue-striped plates. The warm firelight and softly spoked
beams of the Aladdin lit his face and his hands moving tenderly over

the food. Addie glowered throughout the meal, head buried in a book. I sat between them reveling in the femininity which allowed me to glow, undivided, for both.

Addie smoked and brooded while Julian ran to fetch nightshirts from upstairs and I cleared the dishes. The nightshirts were thick and voluminous, patched but scrupulously clean. I changed in the shadow of a barrel that served as a bath and went outside for a pee. The air was brittle with cold now, the moon high and white flanked by chilly streaks of cloud. Shivering, I ran back inside, looking forward to snuggling into one of the brick-warmed beds.

The boys had changed before the fire, Addie keeping on all his clothes beneath the shirt, Julian proud and careless, unbuttoned to the navel, long feet flexing on the hearth as he lifted his flute and blew an impressive stream of saliva through the end. As I preceded them upstairs, commanded to warm the big bed all over, a high, clear melody rippled out, graceful as the shadows dancing from my candle on the wall. With the notes wafting sweetly through the central-heating hatch and faint pops and whispers coming from the fire, I fell asleep very soon.

But not for long.

I woke to see Julian tiptoeing round the end of the bed with a candle and a book in one hand, a pair of slippers, chamberpot and brimming mug in the other. His tongue was curled over his lower lip in the effort to hold on to everything and keep quiet at the same time. But the book was slipping. Pot, book, slippers and light tumbled to the floor, the chamber giving a resounding clang. I giggled.

"Oh!" came Julian's voice, all distressed, through the sudden dark, "I've woken you."

"Don't worry. I've got another candle here."

I lit it and saw that, miraculously, he had managed to save the mug. This he gave me to hold while he searched under the bed for the book.

"Now that you're awake," he said shyly, "would you like me to read you to sleep again with a story?"

"OK."

Perching on the edge of the bed he began to read the tale of "The Little Mermaid," pausing every now and then to take a sip from the mug of hot milk we shared. I snuggled deeper in the bed, feeling very happy and about six years old.

"Aha," came Addie's voice, as he clumped loudly up the stairs, "story time, is it? Right Lucy, you're going to get two stories tonight."

Climbing like a great cold spider into the bed he thumped down a massive volume on the pillow.

"Now then," he announced, "Wittgenstein!"

He opened it at any old page and began to read loudly in a doom-filled prophetic voice. Julian carried on with "The Little Mermaid" as though nothing were happening. I lay for a long minute between the two of them, ears assaulted and hair on end, then wriggled up to a sitting position and cried, "Enough!"

Because Addie refused to stop he was banished to the single bed where his droning bursts of passion continued as a backdrop to the adventures of "The Little Mermaid." Julian finished the story and after tenderly bidding me good night, climbed into Addie's vacated place and fell asleep. His big, cuddly body gave out sighs of contentment and animal warmth in waves. At some point in the night they must have changed places because when I woke with the first stirrings of dawn it was Addie's familiar shape cupped in the dip beside me, long, chilly and concave as a razor shell. The casual proximity of those two masculine but undemanding bodies, in the atmosphere of Mole's End, did more to cure me of post-rape breakdown than any amount of treatment in mental hospital could have done.

The first day at Mole's End formed a pattern which was to repeat itself over and over whenever the three of us were there. I would come down first, light the fire and make porridge for Julian and myself. We breakfasted quietly, yawning and grinning in our nightshirts. Sometimes we plaited each other's hair. Then we would dress and go logging or walk for miles, picking up bits of edible fungus from the woods or climbing the hills to wander among the standing stones of Wayland's Smithy and watch winter set deeper in the valleys.

Addie never stirred in the mornings, lying silent as death with a black shirt wrapped over his face and blankets wound round him like swaddling clothes. We left him undisturbed, knowing that around noon or sometimes as late as three, he would emerge looking pale and exhausted, begging plaintively for coffee. After a while one of us usually remembered to bring some. Dandelion roots were just not the same.

When New Year came I was still under the Mole's End spell. I had gone back to London with Addie, hung around the old haunts for a day or so, then yielded to the quiet call of the Berkshire hills. Julian was there off and on, returning between trips to Canterbury where he was making a recording with some other musicians. My heart always lifted when I saw his cloaked figure striding through the dusk along that by now so familiar stretch of road, but I did not pine when he left again for I was equally happy alone.

Over Christmas—which I acknowledged absent-mindedly by eating nothing but Brussels sprouts out of the garden for three days—I started the reading that was to absorb so much of my time there. Between long sessions with a book before the fire, I went for dreamy walks over the snow-covered fields, picking up kindling and dragging logs on the way back.

I loved the simple rituals of Mole's End life: lighting the fire in the morning, white-faced and goose-pimpled in the cold, holding reddened fingers before the first hint of flame, watching the cloud of my breath grow fainter as the stone room gradually warmed. Sometimes, creeping down at some black, dateless midnight, I would suddenly throw myself on the bellows and blow up a wild blaze from the embers, pumping like Addie with my whole body until the walls were alive with crazy shadows and the roar of the fire filled the snow-muffled night with sound. Then I would dance through to the music room with two hysterically guttering candles and draw long, wheezing moans from the wood and canvas belly of the organ, triple-socked toes slipping madly as I pressed the pedals, chill fingers stiff on the silky smooth keys. When I stopped, and the fire quickly died, silence would close over once more, the little pebble of my actions sinking into the pool of night. Upstairs again, I would leap into the still body-warm cavern of the bed and squirm right down until I was totally enveloped by the lumps and ridges of mattress and bedclothes, snug in the dark as a pit in a prune.

On Christmas Day I climbed to the crest of White Horse Hill and sat there panting, snow melting on flushed cheeks, face upturned to the sky. My pockets were filled with soft little apples and I bit the best from them one by one and spat the bright pips and crimson skins into the snow.

Julian came a few days later and the two of us climbed the hill again, fresh snow sparkling in his beard and building a rich fleece collar on the cloak I borrowed for the trek. At the top we sprawled full length, careless of the melting wet, and finally launched our bodies down the slope like human snowballs, loose sweaters gathering hard-packed layers of snow, boots filling, ears stinging with laughter and cold.

I knew more contentment than I had felt for a long time—perhaps ever—with the fire and the reading, the long, thought-careless walks and the occasional companionship of the boys. But I had not forgotten Massell, and in the second week of the New Year, when the snow had gone, I turned my back on Mole's End and headed toward London, happy and full of hope.

14

The first thing to sort out was accommodation. I could have stayed at 309 but too many times I had gone from that house in unhappiness, too many times returned to find unhappiness there. I wanted to open myself to this new venture as a vessel unstained by the past.

As chance would have it, I bumped into an old acquaintance on Richmond Bridge—Ben, the boy from the bin, who had been the instigator of the runaway truck episode. He was less impulsive now, the horrors which had landed him in the bin having burned themselves out. He told me that he was living with his girlfriend and some others in a house near Felstead on the edge of the Downs. I was welcome to stay, there would be no rent to pay.

The house turned out to be a squat, quite grand on the outside, situated in an old-fashioned residential area, but inside it was little more than boards and rubble. A mattress was found for me and moved into a vacant front room.

The next thing to organize before the lectures began was work, and soon my Young, Strong, Willing and Able notices were pinned up all over the district. There were two replies on the first day, one from an agent looking for someone to shop and clean for an elderly lady, the other from a housewife needing a babysitter, meals provided. I secured both jobs, arranging to babysit at the weekend and do my first stint of shopping and cleaning that afternoon. The agent warned me that Mrs. Browne "could be a bit tricky sometimes."

Mrs. Browne lived in Canton, circa 1923, in a magnificent bungalow with scrolled turrets and ample accommodation for twenty-six servants and a peacock called Bluey. I learned all this within ten minutes of arriving at her third-floor flat in a crumbling block on the outskirts of Sheen.

"What would you like me to get you from the shops, Mrs. Browne?"

"How should I know? What have they got today?"

She was a tiny, compressed figure, concentrating all her energy in her voice. My eyes moved cautiously round the flat, searching for clues as to how her daily life was run. She was waiting.

"Speak up, girl! What are you going to get, then?"

Her hands clasped and unclasped impatiently on the handle of a knobbly walking stick held between her knees.

"I expect you need some food. Does anyone—does anyone cook for you?"

"Cooks, you say? Terrible! Don't talk to me about cooks. Three of them, one after the other, pilfering the silver, forgetting to feed Bluey . . ."

There followed a tirade on the shortcomings of cooks, houseboys, gardeners and maids. I looked at her thin arms, the shrunken cheeks beyond the aggressively quivering chin.

"I'll get you some chicken and perhaps some tins to last until I come again."

She nodded distractedly and waved me away. There was five pounds in an envelope marked SHOPPING on top of a string bag. I had no idea how long it was supposed to last. As I was glancing round the kitchen to see what basics were required she called, "Don't forget my sweets, do you hear?"

It was no good asking what kind.

From a phone booth near the shops I rang the agent who had got me the job. Her reply was brisk.

"Look dear, I get this every time. We've been trying to get her into a home for years but she won't have any of it. We tried sending her meals-on-wheels and she told us to give them to the RSPCA. She's only got her pension so don't let her tell you to buy steak. You're the fourth person I've sent in a month."

I put the phone down, feeling thoughtful. Surely Mrs. Browne wasn't as bad as that?

Pleased with the sensible way I had eked out the five pounds, I returned to the flat in a confident mood. Mrs. Browne was nowhere to be seen. I rustled the packages in the string bag to announce that I was back. She called out from the bathroom.

"*There* you are. Hurry up, I'm all ready."

I thought she might need helping off the lavatory. Instead, I was confronted with the sight of her standing stark naked in a waterless tub trying to hook a shower-cap off the doorknob with her walking stick. I handed her the cap. She thrust it back with irritable fingers.

"Put it on, you silly girl."

It occurred to me that if I were to survive with Mrs. Browne any longer than my four predecessors something would have to be done about these rude commands. Stuffing up my hair, I nonchalantly put the cap on my own head. And curtsied. For a moment her whole scrawny frame froze. Even her shriveled little witch's nipples managed to look furious. I remained demure.

"Cheeky hussy!" she spluttered, "cheeky hussy!" But she cackled as she snatched back the cap and stuck it over her own wispy hair. While I was washing her, trying to treat her frail body naturally, as though this was something I had done a hundred times before, she told me how hers had been the most perfect, the most enviable, flapper figure. She told me in detail what she had worn, finishing with the triumphant line: "It was nothing to me to wear stockings with sequins all the way up the seams—and don't think we didn't have garters to match!"

By the time she was dressed in her old gray cardigan and skirt and back in her chair in the sitting room, she was so exhausted from talking she did not want to bother going through the shopping.

"Next time," was all she would say. So I left out some obvious bits and pieces for her supper and said good-bye. Our worlds would cross again in two days.

I went to 309 before the first lecture. There were some clothes I wanted to collect and it was a good opportunity for a bath. There was no hot water in the squat.

Kay knew by the fact that I left my bag in the hall that I was not going to stay. When I came down with my hair loose and a "new" skirt on, which I had bought in a hospital jumble sale, she asked if I was going to see Addie or Jem. I said no.

"And if they call, is there somewhere they can get in touch with you?"

"No."

My rejection of 309 as a base was also a rejection of her. I was afraid of the lonely turn her life had taken after the divorce and was reluctant to connect my world with hers at all. I sent my love to Marianne but did not ask where she was or what she was doing. It was as if I did not dare learn, especially now, when I wanted only positive thoughts in my head to face Massell. I left with no indication of when I might be back or where I could be found. Still, illogically and with childish cruelty, I was punishing Kay for having let Richard go.

Since the last time I had spoken to him I had read two of Massell's books. One was a paperback on a self-improvement theme, the other a songbook. In the lyrics of one song he spoke of a rare kind of feather which made me think at once of a strange little amulet of woven feathers Botswana Steve had given me. I had it in the bottom of my shoulder-bag now and kept feeling for it as I sat on the bus, making sure it was still there. It was something very precious to me.

On a board in the foyer of the university building, crooked letters said: ADRIAN MASSELL RM 203 4TH FLOOR. I was a little early and I went into an empty classroom to tidy my hair. I did not want to look like a squatter.

I walked into 203 on the dot of 8:00 P.M. As it was the first day a register was being drawn up and students were queueing to hand in cash and cheques. I had no money and my fingers were clutching the amulet. When my turn came, Massell's head was bent over the register, hair in a brilliant red sweep across his brow. He was filling in the name of the student who had gone before. My back blocked off the space between us from the rest of the class and there was the smallest swish as I slid the amulet across the desk and quietly pronounced my name. For less than a second the hand holding the pen hesitated, then he looked up. Green, green eyes.

"Did you phone?"

"Yes."

The next moves were so swift I hardly felt them happen. The amulet was in his pocket, my name written down and I was on my way to an empty desk at the back.

"I'll see you afterward," he had said with a smile.

That was all, but that was everything.

The hour of instruction raced, Massell never once allowing his audience's attention to slide. New words and new ideas were bounced at us in rapid succession and everything he said struck a ready chord in me. I had not been so enthralled since Richard had cuddled close and told me good night stories when I was a child.

When the lecture ended there was a subdued shuffling as papers were stowed into cases, pens which had not had a chance to jot a line were recapped and the first chairs scraped back. The air seemed curiously flat now that Massell's voice was no longer in it. A number of students hung back to speak to him. I stayed by my desk taking a long time to put on my coat. Finally the group moved toward the door, Massell in their midst. He turned at the last minute.

"We are going for a quick Indian meal," he said lightly. "Coming?"

I had only enough money on me for the fare back to Banstead. Could I risk assuming I was with him?

"Yes," I said, shaking back my hair, "I'd love to."

There were about nine of us in the restaurant. The atmosphere was low-lit and full of bustle after the white clarity of the lecture room. A waiter in a red jacket came to take our order, reminding me of the last time I had been in a restaurant—that time I had run out and got caught. It seemed a world away. We were at a long, narrow table, Massell at the head responding equably to the intense interrogation of a bearded young man. I sat on his left sipping a glass of *lassi*. Massell ordered for both of us. He had given back the amulet, saying, "No need for that, we'll sort something out another time."

I hardly spoke during the meal, intent on listening to and watching Massell. I liked the way he broke with confidence the soft, stuffed *parathas* and quested with his fork among the spiced gravies for the most succulent pieces of meat. Once our forks met in a dish of hot chiles and beef and he laughed, gallantly conceding the prime morsel. When he spoke, the muscles below his cheekbones worked gently and small creases appeared under his eyes. His image was printing itself indelibly on my mind.

Toward the end of the meal the young man opposite tried to capture my attention. It was after ten-thirty and he asked if I had far to go. When I said Felstead, he said I would be better to go early in the morning when the buses were more frequent. He offered me a spare room in his flat near by and I felt confused, half thinking it might be wise to accept but not wanting to cut myself off from Massell. He must have overheard for he said easily, "There's always a couch at Bellington Road if you're stuck."

It was awkward, the young man had offered first and was waiting for a reply.

"Thank you," I said, "but Holland Park would be handier for transport I think."

I knew Massell lived in Holland Park, had read it somewhere in the club blurb. The young man accepted the thin reasoning gracefully. There was no competing with Massell.

The party broke up to cries of "see you next week" and I found myself standing alone on the pavement with Massell. It was cold, but with the meal still warm inside and a thick sheepskin coat—another jumble sale buy—I was glowing. We set off toward the square where he had left his car, striding along fast, heads down.

"Brrr," he shuddered, thrusting his hands into the pockets of his thin jacket. "That's a good coat you're wearing. I could do with one like that."

Without any hesitation I took it off and held it out.

"Have this one."

We had slowed down. He laughed.

"Are you sure?"

"Yes."

He shrugged out of the jacket and put on the big sheepskin. It looked good with his red hair, a fox in snow.

His car was dark green and low. Dynamic, I thought, like him. He drove with the same casual precision as Richard. I caught my reflection once in a side window and thought: you clever, lucky thing. He had not offered any of the other students a couch for the night.

His house was small but impressive, all white carpets and brown velvet curtains. There was a built-in sauna and shower unit as well as a sunken bath and a bidet. In the living room was an open fire.

"Know how to light that?" he called, going upstairs.

"Yes," I said with confidence, Mole's End rituals fresh in mind. Two young black cats played languidly around me and ran to rub against his legs when he appeared briefly in a short blue robe ready to take a shower. He was so at ease with his own body he somehow did not look undressed. His legs were red-downed and looked strong.

He was a long time in the shower and I was tired, so I undressed and arranged the cushions and blankets he had provided on a couch near the fire. I lay on my back, arms above my head, completely relaxed. He came down to say good night, a white towel bunched under ears that glowed healthily.

"You know when you rang before Christmas?" he said, "I thought you were one of those bespectacled old frumps from the club. It was quite a surprise matching your face to your voice in class."

He paused, rubbing his neck with the towel, "How old are you?"

"Nearly seventeen. What time do you get up?"

He stopped rubbing and smiled.

"Six-thirty. Breakfast at seven. What do you usually have?"

Feta in Greece, halva in Israel, porridge at Mole's End.

"A boiled egg," I said firmly, "and tea."

"Right then, see you in the morning."

I heard the bedroom door close and rolled over to gaze at the fire until sleep came. Both the cats had gone upstairs with him.

I was halfway through the titles on his floor-to-ceiling bookshelves when he appeared next morning at 6:45. My mind, awake for hours, was buzzing with questions. I began firing them straight away. Did he think the special diagrams he had shown us could be applied to the processes of thought and to emotions? Did he think he thought in words? Didn't it feel more like fast-moving images, clouds of thought reducing to puddles of words? Please could he recommend some reading?

"Good, good, yes, certainly," he said, busy with the eggs. "Try putting all this down. No reason the diagrams can't be used for thought processes. Excellent idea."

I preened inwardly, feeling ready to attempt anything. All night, between short bouts of sleep, I had gone over everything he had said in the lecture. My brain this morning felt springy as an acrobat; it just wanted a trapeze to swing on.

I sat at the table tap dancing a teaspoon over my egg. A pile of books accumulated by my elbow as we talked—Pavlov, Popper, Friedman, Illich, another by Massell himself. He said as I was leaving that I would be welcome to stay the night next week if it helped. I thanked him, bubbling over inside.

"But I don't know why," I blurted. "I mean I haven't got much to offer, have I? I don't know anything—anything!"

His green, green eyes rested on my excited face and the smile I had seen last night as he looked down at me under the blankets reappeared.

"That's just it," he said, "you have everything to offer, the greatest gift of all . . ."

I waited to hear what that was.

". . . An open mind and an infinite capacity to learn."

I danced down the street smiling at every lamppost and stone.

Back at the squat that evening I covered the whole of one wall with a huge Massell diagram. It was ambitious, the central theme being the development of the individual in relation to outside influences from birth. It began with a clear picture of the main character propelled by hollow arrows marked Destiny and Desire, and ended by resembling a dozen spiders' webs inextricably tangled, with the "individual" bound and gagged by the cords of influence and looking far less like a "developed personality" than a hapless fly.

Standing back and regarding it critically, I decided it would look much better in color, and not wanting to stint on materials for future efforts, I resolved to get a third job.

A notice next morning on the board where I had pinned my advert looked hopeful: BLIND GENTLEMAN REQUIRES YOUNG LADY TO READ TO HIM TWO OR THREE TIMES PER WEEK. REMUNER-ATION BY THE HOUR.

I would pop in on him after Mrs. Browne.

A disturbing sense of time frozen closed around me as soon as I entered her flat that day. All was just as I had left it, the food I had laid out for her supper untouched, a bar of soap which had slipped into the bath still skidded up against the plug hole. There was no evidence that anyone had been living there since Monday. I approached the living room door with something like dread.

"Mrs. Browne? Mrs. Browne?"

Silence. I pushed and the door glided open noiselessly. I nearly slammed it shut again as two bloodshot eyes leaped at me with the ferocity of rats.

"Eeou!" came her voice, rasping with fury. And again, "Eeou!"

She was alive, thank God, and bristlingly so.

Knobbly old spine forced straight as it would go, Mrs. Browne was sitting right on the edge of her chair. She was kneading her walking stick so hard it had churned the rug at her feet into a sea.

" 'ook!" she commanded. " 'ook 'ot 'ou've 'un!"

I gazed at her in idiot incomprehension, stunned by the intensity of her rage. What on earth was the matter with her mouth? My immobility increased her anger. Thud! went the stick on the pummelled rug. Thud thud thud! The last thud was so violent it dislodged the stick from her hand and sent it clattering down by the side of her chair. Glad of an obvious move, I bent to pick it up. In a flash she had grabbed it and before I could straighten up, her fingers were hooked under the collar of my jacket. I saw the stick lift out of the corner of my eye and ducked just in time so that it came down over my back and not my skull. Up it went again, with purpose. Grunts and sucking sounds issued from a throat drawn tight with effort. Down came the stick again in a series of astonishingly powerful whacks.

My hands leaped angrily to arrest the flailing arm, wavering in shock as they met the incongruous frailty of tissue-soft skin and baby-bird bones. For a moment we rocked together in a silent parody of combat. Then, for the second time, the stick dropped to the floor.

I stood up slowly. Her fingers were still imprisoned in my own, held together as though in prayer. I softened my hold, afraid she might crumble, but the shake in my voice was an echo of her own rage.

"Mrs. Browne, don't you ever do that to me again."

She would not be cowed. A trapped yellow talon dug into my wrist.

" 'ook!" she croaked, eyes and chin jerking toward the mantelpiece. I looked, and my mouth dropped open.

"Oh God, Mrs. Browne, I'm so sorry . . ."

I felt her relax with satisfaction at my distress.

" 'ere, 'ou 'ee?"

"Oh I do see. I'm so sorry."

The tableau on the mantelpiece told its own tale. After I had left on Monday, Mrs. Browne had evidently looked through the shopping and decided to make a start on the chocolates. I imagined her sharp fingernails ripping open the Cellophane, box balanced on bony knees. She must have thought they were good ones for she had plowed in with a big, gleeful bite.

The big, gleeful bite, chocolate still clenched like a fat cigar butt between upper and lower molars, was exhibit number one on the mantelpiece.

Following this in order of experiment and rejection were all the other items she had attempted to feed herself on over the last two days. But the final word lay in six caramel-colored blobs ranged on the metal cowl of the gas fire. Unable to gain satisfaction from mashing bread and cheese against her upper palate, Mrs. Browne had returned to what was supposed to be her one reminder of luxury: the chocolates. Each melted, tongue-tortured lump added to the weight of accusation in her eyes. I fetched a knife and rubber gloves. It took twenty minutes just to scrape the dentures clean.

There was a tricky moment when I went to put her teeth back in. She still looked suspiciously fierce. I took a risk.

"Mrs. Browne, I warn you, if you bite me I'll bite back."

She mumbled the teeth into place and her hand twitched on the stick.

"You would too, wouldn't you, you cheeky hussy. Now get out of here and buy me some proper sweets."

Later that week I made her some soft fudge on the squat's single gas ring. The vision of her lonely chompings haunted me for years.

With Mr. Geshner, the blind man, I felt I was on to a good thing. I had enjoyed reading aloud ever since making the discovery at school that a small pretense of religious fervor earned the privilege of spending cold breaktimes in the chapel, entertaining my friend Kate with random extracts from the bible. Then there had been the poetry sessions with Jem and later the lively Nietzschean recitations with Addie. Now I had the chance to get paid for it. But first I had to pass Mr. Geshner's little test.

A table in his small flat was covered with old Sunday supplements. Mr. Geshner felt for them with his hands and fluttered one in my direction.

"In zere," he said in a strong, precise accent, "is a pessage on contributions of ze Guggenheim femily to art in ze United States. Read please from ze zecond peragraph."

While I read Mr. Geshner sat with his wiry gray head cocked to one side, rectangular eyebrows raised. On his nose rested a visor supporting two truncated telescopes which he referred to as his "gedgit." He interrupted halfway through the first paragraph.

"Zet's it, Miss Urfin, ze job is yours. You von't believe how many young ladies I hef hed to reject." A nervous bubble of laughter popped in his throat. ". . . Ent all because of a zingle vord. To hear zem get it wrong has been driving me med, med! To me it is qvite simply a metter of stendards."

The word in question was "drawing." If I had pronounced it "drawring" I would have failed the test. I was grateful to Richard for imposing his "stendards" when I was small. It was arranged that I should go to Mr. Geshner twice a week and read articles on the Arab-Israeli war at 50p an hour.

The babysitting at the end of the week went satisfactorily and extended to cleaning as well which made it more lucrative. The only time I felt uncomfortable was when the lady of the house asked me about myself. Her questions were conventional: Did I live with my parents? Had I got a boyfriend? Where had I gone to school? I preferred coping with the idiosyncrasies of Mrs. Browne and Mr. Geshner, neither of whom was interested in my family or past.

Although my jobs were mere satellite occupations around the Massell lectures, it was impossible not to become involved to some extent with each of the different lives I was touching. After the initial hiccups, Mrs. Browne decided that, for amusement value if nothing else, I was better than the usual domestics who tried to boss her into sensible habits. Why should she not eat her meals straight out of a carrier-bag or belabor the TV with a stick if someone she did not like was on? And I think she knew I did not listen to her tales of the past just to be polite. The world her reminiscences conjured delighted me. I was sure I would have enjoyed being a rich Canton flapper with a peacock called Bluey too.

Getting a foot in the door of Mr. Geshner's world took a little longer.

Toward the end of the fourth or fifth session with him my throat felt dry. The piece I was reading on Moshe Dayan went on for another two pages and I knew I would become hoarse if I did not have a break. I asked if I might have a glass of water. Mr. Geshner's attentively cocked head snapped upright and he made gobbling noises.

"My dear young lady, forgif me."

Groping up from the chair he felt his way along the wall to a dresser where there was a jug and some tumblers. Stubby fingers tapped a tumbler rim to make sure it was the right way up before pouring. The twin black telescopes of his eye gadget quested in my direction and I spoke again to guide the outstretched hand. He hovered while I drank, looking strangely anguished.

"Shall I continue?"

"Fun moment Miss Urfin, I vont to explain."

He scratched his gray head vigorously, hesitating, then his words tumbled out in a rush.

"My vife vould never forgif me. Five times you hef been here and not vonce hef I offered you so much as a zip of water. But you see zere was . . . an *inzident*." He stopped and scrubbed at his hair again before going on. "Always I used to offer ze young ladies a cup of tea—even ze ones with terrible accents!—but zen one day, over tea, a girl started to say strange zings . . ." There was a long pause while he spread his hands wide in shock and gobbled, ". . . Ent zen she tried to remove my gedgit!"

The vision was clear as a film clip: Mr. Geshner hopping helplessly round the table pursued by an amorous tart who said "drawrin." If it had not been for the look of misery on his face I would have rocked with laughter. There was more.

"Ent ven I asked her to leave she became abusive—such lenguage! She said vot did I expect advertising for young girls and inviting zem for biscuits and tea? So you see it has been a problem. I am not understood . . ."

His speech trailed off.

"Mr. Geshner," I said solemnly, "I promise that if you were to offer a cup of tea I would not try to remove your gadget."

A wild attack of gobbling dissolved into a shy giggle. Thereafter we always paused for tea halfway through the session and he made a regular little joke as he passed the biscuits.

"Look," he exclaimed, "none of zem has strings!"

His giggles became quite skittish.

*   *   *

The subsequent Massell evenings were no less riveting than the first and when he marked my homework with a flamboyant *excellent* in red I flushed from collar to fringe with pride. I did not mention that I had been playing with word diagrams on my own, wanting to get the wild scrawlings under more control before submitting them for criticism. The meal at the Indian restaurant after the lecture became a ritual.

"It's refreshing to meet someone with such an unashamed appetite," he commented once as I soaked up the last of the meat juices with a *paratha*. "Are you conscious of what you eat in a nutritional sense?"

I swallowed and a small burp escaped by accident. How could I tell him that in the life I led concern over nutritional value took second place to straightforward survivalist opportunism?

"Sometimes," was my cagey reply and then on inspiration I gave him a rundown of some of the wholesome dishes I had prepared at Mole's End. He nodded approvingly and told me he was a great believer in always leaving the table before the appetite was completely satisfied. As I stuffed myself to capacity at every chance, I kept quiet.

The routine of day-to-day survival changed as my circle of acquaintances broadened. Fired by contact with Massell, I spent a lot of time hanging around libraries and ordering the books he recommended. One chilly evening, when the library was closed, I leaned against the warm window of a café reading for so long that a man came out and asked if he could buy me coffee. He turned out to be a heavily Christian social worker who, interpreting my jumble-sale attire as a sure sign that I was on my way to the devil, was determined to save my soul. Unimpressed, I stared boredly over his earnestly bent head at a man opposite, who was covering the menu with fast-flowing handwriting. I laughed irritably at something the social worker said and the man looked up and caught my eye. His tanned face, under a flop of clean brown hair, was almost absurdly good-looking. When the social worker left—to return to his post at a vagrants' hostel in the East End—the man spoke. He had an appealing drawl, reminding me a little of Jorges.

"Seems you didn't have too much to say to that guy."

I smiled and shook my hair back.

"He was dull. He said "have faith" so many times it sounded like an indigestion cure."

He bought two more coffees and later drove me to his flat and gave me supper. He was Canadian, an art historian, and the first person I told about Massell. I did not understand what he meant when he said, "The guy sounds like a real whizzkid type, better watch out."

We talked for a long time, sitting several yards apart on giant tapestried cushions in his lounge. The room was full of interesting things: a fourteen-foot Mexican hammock, fetishes from Africa, Persian rugs and primitive paintings on the walls. I liked it and was interested in his books: Lowry, Neruda, R. D. Laing. In the long, comfortable silences between sentences we listened to an African Mass, the music beating softly from a concealed stereo.

I spent the night on a fur-covered water-bed in the spare room and his flat became another place where I was welcome to stay from time to time. Once, when there were other people using the spare room, I slept with him. In the middle of the night, with the moon shining in on the bed, he put his arms around me and gently lifted me astride his penis. But I must have looked doubtful because after a moment he said, "OK" in his pleasant, easy way and put me down. His name was Michael.

Alf was another occasional doss point. He was a figure I had seen around the Richmond area on and off for years but only met properly that winter. He styled himself as an actor and was always just off to, or just back from, Morocco or Algiers, where he played soldier number X439 in *The Charge of the Light Brigade* and other epics. But he was not *really* an actor, he told me, he was just an Alf. "And you," he said, cuffing me affectionately, "you're just an Alf too."

Until I had read Laurie Lee's *As I Walked Out One Midsummer Morning* I did not know what he meant, but as soon as I made the acquaintance of the lone wanderer under whose pan-rattling wing the young Lee was taken on his long walk from Slough to London, the parallel became clear. Alf was a gentleman of the road who took his ease wherever a pleasing hummock presented itself, the unhurried progress of his laceless boots guided only by the natural rhythms of the year; a being not so much outside society's law as beyond it, definable only as a feature of the countryside who in winter months temporarily became a feature of the town. He referred to himself and all other peripatetics as Alf and despised only those who had failed to hone their vagrancy to an art.

"The only difference," said my Alf, "is that your hummocks are people."

And in this he was right. I drifted from person to person, world to world, perching on the periphery of half a dozen different lives. From the squat to Mrs. Browne, to Mr. Geshner, to Massell, I made my rounds. And in between there were Alf, Michael the Canadian, the babysitting people, Julian and Addie and 309. My days became even more crowded when I took to cramming all earning hours between Friday and Monday so that I could enjoy spring at Mole's End.

There I watched the hedgehogs emerging like tramps from their winter lairs, bumbling with straw still trailing from quills to cross paths with mice just vacating the mattresses. I wandered in woods where scrolled leaves shiny with the newness of birth sang out against wet black bark and my ankles brushed the waxy cups of crocuses. In the evenings I crouched, secure as an embryo, in the big barrel bath and watched camomile-scented steam uncoil among the low cottage beams.

And perhaps it was there, fed by tales of Julian's current romances, that I took to dreaming of a connection with my guru Massell beyond diagrams and a couch in his lounge.

The whole summer would go by, however, before I did something about those dreams, for suddenly a world which under the influence of all the others had lately grown distant, came abruptly back into focus.

Richard contacted me out of the blue.

"I need you," he said.

It was infallible. My answer was instant.

"I'll come."

PART FOUR

Blood

The short season I worked at the hotel that year seemed unconnected with the summers I had spent there before. Arriving several weeks after the rest of the staff made a difference, I was the new girl who had to ask where things were. But I learned quickly and soon had the routine off pat so that I could go through it mechanically, leaving my mind free to wander elsewhere.

Contact with Richard had been thready while I was away and the long, blank patch in the hospital was not something we discussed. Once, I had begun to tell him something of what happened in Greece but I was slow in my lead up and he had looked distant and vaguely disapproving. I was speaking of circumstances outside his world. I dropped the subject before reaching the point and never raised it again. Still loyal, I was back on his ground but this time preoccupied with visions of my own. I did notice, however, that his nails were down to the quick and that Edwina's previously girlish figure had gone very square. Things had changed in their lives as well as in my own.

Waitressing, baking, drying glasses and endlessly Hoovering the dining room, I swung from dreamy recitations of Shelley to the blood-less repetition of Massell's mental agility exercises. Snatched hours off in daylight were spent on the hill overcoming my fear of a new, livelier pony, bought as soon as I had enough saved, and any spare moments before sleep were devoted to colorful entries in a diary kept entirely in diagrams. I seldom wrote in words except in reply to letters from Kay. Addie and Jem were forced to grapple with cryptic messages in thought blobs. Julian and I limited our communication to postal exchanges of heather and Mole's End leaves.

The summer progressed with the familiar dash and grind of hotel life behind the scenes and the ordered, other-worldly passage of the guests. Richard was plotting again. When he was not shut up in the smokehouse with his kippers and terrines, organizing the guests' fishing rotas or guiding their choice of wines, he was down on the croft pacing out land for new developments. Incapable of treating the hotel simply as a business, he was forever throwing some new challenge in his own path. Life without a dream to realize was not worth living. And still, those who could not keep up were left behind.

News of Marianne was not good: talk of doctors, X rays, temporary improvements, frequent regressions. Kay wrote bulletins of the physical ills but nothing was said about the pain in Marianne's mind, the still weeping child mourning the death of family. I skimmed the details of the letters, hanging on to the belief that Marianne would contact me when she was ready—in a space between her "giddy" spells. Richard and I did not talk about what was happening to her. It was too difficult, too sad. We simply turned away and immersed ourselves deeper in the business of our own lives.

Halfway through the season a round postcard came from a Scandinavian town. Massell. The neatly printed message started in the middle and spiralled outwards like a catherine wheel. I twirled it round and round in my hands for a long time before putting it in a drawer with my diary. Apart from Addie's letters, which I only kept because he made such a point of hoarding mine, I generally threw away all correspondence as soon as it was read. Now, for everything that came from Massell, I set aside a large brown envelope marked M. In time, this became A, for Adrian.

Spring at Mole's End and the closeness of Julian and Addie had done much to break down the numbness I had where touch was concerned, but I still had a remote attitude to sex. The incident with Michael illustrates the degree of alienation: I was so far removed that it was almost immaterial whether he penetrated my body or not. But now, fired by an attraction already intellectually intense, mind, heart and body softened and changed.

In the evenings, when work was finished, I would creep upstairs to one of the guest bathrooms, a book wrapped in a towel under one arm. Warm water and secrecy, I had discovered, made the perfect environment for the development of fantasy. While one hand tickled gently at the floating curls between my thighs, the other flicked efficiently through the pages of Mrs. Beeton. Memorizing lists of ingredients, weights, temperatures and timings for everything from Scotch broth to crab soufflé, I was teaching myself the art of cookery for two. For the fantasy was that I was Mrs. Massell.

And it did not stop at recipes. I worked out minutely how my time would be divided between housekeeping, having babies and studying so that I could help Massell. I wrote poems now in the evenings, as well as the diagram diary, and his response was encouraging. Excellent! There was much potential there. That word again.

Cards came from all over the world. Then a score of song lyrics from London, part of a new book he was writing. I read through them twice but their message was beyond me, quite different to verses which came my way from another pen.

Alf had decided that, as fellow Alfs, we should join forces. His poems were flatteringly romantic and with one he even sent a red rose. Touched, although I could not return his feelings, I went to the hotel kitchen for a vase. Edwina handed me one without comment but Richard caught me in the corridor. He was wearing the smart jacket he used for mingling with guests in the evening. He noticed the vase.

"What's that for?"

"I've got a flower."

His eyebrows rose in the slightly suave arch which told me he was already in his guest-mingling mood.

"Just one?" he asked teasingly.

"Yes, one."

Catching his mood I rippled out a secretive smile and added, ". . . From a man."

The arch went higher.

"Anyone—special?"

Suddenly I felt foolish. What was I doing messing about with Alf's rose? Of course he was not "special." I had not said a word about Massell. He was different. He *was* special. A triumphant scenario flashed through my mind: Massell driving me up to the hotel in his smooth green car; me getting out and making the introductions: "Adrian, meet my father. Richard, meet my man."

Later I blushed at my own temerity in thinking this. Apart from a disturbing confusion of faces and bodies in the picture, it was the first time I had called Adrian, Adrian in my mind.

Unconsciously I was taking steps away from Richard. Responding almost unthinkingly to his call: "I need you," I had forgotten all that made life at the hotel uncomfortable: the nonposition as daughter of the proprietor, neither a member of a proper family nor a proper member of the staff. Marianne had found the precariousness of identity intolerable and turned the pain inward, inflicting yet more injury on an already injured self. Unlike me she had no perspective to draw on. I had been far enough away from the struggles of family and far enough into other worlds to know that the wealth of stances from which life could be led was infinite. The idea was daunting but I believed the choice of stance was largely up to me. Despite the complexities of influence, that was the message I read in the diagrams I drew. Comfort and distraction, but not a solution to oneself, might be found in others.

Poring complacently over those two-dimensional diagrams, I was blind to the roots of my own dreams. Passion, in my fantasies, was something very like salvation.

I grew strong that summer, working hard and spending all my time off outside. My body was taut and young, fit without effort, an easy vessel for joy. Carelessly proud, sure of my solitude, I angled every part of me to the sun. And as I stretched out beneath the casual splendor of the sky, the vague yearnings of earlier times were at last defined. I felt magnificent, invulnerable, and I wished Massell had been there, right then, to race me to the next valley and catch me as I fell.

Winter would be in London again and I must plan for it now. No vague job hunting in shop windows, no return to doss points all over town. Both Mrs. Browne and Mr. Geshner had said they would like me back but this time I wanted one fulltime job. Initially I would stay at 309. Kay's letters had been welcoming and it was time to do away with adolescent antipathies. I waited impatiently for the newspapers which came once a week to the hotel and, scanning the columns, applied for a post as a receptionist in the West End. I wanted to be smart for Massell.

Before I left the hotel, Richard suggested I should take on the management of the café next year, have it as my complete responsibility. I was noncommittal, off on a streak of my own. I wanted him to see that there were other things in my life besides the hotel—and him.

I did not recognize then how strong the blood attachment between us still was; how, in the impressive figure of Massell, I was secretly worshiping a Richard with whom I could make love.

Richmond, five months later.

Ah, but the plan had gone awry. Dreams-into-schemes were not so simple and now I was back on old territory, sliding rapidly downhill.

There was rain, no messing about. It streaked the lampposts, slanted at the shop fronts, puddled in the hoisted awnings and ran with the wine down Teddy's beard. Teddy was an ex-binmate; a mate, I had decided, more on my level than Massell.

We had one of those Spanish carafes you have to lift high, holding your mouth to catch the stream like a stone scallop under a fountain-sprouting breast. Jem was the only one who had got the hang of it. Even McAllister, all six foot five of him leaning over me with deadly concentration, could not get it right, spraying an ear by accident, soaking the front of my dress.

"Take it away!" I yelped, batting at his hands. It reminded me of when Kay and I had gone away for a week before the divorce. She in a stiff-cupped swimsuit being wooed by a Spaniard who had carafes like that in his bar. Me not knowing whether to encourage or condemn, finally pretending not to see. Jem started up again, jumbling Pyramus and Gallahad:

> "Oh night, oh night, oh grim-looked night
> Oh night with hue so—*blood red and sliding*
> *down the blackened marsh*
> *Blood red and on the naked mountain*
> *top . . ."*

He had been declaiming all afternoon; he had told the story of Cain and Abel to the park railings, mumbled *The Rime of the Ancient Mariner* into his pregnant girlfriend's hair and, now that it was getting dark, struck poses before the swishing headlamps of cars. Spotlit in the gutter, booed by hoots, he was now Zarathustra, now Hamlet, now Percy Bysshe. Rain streamed from his eye-patch like tears and under his coat he hugged a stolen hassock and a saxophone. We cheered him and ignored him by turns. Teddy ignored us all.

But it was for me he had come. Big mad Teddy with his Medusa snakes of sodden hair, broad body solid as earth and big, wondering hands that held my face as he whispered strange, mad messages to the Queen of France: "Marie-Antoinette, the number is not thirteen!"

I cleaned the wine and rain from the hollows of his throat with my tongue, opened his heavy coat and pressed my head to his chest. There was the distant pat-pat of his paw at the back of my neck and McAllister's giraffe head shaking gloomily beyond, motioning us on. We were about to cross Richmond Bridge.

I ran on ahead, holding up my long skirt, ducking my scarf-swathed head against the rain. It was funny, wasn't it, that here I was, crossing the same old bridge again? Only this time I was with my cronies. Big Mad Teddy, my crony man.

"Come on!" I yelled, laughing at the bedraggled trail in the wet lamplight: Teddy shambling in front, McAllister and Jem struggling for possession of the saxophone, pregnant Josie last, calmly sucking Mackeson from a can. My teeth chattered as I licked in rain. Teddy caught up and I took the carafe from him and poured from the handle end, filling my mouth with sour pools.

Hah!—and I had been so careful that evening after Scotland with Massell, all dolled up in smart receptionist clothes, only taking tiny sips of wine in case I slurred my words or said something silly. Better if I had maybe, better than sitting there like a tongue-tied fool.

And what a fool to think that the mess of adolescence could be swept clean at one stroke, that 309 could suddenly become nothing but a convenient base.

I spluttered, carafe knocking against my teeth, as I thought of poor Kay with her trays of cold food in front of the television, adrift in the wake of Richard's life. And Marianne, slumped across the bed in the studio, hugging a puppy and a bottle. *Who the hell did I think I was?*

Teddy stood behind me, arms around, a cliff against the rain. Jem was tugging wildly at the saxophone, now being guarded by McAllister, who was being sensible, saying, "Be careful, calm down." I passed the carafe back to Teddy and it slipped through his fingers, shattering into curved shards on the road. With a final, twisting effort and dropping the hassock, Jem wrenched the saxophone from McAllister and ran to lean panting on the stone balustrade. Under the bridge the Thames swirled in a heavy, dimpled stream, reflected light shimmering in mud and water whorls.

"For heaven's sake!" shouted McAllister. But he was too late. Powering his throw with a wild, backward swing, Jem spun the saxophone through the air. There was a long second before it landed with a wet thwack just out of the reach of the river's pull. McAllister swore. Punctured, Jem tottered to the curb, sat on his hassock and burst into tears. Josie walked straight past him, absently shaking the last drops of beer from her can. Teddy talked on softly to his voices.

"You're all mad!" ranted McAllister, long legs bounding down the steps to the towpath. Brandishing the saxophone below, he looked like a long, cold ghost in the rain. In the gutter Jem scratched daintily at his wrists and started on "Death, the Leveller."

"Let's go," I said to Teddy, weary of the scene.

"Sure baby, go."

We walked toward the Green, passing a house where one of my old schoolfriends lived. I had been to a party there once and wondered at the way her parents called everyone darling. She would be preparing for university now.

Teddy began to sing quietly in a deep voice full of tobacco ash:

> "If Ah were a cat
> Ah'd be purrin' right now
> If Ah were a dawg
> Ah'd be waggin' ma tail . . ."

I supposed we were going to sleep together, supposed we were looking for a bed. I wanted another drink.

We crossed the High Street, where I had shopped so sensibly in the first weeks back from Scotland: nipping round Sainsbury's on my way home from work, browsing among the fancy shampoos in Boots, reading the whole of *Jonathan Livingston Seagull* in Smiths. Because Massell had recommended it.

Past Alf's place—no light in the window—we roved on up the hill until we came to a pub Teddy knew. He had peddled coke to the barman there. We sat mind-drowned in rock, drinking tequila.

He had been so friendly, too, Massell. Interested to know what I was doing, telling me about a radio series he was making. Had I ever thought of working with kids, getting involved with education at its roots? Mustn't waste all that talent, you know, that potential. He smiled out of those green, green eyes and I just sat there blushing and blushing. I could not look at his face without recalling how I had touched it in my fantasies, could not speak for the bolus of saliva in my throat, could not eat.

"Where's that marvelous appetite gone?"

"I don't know."

"Been writing any more of those promising poems?"

"No."

Glowing with enthusiasm for his own plans he had asked, "What do you see yourself doing five years from now?" Echoes of Richard: what was the plan? Numbly I answered, "I don't know."

There was more tequila, mine in a tall glass. No sunrise was ever that muddy. I gulped it down and reeled off to the Ladies. The face in the mirror was a mess.

"So much," I hissed at it viciously, "for Mrs. Massell."

At the name spoken aloud, I winced and my hands twisted involuntarily on my chest. But instead of feeling pain there, they met warmth, power, the strong, steady beat of a young heart. *Young, fit without effort, invulnerable. Remember?* It was only the feeble mind that was floundering. The body was strong. It would not let me down.

A girl in leather hotpants jumped back against the wall as I shot past and through the saloon. There was a glass of whisky on our table which had not been there before. I downed it in one and spoke urgently to Teddy.

"Have you got change for the phone?"

His blurred, caveman's face broke slowly into a smile, the horizontal scar on his nose curving up like a third lip.

> "Yeah, if Ah were a cat,
> Ah'd be purrin' and how,
> An if Ah were a dawg
> Ah'd be wag wag wag, waggin' ma tail . . . ,

I turned to a stranger at my side.

"Please have you got change for the phone?"

"You've drunk my whisky."

"I know. Have you got change?"

He felt in his pocket and came out with several coins.

"Help yourself." Then with a sidelong glance at Teddy, he indicated the empty glass, "Like another?"

I nodded and went to find the phone.

My forefinger slotted itself confidently into the digit holes. No problem remembering the number. I held the coin poised, thinking I would scream if it was the ansaphone. It was. I did not scream, but beckoned to the whisky man. The message was that Adrian would be in later. *Adrian.*

"That bloke you're with," said the whisky man, handing me a glass, "is he all right?"

I drank quickly, and improvised.

"No, he's not. He's mad. Just out of prison for breaking into his ex-wife's house with an axe."

"You're kidding."

I shook my head.

The man's eyes traveled over Teddy's bulk and back to me.

"Want to go somewhere else?"

"Yes. Now."

He had a car and we went to another pub. It was near the bus route for Holland Park. I checked before we went in.

"What do you do then, when you're not pinching other people's drinks?"

"I'm a char."

Another failure. I had gone back to scrubbing floors.

"What, a cleaning lady? I'd have thought you'd be more like a secretary or receptionist."

"Oh yes!" I said, startling him with my vehemence, "I was. In fact I was *star* receptionist at the Wakeford Corvan fashion salon. But not for long."

"Money" by Pink Floyd ground aggressively from the jukebox.

It all came back, the way I had come down from Scotland with heather in my hair and dreams in my heart and been transformed overnight into the Wakeford Corvan mold. The salon provided the clothes. Real silk blouses and swish tailored skirts. When I was sent out to buy stationery, I got whistled at in the street. But I felt a million miles outside that world. Me an Alf, an ex-binmate, someone who stuck knives into people in bus queues.

Memories and whisky pricked hotly. Nothing would have mattered if things had gone all right with Massell. But I had blown it. Since that ridiculous tongue-tied evening there had been no spoken word. Only a distantly polite postcard in response to three of my own. I left the receptionist job and went to Mole's End. Neither Julian nor Addie was around, but Julian's parents were there and were so kind to me I could not bear it. I went to Felstead but the squat had changed and it was there, among the new batch of drifters, that I picked up Teddy, in whose schizophrenic presence I felt oddly at ease. He did not have any expectations. He never talked about potential.

And then I crossed the Channel with a new Beverly and hitchhiked in the bitter cold as far as Pamplona. I did not know where I was going. Choking on chorizo in a gritty wind, I turned round and came back out of sheer funk.

"Sheer funk," I said aloud to my companion who only got snippets of the reverie. "But the worst, the stupidest of all"—here I stood up and faced him, draining the rest of my double—"was Christmas back in the loony bin."

Back came the drugged, suety faces mumbling and shoveling at the gray travesty of a Christmas meal. Judy, that same Judy, laughing with a sprig of burning holly in her hair.

People in the pub were gaping but I did not care. I said it again.

"Christmas back in the loony bin! And why? Why? *Oh, why not?*"

Shocked at my own bitterness and confusion, I slammed out of the pub and ran.

The rain had stopped. White markers on the road tapewormed away, gleaming, toward town. Up ahead was the red target of a phone booth. Lagging behind the hot drumming in my head, my knees blundered against flapping skirt. Wild with impatience, I ripped it to the thigh and ran on with hectic strides until I stood breathless within the steamy-windowed booth. I dialed and prayed. Hateful slow electronic burr.

"Hello?"

Him. Oh God, pips. Got it. *Now.*

"Adrian-I-want-to-make-love-to-you."

There was a pause too brief for an eyelid to bat.

"That sounds nice. Why don't you come along now?"

"Right. On my way."

My hand, while I was speaking, had made a wild scrabbling print on the window.

The 27 bus took me, locked in wooden astonishment, as far as Notting Hill. Then I was out in the wet streets again, whisky and tequila tangoing through my veins. I swung along fast, holding the torn ends of skirt through the liningless pockets of my coat—that same coat in which I had smuggled the beer for Botswana Steve. A taxi drew up at some traffic lights and I ran to ask the driver if I was heading the right way.

" 'olland Park? I'm running up there misself. Want to 'op in?"

"I haven't got enough for the fare."

"Go on, 'op in. I told you, I'm goin' that way."

I got in and fell back on the cigaretty-smelling seat. My eyes closed as we moved off and the after-image of the street lamps spun. I must have passed out for when I opened my eyes again we were there. Or so I assumed, because we had stopped. The driver was opening the cab door. I moved to get out but instead he got in. There was a smell of spearmint and the rough feel of his sleeve as it brushed my neck. He was opening my coat. His hand was on my knee.

Oh God. It was Tel Aviv all over again; Greece; the cruisers outside the bin. I lunged past him to the door and struggled with the handle. Behind me he swore and rough-sleeved arms tightened and hauled.

"Come on, you little 'ore."

But I had got the door open and my feet were on the ground. I wrestled with the arms that would not leave my neck. He felt strong but I felt cunning. Deliberately, I sagged at the knees and then jerked upright hard. There was a crack as his head thudded into the roof.

Gripping his arms now, and using the strength of my whole body to jerk up and down, I bashed the spearmint-breathing head again and again against the door frame. As I dived away in the dark, I felt with vicious triumph that I had scraped him off my back like a bit of dogshit off a shoe. Foul names bounced meaninglessly off my back as I zig-zagged toward the nearest light.

The street was one I knew. There was the café where I had met Michael, the Canadian. I burst in through the door, drunkenly hoping he might be there. But all the faces were unfamiliar and the place had changed. Candles in chianti bottles, smell of patchouli and lasagne. I stood with one arm up clutching a hatstand, awareness of what was happening washing in and out in waves. A youth with an amiable grin stepped out from behind the cash register and adroitly grabbed the hatstand before it fell. I found myself seated, a glass of brandy in one hand and the youth and another man bending close, looking at me with listening eyes.

Words fell out of my mouth in a lumpy patchwork, some of it woven from dreams. But they established where I was going and to whom. Shortly, when the restaurant closed, these young men would walk me there. Meanwhile there was coffee, which I did not drink, and another brandy, which I did.

"Please," I said, through a screen of bulging clouds, "has anybody got a comb?"

The dressing gown was different but the legs were the same. For a long time they were all I saw. From where I was propped by the bookshelf while he thanked the unknown youths; from behind a mug three times filled with weak tea; from under a toweling robe held out while he dinned in instructions about the showers I was to have, al-ternating with the saunas I was not to have too hot—legs, red-downed, padding about on short strong feet with clean pink spaces between the toes.

I stood in the shower with a hot monsoon flushing my brain, sat in the sauna panting beside a tray of fizzing stones. After the second wetting, moist billows rose until I did not know if it was me or the world steaming and reeling, body or mind enveloped in buffeting clouds. A voice intruded from another planet.

"OK in there?"

There was a distant briskness in the tone, like a vet handling an animal not quite clean.

"Mmmmmmmmn."

I was under the shower again, face right in it. It seemed unthinkable that I should open my mouth and make a hole in the spray. The door opened a crack.

"I said are you OK?"

I nodded with my back to him, head still up.

"How many saunas have you had?"

I flipped a hand up by my bottom, two fingers raised then put down hastily. Rude sign.

"All right, stay just a few moments in the last one, then a cool rinse and out. Shampoo, if you want it, on the shelf."

Back when the door was closed to the reeling and the steam. I breathed in deep, feeling heat tingle in my throat and separate the tiny hairs in my nostrils. Before the final wetting I lathered every inch of my body, swirling soap spirals over my belly, rubbing at my scalp through a mountain of foam. Then I turned the cold on full blast.

"Yaaaaah!"

I had not meant to yell. There was a short laugh from outside.

Moments later, turbaned and robed, I emerged. At once I was shepherded into the bedroom and told that now he was going to take a shower.

Slowly, I sank down crosslegged in the center of the big bed; slowly combed and toweled my hair. With the alcohol receding, my mind felt blank. Stubbornly, cozily, my body glowed. I lay back yawning and wriggled between the sheets. The pillow was the palest green, smelling faintly of him. I gave it a deeply loving practice-kiss—and went out cold.

There were two thoughts in my head when I woke a decade of unconsciousness later. One, I was going to be sick; two, I had blown it again. Prompted by the urgency of the first, I groped a swift course to the bathroom and with one hand screwing back my hair, threw up, stifling the noise. It was not so easy to stifle the shame.

When it was over, I sat on the floor holding my toes. My feet were calloused from all the time I had gone barefoot abroad. Like all the rest of me they felt out of place in the clean, smoothly running world of Massell. I would leave now, never be seen by, never see him again.

I felt calm, beyond the little futility of despair. There would be no more drama, no more dreams.

There was a small blob of vomit on the lapel of the borrowed robe. Quietly, I washed the whole thing, hanging it over a towel rail to dry. I had only to find my clothes now and I would be away.

One of the black cats ran to wind its dainty body round my calves as, naked, I crept downstairs and searched the living room. There was a blank spot in my memory over where I had undressed. Reluctantly, I concluded it must have been in the bedroom.

Upstairs again, very cautiously, I pushed open the door. Muted light from the landing trickled over the bed in a long bar. Massell lay in the center, face in shadow. I could not see my clothes anywhere. What if they were in the wardrobe behind a loud, sliding door? I took a step further in and the cat, fur electric against my legs, trilled out a bright interrogative croon. I stooped to pick it up, to hush its noise, but too late. Massell stirred.

"Keep your claws in, Polydeuces."

I straightened slowly, the cat's purring head warm between my breasts, its soft body dangling down mine.

"Bring him here."

Massell was up on one elbow. I brought the cat close and sat down where he patted the bed. His hand reached out and stroked the furry head in my arms.

"Sleep all right?"

I nodded, head down. His fingers stroked low behind Polydeuces' ears. They were very close to my breast.

"Castor died, you know, so this fellow is a bit lonely now."

A lock of hair fell forward and brushed his wrist. He lifted the strands and laid them half across the cat's fur, half across my skin.

"Nice combination."

He must have felt my heartbeat under the back of his hand. A finger gliding lightly, almost accidentally, over a nipple, caused it to spring, tingling, into bud. Behind the curtain of my hair, my eyes closed. I felt him move up in the bed and gently detach the cat from my arms.

"Go and play, Polydeuces."

My head rode on his shoulder, the rest of me rode in his hands. Hands playing over breasts, belly, thighs, stroking and molding until my hips began to move in a rhythm of their own.

"Excellent. Keep doing that. Now touch here."

Tentative fingers encircling. Power unfolding in my palm. Life pulsing, questing. Unexpected moistenings.

"Good. Now lie back and concentrate all your feelings here."

There was a sudden soundless clamor, a little darting madness that licked at the soft edge of control. I bucked, half sliding away.

"Ha, found the spot, have I? Like it?"

"Nnnnnyes but . . ."

"But what?"

"I feel as though I'm going to explode!"

"That's the idea."

And after I had come, I clung to stay. From his oh-so-welcome entry through the long crescendo of his rise, to the moment when I felt him soar, and a cool drop squeezed from his brow fell on my cheek, I could not hold him close enough. There was strength in my wrapping limbs and a newfound power inside that clasped him as the moist earth clasps the tree. I longed for him to spill deep into my ready womb.

But modern man responsibly withdrew and it was my navel that overbrimmed.

"I presumed you were not fixed up."

"No."

"Will I sort something out or . . . ?"

"I'll make an appointment today."

I felt I could sort out the universe now that I was sure there would be a next time.

Within a fortnight I had moved into a flat less than two miles away with two jobs to pay the rent and save. To celebrate the installation of an intrauterine device I went out for a meal with Chris, the boy who shared the flat. As a flatmate he was conveniently self-effacing, although had he been otherwise I would not have noticed, for I existed on a tightrope five miles high, breathing in the rare altitude of bliss.

Whether it was weighing dried fruit in the health food shop where I earned my daytime wage or taking messages as a receptionist at night, I found pleasure in everything I did. Walking down the High Street was a joy; catching sight of myself in a shop window and pausing to readjust my new feminine glide. Every roll of the pelvis was a celebration of how good it was to be young, female and tinglingly alive.

"What do you think of that?" I would cry, prancing in to a startled Chris in some new exotic robe which, flung aside, revealed a clinging sheath of softest see-through stuff. I had suddenly become acutely aware of the subtleties of texture and wanted only to wear things which felt voluptuous against my skin.

Or else I was flourishing my latest culinary creation, which Chris was never allowed to touch until it was a day old, in case Adrian dropped by. Experimenting with homemade beauty aids, I suffered delicious terror that he might turn up when I had just daubed oatmeal and honey all over my face. Chris had strict instructions to employ delaying tactics in such an event.

Adrian. I hugged the name to myself, whispering it into the brush and pan as I worked to make the dreary little flat immaculate, kneading it into the wholesome loaves I baked—just in case. I longed to murmur it into his ear but the cries he drew from me were sounds without form, springing from regions of the woman in me that had no use for names.

Happiness was infectious. It made strangers in the street follow me with their eyes and broke through the suspicion of two elderly Russian sisters in the flat below. They heard me singing as I swept the communal stairs and invited me in for tea served from a samovar in an ornate silver stand. I brought them treats of halva and figs from the health food shop and liked the way they nodded significantly whenever I mentioned Adrian's name.

And safely out of the neighborhood of 309, I found myself responding more sympathetically to Kay. Always shying from contact in the past, I now telephoned her regularly and chatted for hours without strain. As for Marianne, when I looked into her unhappy face, I ached to be able to offer some share in my joy. For a while we fell back on old patterns, with her thrilling vicariously to accounts of happenings in my life. The adventure now was a man.

It did not matter that I only saw him once or twice a week. I loved the urgent animal frisson which shook me when the phone rang and there was his brisk, sunny voice saying, "Tonight?"

I had made sure the hours I worked in the evening were flexible. After he had rung there would be a frantic twenty minutes in which to bath and dress. Whatever I put on was for him to take off. Time and again I went over in my mind that moment of total trust, when I would stand before him naked, offered with no holds barred from the crown of my head to the tips of my toes. The cool phrases he uttered while running eyes and hands over me echoed and reechoed in my brain, heightening the pleasure of the fantasies which sustained me when he was not there.

If we met before nine-thirty in the evening he might take me out for a quick meal, but more often than not, he called me straight to his house. I ran to his call as surely as a turtle hatched in dry sand scuttles to the sea, and, absorbed as I was in the joy of everything newly roused in me that was physical, womanly, I paid scant attention to the further Massellian development of my mind. Echoes back to the days when lover Adrian had been mentor Massell had little meaning.

"You should think about becoming one of my lecturers. Once trained you could tour abroad—go all over the world."

I shrugged the idea away and nestled closer under his arm. Why would I want to go lecturing abroad when I had him here? Procreation was the name of the only brilliant career I wanted; to be the perfect vessel for his seed.

Riding so blind, I could only be heading for a fall.

I fell all right. The dream backfired. But, as I had blocked off what happened in Greece, so damagingly and for so long, I blocked off what happened with Massell. Faithful to Richard in the idea of turning dreams into schemes, I had overlooked the fact that where other people's emotions are involved, one is no longer in control. It was Addie who got closest to pinning down the problem: "So he just wanted to screw and you thought everything else was involved."

I thought how I had fallen, head first, body last, heart somewhere in between.

"Yes."

"And you made a bloody fool of yourself?"

"Yes."

"Well, you kept pretty quiet about it."

"Not inside."

No, the firecracker joys and pain I had learned through Massell would not end on a note of fizzle. But for the time being I pushed it all to that undefined region at the back of the mind where thoughts do not come in words. There it fermented dangerously, as the rape had done before I knifed the man in Tel Aviv.

And that year another major affair in my life came to a head. I gave up the flat in London and spent the summer in Scotland, half reluctantly back in Richard's world. With the end of the hotel season came the first painful opportunity to brood.

The old room near Richard and Edwina's had been made into an office and my accommodation now was a caravan, one field away from the sea. Because it stood up to the roughest batterings of the wind and was a small, pale oval nestling alone, I called it my egg in a storm. Out of habit I still went down to the sea each morning, as I had all through the working months when it had been my only outside glimpse of day. I watched the islands change from sunlit brown hummocks to ice-blue clouds in an ice-blue sea and sky.

As a baffle to the ache I had brought with me from London, I had thrown myself at the challenge of managing the café with an all-absorbing will. And it had been a success. All the things I planned to display on the counter had appeared. Pride and insistence on doing all the cooking myself made the job formidable, but that was what I wanted—one demanding occupation to stretch me to the exclusion of all else; distraction from thoughts, memories, dreams.

There were times when from the moment the café doors opened until the last mackerel had been grilled for High Tea, there was no break in the flow of customers. Wanting to please, hating to say "run out" to anyone, I worked and worked until, as Richard put it, my eyes hung out of my head like Davy lamps.

But others were stretched to the limit too. Up at the hotel Edwina never stopped. There was no such thing as time off for her. When there was work to be done she was busy and there was always work to be done. Although there was little communication between us, I admired her—it was impossible not to—and she must love Richard very much to work that hard. When, at the end of the season, faced suddenly with the shock of my own emptiness, I went badly to pieces, I even respected the way she washed her hands of me. In her world there was no room for weakness.

Weakness was cause for dismissal in Richard's world, too. People who fell in his wake became material for odd, nostalgic ponderings, nothing more. I had seen it happen to Kay and to Marianne. When it looked as though I were next in line, a solid nugget of determination set in my otherwise floundering mind. The woman in me, rejected by Massell, reverted to being an angry and frightened child.

That winter the storms were brutal. Boiling and massing, the sea sucked back to surge with hooligan violence on the land, slinging boats in splinters over the fields. The hotel speedboat was smashed to a blue and white nothing. Its dismembered parts lay with the sheep's bones and Squeezy bottles and I salvaged what was left of the seat to make stepping stones to the caravan.

Richard surveyed the havoc wreaked on his new horticultural tunnels with deadened eyes. He moved about as a distant figure, stooping in a field to wrestle a carrot from the frozen ground, building ramps to deflect the rush of water which would otherwise flood the hotel when the thaw came. Beneath the woolly rim of a bobbleless bobble hat his face was papery pale and there were thin gray feathers in his hair which had been so black. Edwina, duffel-coated, paler than he, carted the heavy buckets of swill down the pig field. Neither of them came to the caravan and we led very separate lives. Then, at the end of November, when Edwina went away for a fortnight, I went up to the hotel to housekeep for Richard.

The first few days went smoothly enough. Maintenance work was being carried out on the hotel and Richard was busy with his small labor force. In the evenings he was glad to slump into a deep chair in the smoke lounge with the dogs pressing around him in jealous adoration and a plate of supper balanced on his knees. I served him quietly, with a veneer of casual competence which belied hours of dithering indecision in the kitchen. The rest of my life was so bungled, it seemed quite probable that I would suddenly make a mess of a simple stew. And I did not want to keep asking Richard how Edwina did things.

Since the café had closed, all my confidence had gone. I knew I looked a mess but refused to care. Once, I had hung a cloth over the caravan mirror to dry and, intentionally or not, left it there. I lived in Richard's old pullovers and wore a scarf over my hair so that I did not have to brush it. I never wore it loose now or wrapped in soft phones around my ears as I used to for Massell. I looked forward to when Edwina came back and I could retreat once more into my egg in a storm.

When the workmen stopped coming toward the end of the first week, Richard went back to his usual winter occupations of nail-gnawing and plot-hatching. I could tell how the plots were progressing by the way he moved: a heavy, knit-browed stride meant he was grappling with an awkward, possibly insoluble problem; a hesitant uneven step that he was teetering on the edge of vision; and a fine, upright swing that he had got there and had only to match the plan with action, which he always did in the end.

And although I had seen him look diminished beside the steamroller of Edwina's earthy strength, had seen him lost and in the way in the heart of his own enterprise, I knew that he was still the life blood behind it all, the power that planted the seed. Feeling my old love for him revive, my own vapid wallowings seemed even more despicable. I was more directionless now than ever before, more than ever lacking in a plan.

I spent one afternoon swabbing the barroom floor and was descending the concrete steps to the back door, armed with mop and bucket, when Richard's voice arrested me. He was standing by the animal steading, arms akimbo, brow crossed.

"Lude"—it was his old pet name for me—"have you seen yourself recently? You look frightful."

He said it again, shifting his foot almost as though he would stamp, "Frightful!"

I set down the metal bucket and squeezed out the mop before putting it away.

"Well, it doesn't matter, does it, when I'm only cleaning out the bar?"

"It *does* matter. You look a disgrace. Why are you wearing that ghastly scarf? What's happened to you?"

I felt as though he had a pin stuck through me and was pulling off my wings.

"It *doesn't* matter. You're the only person who sees me."

"But you look dreadful, frumpish, worse than I've ever seen you."

"So what?" I was shouting now. "I'm your daughter not your lover!"

"What's the difference?"

I had nothing to say to that. It was not so simple to dismiss his words as senseless. The question was one that had been simmering between us for years.

Later he was gentler, praising the supper I had prepared.

"Mmmmm, this turbot is very good, Lude."

I felt myself preening, as Marianne would have done, at this tidbit of a tribute to my efforts to please. I was frightened to see myself behaving like her.

Usually I went straight down to the caravan after clearing away. But tonight I was restless. I would go for a walk in the wind. Richard watched me pulling on oilskins.

"Going down already?"

"No. A walk."

"I could do with a walk too."

It was dark and damp and the moon was hiding so we walked on the road. If it was a wilder night than we had realized, neither of us said so. Heads bent to it we strode, moods and booted footfalls matching.

Where the road forked we turned inland and walked on with the wind driving at an angle against our backs. The single-track road cut through flat bogland, rumpling away on one side toward the sea while on the other, close to in their blackness, the mountains crouched, nudging bony shoulders against the void. I would have liked to describe to Richard the way darkness fell at Mole's End. I knew he would like it. But somehow I never talked to him about those things.

The "void" was on my mind. I liked the eggy vacuum sound of the word and the images it conjured—black, blank whirlpools of nothingness; oblivion. We tramped for a long time without speaking. It was a night for thoughts whirling down dark holes.

There was a loch to our left, black water trembling, so wind-whipped it lashed neither one shore nor the other but stood poised all over the surface in quiffs. Glimmers from a cloud-shredded moon caught a breaking wavelet here and there.

"Have you thought what you're going to do, then?"

Richard's words, the most dreaded, broke into the void.

I shook my head, but it was invisible within flapping oilskin hood and I had to call out loud.

"No!"

It sounded like a wail, against the wind.

"You can always do the café again next season. You didn't do badly for a first go."

"No, I'll . . ."

"What? I can't hear."

Why was his voice so clear and I had to shout? I jumped round to his other side.

"I said, no, I won't do it again."

Now my voice was clear. His words came back wind-punched, vexed.

"Well, what *are* you going to do then?"

"I don't know! I don't know!"

I jigged around in a circle, let the wind box my other ear. We had reached the end of the second loch. Time to turn back.

Facing this way, it was impossible to talk. The wind shoved at our faces, worried our trousers round our legs like juddering leaves. We threw our bodies into it, sharing the exhilaration of our two small strengths pitted against a far greater one. We caught our breath in gulps, bent almost double. Thought was blown away. Sheltered for a second in a dip before breasting the last wind-beaten lap, Richard gave the wild weather yowl I knew and loved. Our shoulders biffed together and he grasped my hand. Half running, hands tight, we charged all the rest of the way, only letting go at the top of the caravan field.

"Come up for a hot drink," he mouthed, shrugging toward the hotel.

I beat him to the top of the bar road and stamped into the kitchen, puffed out and tingling from the wind. Caillach, the black labrador, thumped her tail on the floor, then laid her head back on her paws. She was missing Edwina.

Richard stood by the stacked chairs and tables in the dining room looking out on to the roaring night through big picture windows. I came in carrying two mugs of coffee. He was ruffling his hair with one hand, a gesture which brought a sudden memory picture to mind: me and Marianne, each in possession of one knee and one side of his parting as he sat in the lounge at 309. She was putting in curlers, I was making Indian plaits. Kay was somewhere offstage cooking mince. It was a way we often spent Saturday mornings and what Marianne and I liked best of all was when the doorbell rang and Richard, unperturbed, got up and answered it as he was. We would hide behind the bannisters clutching one another and hissing to remind him to walk carefully or the pins and ribbons would fall out. He did not seem to have aged at all since then, except for the feathers of gray.

"I enjoyed that," he said, meaning the walk. "Need something like that from time to time. You look better for it too—less 'blanched turnip.'"

Richard had never been one to sacrifice a witty description for the sake of tact. Smarting inside, I moved nearer the window, blowing waves across my mug.

"You know, I've been thinking," he said, taking short steps and pausing in the middle of the room, "you could do a lot worse than spend another season in the café. You could use what you've learned from this year's experience to make improvements—might even organize yourself some time off."

This last was said lightly. As family, I was not expected to want time off.

"I've already said I won't be doing the café again."

Indoors the statement sounded different, as though I were taking a stand against him. He looked up irritably and I said defensively, "There are things of my own I want to do."

"Mmmm?"—he was prepared to listen—"like what?"

The void was back in place. My words bounced feebly off its sides.

"I might go abroad again . . ."

"What, just bumming about?"

He tossed the expression at me like a dirty dishcloth. That was how my time in Greece and Turkey and the desert must have looked to him.

"No! I'd probably work for a while in London first."

"Seems to me you don't do anything very serious there."

No, I thought, floor washing and a bed scene with Massell flashing through my mind, *I don't do anything very serious there.*

Richard started walking about again, little finger neatly cocked away from the handle of his mug.

"You know, I've been watching you this winter, Lude . . ."

Rubbish. You've only just noticed me.

". . . And I must say I have been surprised at the way you've let yourself go."

The wind worried at the windows, Richard at his nails. He was saying he was disappointed in me. *Surprised and disappointed.*

"It's not like you to be lazy, but as far as I can see all you've done since the end of the season is sit around on your backside."

My thoughts batted about angrily. How could he speak of what was or was not like me? He knew nothing of my other lives, my jobs, my travels, my friends . . . But the inner protests rang hollow. I saw all too clearly the fragmented mess of all my little lives.

"Oh, shut up!" I blurted—and it was "not like me" to be rude to him—"lecturing doesn't suit you and you're not telling me anything I don't already know."

"Well, you need something, don't you, or do you mean to go on like this, wasting yourself, becoming a misery . . ."

He would have gone on but I cut him short, tension making my voice shrill.

"Do you think I like being like this? I wish I could just 'pull myself together' but I can't. It's not as simple as that. Sometimes . . ."—I moved near enough the window to feel the rage of the darkness outside—"sometimes I just feel like jumping off a cliff!"

It sounded pathetic, ridiculous, even as I said it, and I might have laughed if it had not been for his reply, which was instant and studiedly derisive.

"Oh God, Lude, you are beginning to sound like Kay."

You shit, I thought, *you shit. Like Kay. Oh my God.* I had been relegated to the order of mistakes he did not have to live with.

It took four steps to cross the room to where he stood, four words to point the mockery of his promise of home.

"I hate this hotel"—the mug shook in my hand—"and I hate you."

And to stop another impossibly clever reply, I threw the hot coffee in his face.

I was frightened as soon as I had done it. But it was too late to regret or run away because Richard had caught the throwing wrist in mid air and was propelling me backward, wet slicked jaw rigid with rage. I did not see his right fist coming. It slammed in just below the browbone and I thudded full length to the floor.

Richard was on top, instantly pinning down legs and arms. I writhed, blind. It was familiar: Cape Sounion; the hospital. If he had let me go then, I would have attacked him with anything to hand. My heart seemed to be punching holes in my brain.

Then sudden still and his voice, very quiet, very full: "Oh my love . . ."

I stopped moving and looked up to the echo of his words. His face hung above me, the skin under his eyes faintly lavender, trembling. As we looked at each other one tear popped out and slid away down a crease. I thought: he is older, after all.

There was a long, long moment before either of us moved again. The storm outside went on raging as ours gradually died. When at last we drew apart it was as though, in breaking bodily contact, our visions of ourselves, which for a moment out of time had been without civilized judgment, animal blind, fled to the corners of the room. Dazed, we fumbled our way back to normal perspective, across the safe border of the everyday world.

I fetched a brush and bucket to scrub away the coffee stain on the carpet. Richard got out the best piece of steak in the fridge for my eye. Then we ate it, like a sacrifice, almost raw. But neither of us knew to what god.

The bruise had gone by the time Edwina returned and the era of the egg in a storm was at an end. I said goodbye to the wind-scuffled hills and spent a last, long, goose-fleshed afternoon wedged in a rock crevice by the sea. Eight years of waves infinitesimally smoothing the sides of that crevice would go by before I came back to wedge myself there once more. And by then, I would have been seduced by another sea, and Richard would be a different man with a new love whose birthday fell on the same day as mine.

17

If ever I did any "bumming about," it was that year in Bristol. I twirled a finger on a map of Britain and that was where I landed, exchanging the egg in a storm for a cellar in the student quarter. Addie joined me shortly, at the end of some private era of his own. He arrived wrung out and haggard, climbed shakily into bed without removing his clothes, and stayed there for ten days, filling the air with stale farts and Dostoevsky.

During the weeks that followed, when he got heavily into West Country cider and Stockhausen and I hovered uncomfortably on the edge of the student crowd, we chewed the sap out of our relationship, finally reaching a stage where all we could say to each other was:

"Oh God, Addie."

"Oh God, Lucy."

"Oh God, Addie."

It was Julian, bursting back into our lives with the first daffodils, who rescued us once again from ourselves.

He came from the Black Forest via Mole's End, carrying compost under his fingernails, dried mushrooms in his flute bag and a dozen new loves in his heart. Shy before us for a moment, he stood like a choirboy, one sherpa-booted leg shuffling against the other. Addie and I were more than ever effete pressed flowers before a field of shining corn. But it was Addie who opened his stringy arms.

"Julian," he said, "thank God. You don't know how badly we need you."

That night all three of us slept in Addie's attic room. Julian rhapsodized about his latest love and we decided to go busking in the Antique Market next day so we could buy her a present. We did not know it then, but it would be the last time we would all be together for years.

The expedition got off to a prompt start. While Addie slept, I cooked porridge on a paraffin heater and Julian darned his breeks and plaited his beard. We left a note telling Addie to meet us at the Coronation Tap midday.

Julian and I walked with arms linked. We stepped lightly, feeling beyond the cool residue of night the promise of a sunny day. Stopping by my cellar, I collected a bright patchwork clown suit and leather gaiters. I felt like dressing up.

The stalls of the Antique Market were set up and starting to trade by the time we arrived. Large women in holey cashmere served smaller women in Laura Ashley. Trivets and candelabra passed from hand to hand. Julian floated through the cluttered aisles absently bestowing and receiving smiles. We found a place for him in a section of the market devoted to paintings. Here, against a backdrop of somber oils, all russet and wine, he ejected a streal of saliva from his flute, threw his head back, and began to play.

I stepped back, disassociating myself for the pleasure of watching people watch Julian. Within minutes a semicircle formed, one, two, then three rows deep. Julian, eyes closed, played on oblivious to all but the heart of his theme.

At the end of the third piece, he paused. The audience had shuffled closer to make room for more at the back. When Julian opened his eyes, he blinked wide with astonishment and burst out laughing. Palpable droplets of merriment landed in a light spray on the shoes of the front row.

"Ooops, sorry," he said, and bent to wipe it off with the hem of his tunic.

When he started to play again, coins tinkled at his feet and by the time he took his exit bow there was enough silver for half a dozen gifts. Julian expressed his pleasure by lifting me up and waving me around in my clown suit like the fairy on top of a Christmas tree.

"It's funny I've never fallen in love with *you*," he said suddenly.

"Don't be daft," I said, hugging him hard, "that would be incest."

And truly that was how it felt. There was still no meeting in my mind between lovely friends and friendly lovers. Perhaps if there had been, I would have accepted more easily the end of the affair with Massell—and punished both him and myself less painfully.

We arrived at the Coronation Tap a little late. Addie may have thought we had deserted him. He was certainly cross. Emboldened by my own good feelings I wrapped my arms round him. It was like cuddling an iron spike.

"Oh God, Lucy, you smell happy. How sickening."

"Not really," I said to comfort him, "just snatching a few sweet flowers before plunging into the abyss again. Are you drunk?"

"*Ish*," he said, brows ferociously knit, "drunk-*ish*."

He hunched over to roll a cigarette and I noticed behind him a very large black bag. There was string in places, dividing it into irregular bulges.

"What's that?"

"It's not a what, it's a her. The new love of my life."

I would not have put it past Addie to tie one of his girlfriends into a bag. He liked to feel in control.

"Can she breathe all right?"

"Doesn't need to. She's only got two functions in life. She screws and she sucks."

Julian winced. He was always uncomfortable when Addie was in a black mood.

"Feel her. Go on. She won't bite."

I reached past him and pressed tentatively.

"Harder."

I increased the pressure and all of a sudden a loud, squeaky fart came out. I snatched my hand away but the fart went on and on, piercing as a cat's meow. Every eye in the pub swizzled in our direction.

"Oh yes, I forgot," said Addie loudly, "she's pretty good at those as well."

"What is it?" I hissed.

"*Her*," he growled and his voice rose like a salesman's. "The only woman in the world for me, guaranteed orgasm every time with the hiccup of a dying cow. What shall I call her, Lucy?"

"Jemima," I said quickly, wondering if I could snatch her and get outside before he caught me. I knew he was going to start untying the bag any minute.

"I know! Let's play Tanks outside with Jemima."

"She'll deflate."

"Come on, we can try."

I plucked the bag from behind him and ran to the door. Jemima emitted her protest from several directions. She must be well endowed with orifices.

"Bitch! Traitoress! Coward!"

Addie clambered grimly over heads and tables, taking the shortest route. Behind him I caught a glimpse of Julian righting pint pots and staunching the flow of spilled beer. I was almost back at the Antique

Market before Addie brought me down with a flying tackle. He landed on top of me and I landed on top of Jemima whose toeless plastic foot burst through the bag, splitting it open to her waist. Plump pink legs flew apart and stuck up in the air. I twisted my head round and gasped.

"Addie, she's dribbling!"

He panted, flushed face resting on my belly.

"Yes, well, I thought she'd make a handy water pistol, too."

Julian cantered past, ignoring our tangle *à trois*.

"There's a fair," he cried, "with goats and everything, on the Green."

Slowly we picked ourselves up and dusted off Jemima. To keep her under control we tied her legs together with string and plugged the poised "O' of her mouth with a scarf as though she had toothache. I covered her bombnose breasts and gaping vagina with strips of the plastic bag; making a kind of bikini. Addie told me her history on the way to the fair.

"Found her in Leigh Woods, near where you go walking. She was stuffed into the hollow of a tree. But I'll tell you what was really peculiar. Beside her, all neatly wrapped up, was a gas mask, a duster and a little tin of polish. Put your imagination to that."

I did, and decided not to go walking alone in Leigh Woods any more.

We spent the afternoon at the fair. Julian won a bottle of fizzy cider by hitting a weight with a hammer and ringing a bell. Addie cut the *ish* out of being drunk and insisted on having a game of Tanks in the middle of the fair. He held my ankles and I held his and we rolled head-over-back-over-legs-over-head making a giant human wheel. Julian found the tube from a Hoover and coaxed a range of musical notes from it to accompany us.

"Not so much Bach's Air on a G-string," I said to the laughing onlookers, "as Julian's air through a vacuum." I was mildly tipsy too.

The sun went in and out and the day drew to a close. I waxed sentimental and told my boys I loved them. Addie burped and pressed a fart out of Jemima. Julian hugged me and said, "Come to Mole's End." All three of us went as far as the hitching point and then Addie slouched off with Jemima in a state of semitumescence under his arm. He said he was going to sell her for fifteen pounds and buy a scooter.

He did, but my life would turn a whole new set of somersaults before I had the chance to ride pillion.

18

It was good to be at Mole's End again, especially in the spring and with Julian. We played games, made music, planted herbs and danced. But beneath the superficial contentment I fretted; the old, old questions still floating around unanswered. Where was I going? What was the plan?

Then, tearing up newspaper to light the fire one morning, I saw the possibility of an answer, at least in the short term. Vacancies were being advertised for students on a full-time contemporary dance course. Why not? In a way it hardly mattered what the course was, so long as it was something definite, with direction. And I had always enjoyed expressing myself physically.

Julian kissed me goodbye on the day of the audition and stuck a cowslip in my lapel for luck. Once more I headed up the M4 to London with high hopes for the future.

Five hours after the audition, which to my amazement I had passed, I lay chin deep in a warm, cozily lapping bath. Three strands of hair, subtly intertwined, drifted on the surface like a tiny ship. I imagined that the white marble sides of the bath were cliffs and the streaky red stains in the water reflections of a setting sun. Idly, I poked the hairs with the tip of a finger and they clung. His, not mine. I let my hand sink and the tiny ship bobbed up and floated away, crisp and brisk, just like him.

I had come to tell Massell the good news of my belated return to the rails. He would surely be impressed. But unfortunately he had not been in and I had had to break a little window to get into the house and I had cut my hand.

It is funny how coincidences can slide one into the other until they form a new entity unfurling slowly in the mind like a warning flag. Stop Go Stop. I saw the flag unfurl before I reached Holland Park,

late and in the dark and rain, but I did not heed the warning on it and
the pips on the public telephone obscured the message on the ansa-
phone. The same way womb wonder in me had obscured the message
that he just wanted to screw.

"I'm sorry about this mess, though. I'll clear it up before I go."

I said it aloud, even though he was not there. I felt like chatting to
somebody and Polydeuces no longer seemed to be around.

When the pink bathwater began to cool I got out. I was dizzy so
decided to fix something to eat before sponging down the paintwork.
Breakfast at Mole's End was a long time ago. But perhaps I ought to
take my shirt off first. Its white front was dyed scarlet from neck to
hem and now it was dripping water as well. But my left hand, the blue
woolly glove a black clot, would not go through the sleeve so I left it
on, squeezing the worst of the wet into the bidet and running cold water
to wash away the red. It was a nuisance about the glove, but it had
been chilly when the rain began.

In the bedroom where I went to look for a robe—that sheepskin I
had given him would do—I found instead a bright bikini. I took it off
its hanger and held it against me. Red smeared the mirror where I tilted
it and dripped in small amoebic blobs on the dressing table. The bikini
was about my size.

On the way he had been the old Massell to whom I was bringing
the news of the rebirth of Lucy as potent shell. No more floundering
or emotional nonsense. Briskly forward from now on like a positive
arrow in one of his diagrams. But he was back to being Adrian now.

"Look at that torso," he had said, *hands appraising the velvety*
nipples as I sat astride his loins.

Now the stain there was turning from scarlet to brown. I felt light-
headed but aware of a need to be practical. Must get a cloth to wipe
the skirting and the light switches. Little blood goes a long way.

Downstairs I poured myself a glass of green Chartreuse. He had
given me that the last time I was here, the time he had not invited me
upstairs and I had lain all night on the old couch in the lounge staring
at an art deco lamp. Colored bubbles in it floated and rose, merged
and fell apart.

" 'All is vanity,' " *I had thought, misquoting Nietzsche,* " 'vanity
and colored bubbles.'"

Comprehension had crept up slowly on my comfy couch in exile but
it hit with the finality of a club. He did not want me any more. My
body, my "potential" even, had outgrown its appeal.

Drawing a diagram with my blood on the mirror I recalled how it had been once when I had come.

"Do you remember? I wrote a miniature word song about it? And your fingers made it happen while I sang. And then your tongue."

```
Girl coming
     o
     m
     i
     n
     girl

   co-mingle   co-mingling
                    i
                  cling
                  k

                  Lick
                   l
                   i
                   n
                   g
```

"It wasn't very good, was it? But you were my lickling then, all right."

I drank some more Chartreuse before going back into the hall. It was a shock to see what I had done to the door. No wonder they thought it was a crowbar at the trial. I kept saying it was a small gray umbrella but I don't think they believed me any more than Kay had over the lacrosse stick business years ago.

I had found the umbrella in a green litter bin attached to a lamppost. The handle was broken but the spokes and canopy were fine. I had walked along twirling it, spinning off the rain. It had been disappointing to see no lights on in the house. Even though it was garbled by the pips, I had thought the message on the ansaphone said he would be back later. And I was not drunk this time.

As soon as I got in I had made a mental note to buy putty for the window and a seven-inch-square pane. I could not write down the measurement because of the pain in my hand. The glass must have got pushed in deep while I was making that great hole, deep into the soft mound at the base of the thumb.

It had been a surprise to find the inner door locked as well. The wood was tough, with a honeycomb of insulating material at the center. I had to use my feet in the end to knock out a space big enough to crawl through. When at last I reached the other side, I could not remember why it had been so important to get there. I sat dripping for long moments on the thick white pile before thinking of the phone. Then I was in that little room where he had poured me the Chartreuse. He was wearing white trousers that day and a silky green shirt which I longed to put my hand inside. He stood with his back to me at the drinks cupboard, talking about a friend of his, a girl, who was gaining an important position in the world of contemporary art. It seemed that most of the people he mixed with were in important positions. I looked forward to the day he would introduce me to them.

There was a little red light on the phone. More, duller red lights when my hand had rested there a while.

The first time he had pushed my head down I had not known what to do. So I kissed him because I loved to kiss him anywhere and my breasts nestled around his thighs. He told me to take him in my mouth and as soon as my lips were round him it felt right. Wanting more contact still, my hand sought for his on the sheet, but it was not there. His arms were behind his head and his eyes were closed. So my tongue and lips made discoveries for themselves and I must have done something right for after a while my hands, massaging, felt a familiar tightening and, as though from another world, I heard the crow of his imminent come.

I was back through the hole now and opening the kitchen cupboards, looking for something quick and comforting. There were Japanese things in tins, cartons of Longlife milk, a whole crate of dried bananas. His pots and pans were in top-heavy stacks on the lower shelves. I would have arranged them better than that. I would have arranged them beautifully. While I sat there on the floor, feeling childish with the pans in my hands, echoes of Addie saying: "*Do it beautifully*" floated round the room.

I stood up, the liqueur chasing giddy spirals from belly to head. I emptied a can of abalone into a pan. It looked wetter than I expected and less appetizing. I tipped in another can, inadvertently adding a squirt of blood. The second can was a mistake, something white and glutinous like semolina, so I abandoned the idea of a meal and gnawed on a block of dried bananas. It amazed me that eleven of them could be so compressed. They would have made ideal Beverly ballast for the old days on the road. Then, when I crawled back through the hole again, leaving the bananas, I remember that I had forgotten to bring a cloth. But the most important thing now was to put on some music. I could do anything to music.

I knew now what I had done wrong but I did not understand at the time.

When I felt he was about to come I took my mouth away because I thought he would want to come inside me. I wanted him to come inside me. It was a bad mistake. The crow turned into a groan and then he shouted at me to grab him.

"Grab him! Quickly!"

Flustered, I took hold of him, hands forming a tunnel.

"Tighter! Whoa—not that tight!"

It was the first time I was glad when it was over. When he came back from the bathroom he said, "Why didn't you swallow it?"

I gaped at him from the pillow.

"I didn't know you could."

What a fool. Didn't I remember that word the doctor had used in the bin? Éclairs?

I promised I would get it right in the future. And all the other important positions.

There was Handel and Beethoven but no Bruckner or blues. If I wanted something familiar it would have to be the "Eroica" or the "Royal Fireworks." Both too grandiose. This was more like it: The Who. I recalled the lyrics of Tommy's most poignant plea and sang it while fiddling with the switches.

I put on the headphones because I could not work out how to make the sound come out of the speakers. The needle scored fresh leaks of blood in the grooves when I set it on the beginning of the track again. Pain yanked at my thumb and after a moment I pulled the phones off and let blood pool in the black padded cups of sound. I was not Imogen, had no plans to die to the "1812"—or The Who.

It was the vision of Imogen dead, cheeks translucent under the tangle of black hair, that brought me to my feet. I had to phone. The mess had gone too far, was too much for me to clear up alone.

The spattered staircase rippled upwards, the carpet seeming to dance my own red spots before my eyes. I stepped back, groping for solidity. Pain whistled through my teeth as my left hand hit the edge of something square hanging out from the wall. I turned round and held on to it, staring close up at softly symmetrical fusions of color on canvas. Sliding carefully to the bottom of the stairs, I looked up and saw that blood destroyed the symmetry. In the lounge there was another painting. Somehow blood had got on that as well.

I crouched, animal still, as the phone in Michael's flat whispered cool couplets. Please, please be there.

"Hello?"

His Canadian accent was tousled with sleep.

"Michael? Michael? It's me. I'm sorry to bother . . ."

"Who is this? Do you know what time it is?"

"No, but I know it's late and I'm sorry to both—"

"Look, this really is not convenient. Could you call back another time?"

I held the damaged hand against my chest, knees drawn up close so that it only dripped into my lap. My eyes, skittering from the streaked carpet to a rainbow cascade on the wall, caught on the splintered wood in the hall.

"I've cut my hand."

His voice, sleepy, unseeing, pressed from me a disjointed recitative in which the broken pane, Massell's name and a bloody umbrella stabbing through a hole featured like cryptic clues in a thriller. Michael said he was sorry I seemed to be in some kind of mess but it all sounded a little crazy and he really was not sure why I was phoning him. There was a pause before he pronounced the four short words which explained why he could not help.

"I am not alone."

Again I apologized for bothering him. But now I was afraid. My own fragmented portrait of the scene in which I sat had brought it abruptly into focus. I saw the blood, I felt the pain. Weakly, I spoke again of the mess, saying—and feeling a numb kind of surprise at the truth—that the hand would not stop bleeding. He said maybe if it was that bad I should call an ambulance. It gave me a lead, something to think about when the phone went down.

I pulled myself over to the window and leaned my cheek against the pane. Outside the rain and the darkness seemed like old friends. But I could not go to them because my legs would not work any more.

And when it came, a long time later, to the rolling, tumbling, spine-whacked-in-the-grit and the wrought-iron spirals and the elegant fleurs-de-lis, there was no heart pounding and the grit was all in the palm of my hand.

19

It was a shock to see my old bush jacket, with the wilted cowslip still in the lapel, in a polythene bag labeled Prisoner's Effects. An officer from the CID interrogated me after the blood transfusion. Standing by the side of the bed—this scene was somehow familiar—he went straight to the heart of the matter.

"Why did you do it, then?"

"I don't know, really."

"Now come on, Lucy. You go to a bloke's house at dead of night, break in and start laying about the furnishings with a crowbar or something similar. Blood all over his nice carpet and halfway up the walls. Not to mention a couple of paintings worth more than a couple of quid. And now you tell me you don't know what it was all about. Come on, girl, pull the other one."

"I . . ."

"Sex, wasn't it? We get cases like this all the time. What did he do, throw you over? Well, you can't go round beating up private property just because it suits you. You, my girl, are in big trouble."

I was. My ignorance of the value of the paintings was no defense against what the C I D saw as an act of premeditated destruction. There remained only the question of whether self-destruction had been intended as well. I told the truth: I had no idea there was an artery in the base of the thumb. But I had called the ambulance, hadn't I? Surely that meant I did not want to die?

As to *why* I did it, the officer was, in his crude assessment, more or less right. Only I had not fully understood at the time that I was deliberately punishing Massell. And there was more to it than that. I was, once and for all, exploding a dream; crushing a misplaced ideal. Richard was a hero who turned out to be only human; so, in a different way, was Massell. I had to take my frustration out on someone and unfortunately the ideal sacrificial victim—the Greek who raped me—

had long since got away. Now I had to face up to the consequences of my actions and, ironically, this turned out to be one of the best things that ever happened to me. It was a while, however, before this positive side of things became apparent.

The months before the trial passed like a summer in the dark. On bail of £500 I haunted the M4 between London and Bristol like a soul shuttling back and forth in the shadowy zone before judgment. Yet I had no sense of being damned, only an awareness that whatever happened at the trial, my immediate future would be structured by agents beyond my control. This knowledge produced a feeling of security not experienced since the days before I walked out of school. By a small act of chaos I had reentered the world of established order where choices were clear and options limited.

Because no one knew about the dancing plan, no one said what a pity the trial was so near the beginning of term. But in the face of that black night of blood and all that followed, passing the audition now seemed no more than a pretty memory belonging to another place, another time. I let it go and looked coolly toward the prospect of prison instead. At the time, it seemed no better or worse than any other option.

My defense lawyer was hopeful of a light penalty on the grounds of diminished responsibility. The hospital to which I had been rushed in the early hours submitted helpful evidence of no recordable pulse. Sustained loss of blood was known to do strange things to the brain. I had no memory beyond the phone call to Michael. The lawyer advised me not to mention that I was conscious of what I was doing from the moment the artery was severed. The hospital said that but for my glove, which made the difference between swift spurt and slow leak, I would have passed out long before. And died. It horrified me to think that Massell might have come upon me like that, all leaked out on his white pile like a deflated Jemima.

As far as the police were concerned the case was simple: young woman with history of truancy and antisocial behavior forces her way into home of ex-lover and wreaks bloody vengeance, committing a crime in the process liable to a two-year prison sentence. Hell hath no fury, etc. But as Massell did not press charges they were obliged to take me to court on a charge of common burglary, a label which covered the act of forced entry, even though it was acknowledged there was no theft intended.

Here, the lawyer warned me, was the stumbling block. Even if the court allowed that owing to loss of blood I could not be accused of malicious intent once inside the house, why had I broken a window in the first place, thus damaging both myself and the property? I had no satisfactory answer. So the lawyer delved into the past for material to support his case and as files appeared and psychiatrists were consulted, I felt myself sink further and further into an apathetic daze.

There was a time when I wanted to stand up and cry: No, this has nothing to do with the past. Don't take me back to it. Treat me as a criminal and punish me as such but don't saddle me with the burden of resurrected memory.

But I could not escape being me. And because I was me, I got off lightly. Two years' suspended sentence. There were, however, conditions. One, I must cease forthwith to be of no fixed abode. Two, I must consent to psychiatric treatment.

The matter of stabilizing my address was not difficult, although I felt choked with the irony of it all as I wrote down the number 309. It was like being sent back from Littlehampton all over again, back to what had made me run in the beginning. A term in Holloway would at least have been breaking new ground. But I knew it was for official purposes only and there was no reason why my independent meanderings should cease so long as I reported in from time to time. And Kay's unquestioning loyalty from the moment of her involvement on the morning after the crime made me feel ashamed of the offhand way I had treated her in the past. She said as we waited for the bail documents, "I'll stand by you whatever happens."

Richard would never have made such an unqualified statement.

On the way to 309 Kay had to stop the car twice to blow her nose, stifling sobs caused by a mixture of relief that I was alive and bewilderment at what I had done.

"*Bloody* man," she said once, anger cracking the words through tears.

I was not sure who she meant—Massell or the aggressive CID officer.

"That—whatever his name is—Adrian."

I looked out of the car window.

"No," I said, "he's not a bloody man."

I knew now that Massell was not to blame for anything. He was just a scapegoat; victim first of fantasy, then of reality. Kay was sobbing again.

"I don't care what you say, he *is* a bloody man. *All* men are bloody."

Somewhere around Richmond roundabout I glanced at Kay, her hands nervous on the wheel, profile still pretty but lined, and imagined how she must have looked twenty years ago when she and Richard had run off to Ibiza and lived on love and rice pudding for six months before getting married. The legacy of that love was one daughter who was an alcoholic—Marianne's "giddy" spells had at last been correctly diagnosed—another who had just been pronounced a criminal, and a son who was embarrassed by her because she turned up at his school plays dithery with nerves. Of all the family dreams, hers must have been shattered the hardest.

Strange that at such a nadir in my own life I felt big enough for the first time in years to look at my mother with genuine love.

The second condition set down by the court caused a private anguish from which there was no escape. That first day I reported to the psychiatric clinic is splurged on my memory like a nightmare Rorschach blot.

In dread of meeting any of my old Richmond cronies—Jem, Alf, McAllister—I went a long way round, eventually emerging on to the clinic road from under the fence of a golf course. I could see the patients going in from there and a bolus of nausea lodged between stomach and brain as I recognized the old gait, the unmistakable loony bin shuffle.

Beyond the wheelchair ramp and the outer door was a short corridor painted ice cream green. A receptionist screened off by a long glass window roved languidly among bays of stacked files. I had to clear my throat several times before she came to the speaking grille.

"Yes?"

I spoke quietly, willing her not to be loud in return.

"I've come to see Dr. Stewart. I have an appointment for one-thirty."

Her face remained blank.

"Which department is that?"

My eyes darted to the end of the corridor where people were sitting in a row. Not bin types.

"Psychiatric," I said, very low.

Her words jangled back like coins in a cash register.

"Psychiatric, did you say?" She ran a thumbnail down a list. "Oh yes, that will be Lucy Irvine for Dr. Stewart. On your left and straight through. Take a seat and wait to be called."

I hated her for her blank face and loud, uncaring voice.

On my left and straight through was a general waiting area. Two blocks of joined plastic chairs faced another green wall, this one crookedly patched with smoking cautions for pregnant women. I noted the slumped poses of patients in the farther block. That was my lot. None of the heads were up but I recognized two ex-binmates at once. One was a greasy-haired girl who had a phobia about hygiene, the other the unhappy boy who had been my partner in the restaurant meal escapade. That was four years ago but he looked exactly the same. I hoped I did not. There was a refreshment counter at the nonpsychiatric end of the room. It was closed but I went and stood by it anyway, just to keep my head turned away.

At one forty-five a community nurse emerged from the glass cubicle separating the waiting area from the consulting rooms. He had a copy of the receptionist's list in his hand and was glancing over the patients. I covered the distance between us in four strides, grabbing his wrist before he could shout out my name. His face was familiar too. The whole scene, unchanged, perennial with its props of plastic chairs and slumped bodies horrified me. The only difference I could see was that the walls were green here instead of lamb chop red.

The nurse greeted me casually as though I had been coming every week for the last four years. He said there was maybe an hour to wait before my turn, the doctor was a little behind today. Of course, the endless waiting was all part of the scene. Saying I would be back, I hurried away.

There were shops at the end of the road, one of them a bakery. I bought cakes, including three éclairs, and rammed them down my throat one after the other, staring at a fishless aquarium in a petshop. If everything was so the same, then I would be the same too. I was not going to talk to Dr. Stewart about Massell. Let him grapple with the old red herring of compulsive eating and stick on the same old labels of insecurity and maladjustment. I stood in a telephone booth for the rest of the waiting time, chewing and choking furiously.

Beyond a loathing of the mechanics of the appointment, I was afraid the doctor was going to attempt to analyze my behavior, and by defining it kill both the cause and all the feelings arising from it. For all the trouble it gave, I valued that dark region of the mind where thoughts did not come in words. It was the most fiercely living part of me.

But my fears were unfounded. I emerged from the clinic with a selection of pills designed to relieve current symptoms of distress and curb any further off-the-rails behavior. Some I took, some I disposed of quietly on the underground market.

All I must do now to comply with the terms of the suspended sentence was be good for two years.

PART FIVE

Being Good

20

And I was good.

After a while that suspended sentence became, instead of a sword of Damocles, a personal challenge, and when the two years were up, I continued to impose my own discipline from within. The age-old "search for identity" was still on, but I now became very methodical in my approach to it.

I began by saying goodbye to 309 for the last time and finding myself a room. Wedged four flights up under the eaves of a narrow house overlooking a railway line, it streamed with condensation in the winter and turned into an oven as soon as the sun shone. But, cut off when I needed it to be from the rest of the world, it was mine and it was home.

Over the next four years I emerged from that room in a dozen different guises. As in the past I had tried on hats in a mirror, I now tried on a whole series of images. I recorded some of my experiences in a diary, this time with no Massell diagrams.

Sticking cautiously at first to a sexually anonymous role, I bought an all-concealing boilersuit and took a job as a stonemason's mate. This entailed lugging gravestones in and out of the back of a plaster-caked van and laying cables around churchyards for electrical tools. My boss cut IN LOVING MEMORY messages on the stones, adding the names of the newly dead to the old, but he was also a sculptor and one day, when we had had to call off work because of impossible weather, he asked if I would pose for him. Ready by then for a change of image, I said I would give it a try.

Dan has nearly finished the life-sized sculpture. It sits in the middle of the room, eyeless and nippleless but otherwise entirely me in gray clay.

When he is working I always look at the same tree outside the window. It was bare and spindly when he started, like the wire ar-

mature under the sculpture. Now it is gradually unfolding into a new soft shape, rounded out with hundreds of little leaves. When I go into a dream, Dan and the tree become blurs. It is a surprise sometimes when I come out of the dream to see that he has suddenly completed an ear or given me a navel. He has even got in my bunions and the funny way a bottom squares off sitting on a stool.

It disturbed me that from one side the face of the sculpture could almost have been Marianne's. Dan had never met her.

Thoughts of Marianne made me afraid. Her whole world, as far back as the days of divorce and anorexia, had been one of shadows, fantasy and pain. We had little contact now but the few words and gestures which did pass between us told me that beyond the baffle of exterior symptoms, Marianne was still the same proud, beautiful girl with whom I had shared every thought as a child. And that terrified me because essentially we were so the same. Every time I heard of some new manifestation of her despair—shameful alcoholic episodes, overdoses—I thought: There but for the grace of God go I.

And as if the injury to heart and mind was not enough, her body continued to betray her as well. While I was being sculpted—strong, whole and still, for all my ups and downs, an easy vessel for joy— her womb was being scraped away. Through the nightmare of the alcoholic void which followed she sent one message: *Scream. Long black howl.*

I resolved then that, should she ever claw her way back through that long black howl, I would one day carry children which in some way would be shared with her. I wanted a tribe, a great big close loving tribe, to somehow balance the splintered nucleus which had been our own experience of family.

Meanwhile, after one or two futile attempts to wrench her back by the imposition of my own will, I left her to fight on alone and went on creating and demolishing images in my own world.

Spent the day with Dan plastering the sculpture. We started by flicking the plaster on to the clay with brushes. Soon the whole room was covered in splashes like enormous seagull turds. Dan could hardly wait for the plaster to dry so that he could break off the molds and get on with the final stage.

But something went wrong. All the molds cracked. Dan just put his head in his hands when he saw the torso go and said, "Oh shit. Shit shit shit shit."

Half the semiset clay had come off with the plaster. Half a face on the armature, half on the floor. One breast was sort of hanging. Dan sat there for ages with his head in his hands and I did not know what to do. In the end I picked up a piece off the floor and said, "Never mind, at least you're left with a shoulder to cry on."

He held the shoulder and I thought he really was going to cry but after a minute he giggled instead. So did I. We dumped the pieces into three big bags and took them all the way out to the Civic Amenities dump at Mortlake. There, instead of just leaving the bags, we took out all the bits and broke them against a wall. What was left of the head split quite neatly into four. Dan and I got almost hysterical laughing at the waste and madness of it all.

Trying out a new face—this time ministering angel—I went to work next in a home for young disabled people. It was only temporary, filling in while someone was away, but it opened my eyes to a world I would never forget.

They call the things that dangle down their legs sporrans. I am always afraid to jog them in case the plastic tubes tear out from the other tubes inside. But the "wheelies," as they call themselves, are quite matter-of-fact in dealing with their own bodies.

Once I nearly fell over William backing out of the lavatory with a soiled glove still on his hand. His face went red behind his glasses but his lips pulled themselves into a smile. Turning to face me, he held up the glove and waggled the finger like a puppet.

"Nasty, isn't it?" he said.

I suppose a proper nurse would have said: "Oh, go on with you" or something. I just said, "Yes." William's neck was red too and the triangle of chest above his shirt, but the brown fingers went on waggling.

"Can you steer with one hand all right?" I asked. I thought he might want me to wheel him to the dustbins.

"Like Jackie Stewart," he said. "Haven't you noticed something?"

His eyes, big behind the glasses, were challenging me to understand. I looked at the waggling hand and its meaning suddenly clicked.

"Hey, that's great, William—the middle finger is working!"

He had not been able to move it independently of the others before.

"Yes, great, isn't it," he said, spinning the chair away so fast that his withered pipe-cleaner legs slapped against the arm rest. "Think what fun I can have now!"

We had a birthday party one day for Joyce, a quadriplegic. By four o'clock all the wheelchairs were assembled. There were seven "wheelies" and three ladies from the Home committee at table. One of the ladies cut the cake and another opened Joyce's presents for her, blushing when William's fell out. It was a tiny pair of silk briefs with "Where there's a will there's a way" stitched in crazy letters on the front. Joyce's face lit up and her boyfriend, in an electric wheelchair, clapped William on the back so hard his glasses fell off. While I was groping for them under the table I noticed that the stopper had come out of someone's sporran and a pair of smartly shod feet stood in a pool of urine. The youngest committee lady's face looked down as I looked up.

"Oh dear," she said, embarrassed. "I think someone has had a little accident."

I could feel William smirk. As I emerged from under the table he said, in a polite tea-party voice, "An accident, yes, but that's something we don't talk about much round here." He paused, glancing pointedly at the assortment of twisted bodies around him, " . . . Do you think it was God, or the other fellow?"

The silence that followed was broken by some brave soul starting "Happy Birthday."

At six the party broke up and only a nucleus remained: Joyce, her boyfriend and William. The boyfriend produced a bottle of wine and insisted I stay to help them drink it. After a while Joyce and he stopped talking and just stared at each other. William said, "Why don't you two disappear?"

It was clear that was what they wanted to do. I wheeled Joyce to her room and her boyfriend followed in his chair.

"Will you mind if we have to buzz for you?" he asked.

I told him of course not and left.

They did have to buzz. Twice, while William and I sat finishing the wine, I got up to answer their call. William's eyes behind his glasses watched me go and watched me come back. He smoked, sometimes missing his lips.

After the second time I came back—the two bodies still clear in my mind, the way his arm shielded her breasts so gently as I helped with their helpless legs—I accepted a cigarette. William leaned forward to light it, daring me to trust the flame in his dangerously flicking fingers.

"Come here and help find my cufflink," he said. "It's dropped down the side of my chair."

As I bent down, William pulled the pin out of the leather slide holding my hair. He wheeled his chair forward as I drew back.

"Don't panic, this is hardly going to be rape."

He had one arm looped round my neck and was reaching up with the other.

"Oh William . . ." I said feebly and remembered Addie mocking voices which were always saying to him: "Oh Addie . . ."

The second arm was misbehaving. Each time he flung it up it spasmed at the shoulder. If I pulled back now I would make him lose his balance altogether. If I yielded I would be clinched in his arms. I could picture already the small, hunched body pressed to mine.

"Do you realize," he said angrily, "what it's like to be a 'wheelie' but still have the feelings of a man?"

By now he had both arms in place and all his weight was round my neck pulling me down like a giant human collar.

"William, I don't know what it's like to be a 'wheelie' and I don't know what it's like to be a man but I do know what it's like to be a girl and you're making things impossible for me now."

"Impossible, huh? You'd know what impossible meant if one day your legs packed up on you and you were suddenly reduced to a *thing* in a chair."

The tops of his glasses were bumping my chin. Only his feet, little flopping things in shiny shoes, remained in contact with the chair. I had no idea what I was going to do.

Then, searingly loud, the buzzer went.

The urgency drained out of both of us like a pulled plug. He hung, a dead weight, and his lips curled wryly against my throat.

"Ha ha ha. Saved by the bell."

"I'll have to go, William. Unwind."

He let go slowly, feeling for the chair behind.

"Oh God," he said, sagging into place, "my heart is as full as my sporran."

Both of us giggled.

Later that night when I came down to help Joyce pee, William called softly through his door.

"Hey—I've been thinking about you. Does that repel you? Where, oh where would man be without his dreams?"

My dreams these days were being kept firmly under control. I worked, went jogging every morning whatever the weather and spent my evenings alone, reading. I rejoiced in the self-imposed order of my days. Discipline was the keyword in my existence now and if ever I felt the

old longings revive—to be tender and feminine, to hold and be held—
I stamped on them hard. Things were going all right at the moment. I
was being good. Passion, once associated with salvation, now looked
more dangerous than alluring. After all, where had it led before?

The various jobs I took reflected the images with which I was experimenting. Back in a boilersuit, I worked for a while painting boats
in Oxford. Then I became a nanny, taught conversational English to a
Japanese and filled in any spare hours with life modeling. But, as the
power of the suspended sentence came to an end, although I stuck
unwaveringly to my own guidelines for discipline, the contrasts between
the images became increasingly extreme.

WANTED: Caring and responsible person to look after elderly
disabled lady. Weekends only. £6 plus meals.

WANTED: Topless hostesses for gentlemen's luncheon club.
Earnings from £20 per session.

I took both jobs. My interest in learning to understand the problems
of the disabled had continued and, in taking on the role of club hostess,
I seemed in some way to be finally evening the score with the Greek
and Massell. Now the shoe would be on the other foot. I would be the
user, not the used.

I kept track of my progress in a tiny notebook which fitted as snugly
into a stocking top as into the breast-pocket of my nursing overall.

> *An insignificant arrow in club colors pointed down an alley to a
> black door with a judas hole in it, just like those in the bin. Beyond
> the door a soft-carpeted stairwell led down into a red-illumined in-
> terior where a woman with dyed blond hair whisked me into a booth.
> I had a quick glimpse of more booths and a small, dark bar.*
>
> *The blond woman handed me a bundle with a chit pinned to it
> saying New Girl. She smiled and said in a foreign accent, "I ham
> Madame. Chour name is Zsa Zsa."*

> *The changing room reeks of scent and hot bodies. Big Mona clouts
> people who get in her way with her enormous black breasts. Someone
> is always screaming for a Tampax and everybody uses each other's
> makeup, lipsticky mouths muttering through hairgrips, painted eyes
> flashing signals in the mirror.*
>
> *My tiny skirt keeps riding up over the flounces of my knickers but
> Big Mona says, "It's OK honey, it's meant to be that way."*

She told me to hide anything private down a boot because Madame goes through our bags when we are out front.

I liked Big Mona. She turned up every morning at the club in an old white mac and flat shoes, looking like the cleaning lady. But when she put on her wig and stockings and smoothed the Kleenex-sized apron over her great rumbling belly, she was magnificent. Her breasts, with long purple stalks, seemed to boom out in front of her like foghorns and her vast, jutting rump made mincemeat of the tiny skirt, chewing it into a crumpled belt over knicker flounces which barely spanned half her buttocks. From time to time Madame scolded her for the disorder of her uniform, but Mona just snapped a big bubble of pink gum in her face, rolled her bulk languidly and answered, "Anybody—Ah mean anybody—can see Ah ain't *designed* for dis gear. Ya got any udder complaints?"

Madame had not. Big Mona made her a lot of money.

Occasionally we would go for a meal together after the club closed: Mona in her cleaning-lady gear again, steak and chips vanishing between her broad lips like small change into a carpetbag. She told me she was just filling in time before taking a cruise to Las Vagas.

"Won't that cost the earth?"

"She-oo! You green or what? Double trade all de way, honey— crew for de short-times, first class for de dee-luxe nights."

I was green. It took me a week to realize that I was the only girl in the club not "going case." While I was pulling in a steady £20 a day—the fee a client paid for my company while he drank champagne and I trickled it into the carpet—the others were making assignations for after-hours which earned them anything up to £100 a throw.

This knowledge rolled around my head disturbingly as I looked after Dr. Carew, the disabled lady, at the weekend.

She has to have four lots of medicine through the night and I turn her three times. Her poor body, each limb a grayish, powdery branch attached to a grayish, powdery trunk, is not always easy to shift, but she never complains. She just seems relieved when the TV programs end and it is time for her first dose of oblivion.

The last time I saw Jem he gave me a funny little poetry book called Archy and Mehitabel. *In one poem a cat dances in the catacombs, describing the once-full lives of the bones that lie beneath and saying at the end of each verse:*

"All men's lovers come to this."
It's true. Dr. Carew, Big Mona, Richard, Massell, me—that's all
we really are in the end, bones.

This distant and no doubt past-colored way of looking at things made
the issue of morality seem irrelevant, and with my habit of taking things
to the limit it was inevitable that one day before leaving the hostess
club I would try "going case."

It happened one Monday lunchtime. I was tired after a particularly
painful night with Dr. Carew. She had not been able to sleep and lay
all night staring at the ceiling through pain-bright, exhausted eyes.
Beyond the small promise of a grandchild's visit and tea in the garden
when the sun came out, she was only waiting to die. As I shrugged
out of my nursing overall and started to apply makeup for the club, I
felt angry and confused at the seeming futility of it all. And by the
time I had got up to town I was in a strange, hard mood, ready almost
for anything.

He began by ordering a bottle of Krug. I sat across from him, face
and upper body in three-quarter profile, which displayed me to advantage and at the same time allowed me to keep an eye on what was
happening outside.

He said, "Aha!" heartily as the cork, expertly thumbed off by
Madame, made a soft, steamy pop. We raised glasses and sipped.

"Mmmmmn," I murmured appreciatively, "my favorite."

"Jolly good," he said stiffly, looking at the wall a few inches from
my breasts. "Smoke?"

He offered a packet of Players and I refused politely. He lit one for
himself, then waved it around awkwardly.

"I say, I'm sorry—do you mind?"

I had to decide quickly whether this shy formality was a pose or
genuine. I tested.

"*I* don't mind, but it probably isn't very good for you, is it?"

He hesitated, a little startled, and eyed the cigarette shyly.

"I know I shouldn't really—but am I allowed just one?"

I was home and dry. Holding his eyes with mine and leaning forward
deliberately, I passed a hand under the table and dribbled away the first
glass of champagne.

"Oh, I might let you get away with that," I said, " . . . if you are
a good boy in other ways."

His cheeks went pink and he gave a bashful smile. Definitely a case of spankypoos.

Two bottles of Krug later, my middle-aged schoolboy was looking more relaxed. His pure new wool tie was off center and two fingers of mousy hair stuck straight up over his forehead like devilish horns. He was telling a long, complicated story about how he and someone called Crowther had once got lost in the backstreets of Cologne and ended up being taken in by an extraordinary woman.

"Ix-*straw*dinry," he insisted, screwing up his eyes at the memory. "Old Crowther and I had *such* fun."

He was squeezing the cup of his champagne glass and twiddling the stem incessantly.

"*Stop fiddling* while you're talking," I said sharply.

His eyes flew open and glanced guiltily at his hands. We both smiled and a warm palm came wobbling hopefully across the table.

"*Bad* boy," I said, swatting it lightly just before it touched. "Come here and let me straighten your tie."

He began to shuffle quickly round the table.

"But wait a minute"—I held up the latest empty bottle—"what about this?"

Madame caught the signal and bustled into the booth within seconds flourishing a new one. She wrinkled her nose at me delightedly. I was "being good" at this game, too. When she had gone I moved up and straightened the man's tie. He had drunk a great deal very fast and there was a film of sweat over his face. As my breasts accidentally brushed his lapels he whispered breathily, "I say, you are going to come with me, aren't you, and let me, let me . . ."

I gazed blankly for a moment at the curtain. Did it really matter, after all that had happened, what I did with my body now?

It did matter, it always would, but caught up as I was in this role, this game, I said, "Yes . . . only with a friend."

We arranged to meet outside the Café Royal, where he would have a taxi waiting. In the changing room I made a deal with Suzanne, a thin, businesslike girl. We shared a chocolate bar as we walked to the rendezvous.

The man had already booked a hotel room by phone. Suzanne, muttering about having to be quick because she had to collect the kids from school, stripped down to stockings and suspenders and sat on the edge of the bed, thin legs apart, breaking open a packet of condoms with her teeth. She smoked a cigarette while I undressed as far as the club uniform and pushed off the man's coat. He stood dazed and grinning as I removed his tie.

"Drop your trousers," I ordered.

He did so, staggering a little, and Suzanne's expert hands shot out to work on the half erection pointing up the cloth of old-fashioned Y-fronts.

"Bend over," I said and he bent over, flushed face close to her lipstick-reddened nipples. Still working on him with one hand, Suzanne stubbed out her cigarette and spat on her fingers, moistening herself before hooking up a condom on a long red nail and rolling it on to him. He was still not fully erect and I gave an experimental whack with the flat of my hand. He lurched lower over Suzanne and the Y-fronts slithered down. His feet, in neat red-patterned socks, danced around at the edge of the bed. The whole scene was like something out of a third-rate film but someone had to go on directing it.

"Kneel here," I commanded, smacking the bed between Suzanne's thighs and flipping up his shirttail to expose white, loose-skinned buttocks. My hand flashing down left a mark like a pink exploding star.

"Oo ow!" he cried, sounding like the villain in a Batman comic getting his comeuppance, and then: "Oo oo!" as Suzanne pulled him into her. She grabbed a pillow from the top of the bed, whipped it under her bottom and clamping her legs high up on his back, sucked at him like a drain plunger.

"I'll give you Oo," I heard her growl between gritted teeth, "fucking bastard, fucking prick."

I peppered another series of slaps on his blotched buttocks as she went on drain-plunging, bony spine lifting clean off the bed in the effort to hurry him on. His hair was now little devil's horns all over, but the rest of him was beginning to sag.

One hand that had been trying to hold a breast fell off and groped for purchase on the counterpane.

"I'm afraid I've had a drop too much to drink," he gasped.

Suzanne stopped in mid-plunge and unwound her legs. She was up and dressed before I had got the pillow out from where he had flopped and placed it under his head.

"Well, can't say we didn't try," she said cheerfully, tucking away the fifty pounds I gave her off the top of the television. She blew me a kiss as she went out.

"Thanks for the biz, darl. I'll do the same for you."

I sat on a chair before the dressing table, slowly pulling on my clothes. The face on the pillow looked empty; the legs, still with socks on, white and sad. I thought he was asleep. Brushing my hair, I saw in the mirror the rest of the money on top of the television, another fifty pounds. I thought of the woman on the canteen steps in the bin opening her doughy legs for two cigarettes. The way she had screeched when the whitecoats dragged the man off and one of the cigarettes got broken.

"I say, you're not going, are you?"

The man was sitting up, pulling the counterpane over his legs.

"I must," I said. "Why don't you get into bed properly and have a sleep? You don't look too good."

"Can't. Train to catch."

He looked around him unhappily, taking in the rumpled bed, his tie and the Y-fronts on the floor.

"Did I—did you pay that other girl?"

"Yes."

I went into the bathroom and came back with a glass of water.

"Try that."

Looking at his embarrassed face I thought how happy and excited he had been chattering about his friend Crowther in the club.

"Do you still see Crowther?" I asked, peering curiously for a moment into his world.

"Crowther? Why, yes. Matter of fact I was supposed to be meeting him today. But he canceled at the last minute. Can't think why."

He looked disappointed now, as well as hungover and embarrassed.

"I say, I've made a nitwit of myself, haven't I? What a shambles."

I went and sat beside him on the bed.

"Couldn't even . . ."

"Shush," I said firmly and unbuttoning my dress took out a breast for him to lean on. As his hands came up to touch, mine went down to him. Somehow this experience, like everything else in my life, had to be seen through to the bitter end.

He came quickly and kept his arms around me until I gently pushed him away. I realized then with a shock that this stranger had touched me more tenderly than my onetime dream man, Massell, had ever done. It made the power of illusion—or self-delusion—seem stronger than even the crudest reality.

But once was enough. I never went back to the hostess club and the following week began work as a clerk in an Inland Revenue sorting center.

From 8:30 A.M. to 4:30 P.M. I sit inside a giant shoebox built by Italian prisoners of war. Light hums from fluorescent strips ranged evenly over long, meccano-gray bays, each housing hundreds of lettered pigeonholes. Corrugations divide the meccano into blocks and in front of each block sits a man or woman in a high chair. If you wander up the bays during work hours all you can see are rows and rows of bent heads and pairs of arms moving up and down like sluggish pistons, each with a white slip of paper on the end.

Every now and then someone gets up and ambles to the end of their bay to fetch a fresh mailbag, settling back into position quietly, arms resuming the interrupted rhythm. There is the occasional cough but otherwise the only sound is the rustling of countless hundreds of letters about tax. If you close your eyes you can imagine it is the sound of surf riffling a shoreline of fine pebbles.

I stayed in that job for nearly two years, enjoying the role of being "ordinary" for once. It was almost like sending myself back to school. I, who had rejected all early forms of structure in my life, now welcomed it, and the proof that I could stick to the tasks I set myself made me feel strong. The fight was after all not with the outside world. What I did was up to me.

But whatever I did, however immersed I became in one role, I could never escape the knowledge that there were a thousand other avenues open. Gazing beyond the pigeonholes in the Inland Revenue sorting center, just as I had gazed out of a window in a Latin lesson years before, I knew that I was only waiting for another sunny day to walk out into the blue.

The time had come to go beyond all images, all roles.

At the beginning of January 1981 I started spending all my lunch hours in Richmond library, scanning lists of single airfares to places as far apart as Africa and Greenland. I wrote away inquiring about jobs in Leningrad, Peru and Singapore and looked into the possibilities of overlanding, joining the armed forces and crewing on round-the-world yachts. Some of the replies I got were encouraging but still I hesitated. What I wanted now was a personal challenge of such dimension it would almost be a case of kill or cure. Trying to pin down my desire, I had a vision of being dropped by helicopter into the middle of some nameless land and grappling the means to survive out of the earth. I wanted to scrape away the superficial layers of my environment—and of myself—until I was right down to the raw stuff of existence.

This dream, ironically, was probably easier to realize than any I had had before. All I had to do was answer one more advertisement: a writer was looking for a "wife" to share a year-long survival exercise on an uninhabited tropical island.

I went.

EPILOGUE

The year on the island proved to be one of the richest, and most instructive, experiences of my life.

Just before setting off I went to see Marianne. At that time she was still in the grip of past unhappiness, hiding away in Richard's old studio at 309 surrounded by crumpled family photographs.

"Hello, duck," I said, using our old greeting, "I'm going to live on an uninhabited tropical island with a stranger for a year."

She smiled and settled back as though I were about to launch into one of Joey's adventures from our childhood game of Chatter. When I shrugged and said: "That's all," she asked seriously:

"Do you think you'll ever come back?"

"I don't know."

She nodded, understanding everything.

"If you do, will you promise to tell what happened?"

"Yes."

I kept that promise by writing *Castaway*. And while I was doing that Marianne was fighting her demons. I am proud to say she won and is now, amongst many other things, a very special Auntie to the latest adventure in my life—a son. Kay, too, now leads a full life of her own and the unhappy days of family strife are long gone.

But real life, unlike fiction, does not wrap up neatly at the end of a scene, and it would take another volume to describe what has happened to all the other people mentioned in these pages. Our lives go on and in some cases they touch and in others they slide by a long way away.

Richard remarried and now has a son the same age as mine. We live on opposite coasts in the highlands. On the way back from bringing the two babies together for the first time, I stopped off and carried mine part way up a favorite mountain. He was asleep and I laid him down under the shade of a clump of heather and turned away to watch the play of light on a loch below. After a while a small sound made me look round. There was my baby, eyes wide and calm, gazing at the sky through a pattern of twigs. And his little hands were reaching toward the sun.